# The Wolf Almanac

## A Celebration of Wolves and Their World

REVISED AND UPDATED

ROBERT H. BUSCH

Foreword by Rick Bass

THE LYONS PRESS
Guilford, Connecticut

An imprint of The Rowman & Littlefield Publishing Group, Inc.
4501 Forbes Blvd., Ste. 200
Lanham, MD 20706

Distributed by NATIONAL BOOK NETWORK



British Library Cataloguing in Publication Information available

**Library of Congress Cataloging-in-Publication Data**
Names: Busch, Robert (Robert H.), author.
Title: The wolf almanac : a celebration of wolves and their world / Robert H. Busch ; foreword by Rick Bass.
Other titles: Celebration of wolves and their world
Description: Revised and updated third edition. | Guilford, Connecticut : Lyons Press, [2017] | Includes bibliographical references and index.
Identifiers: LCCN 2017057201 (print) | LCCN 2017057671 (ebook) | ISBN 9781493033768 (e-book) | ISBN 9781493033751 (paperback : alk. paper) | ISBN 9781493033768 (ebook)
Subjects: LCSH: Wolves.
Classification: LCC QL737.C22 (ebook) | LCC QL737.C22 B865 2017 (print) | DDC
599.773—dc23
LC record available at https://lccn.loc.gov/2017057201 ISBN 978-1-4930-3375-1 (paperback)

∞™ The paper used in this publication meets the minimum requirements of American National Standard for Information Sciences—Permanence of Paper for Printed Library Materials, ANSI/NISO Z39.48-1992.

Printed in the United States of America

**This book is dedicated to all those people who fight to save those who cannot speak for themselves.**

# ALSO BY ROBERT H. BUSCH

*Wolf Songs: The Classic Collection of Writing About Wolves (ed.)*

*The Cougar Almanac*

*Gray Whales: Wandering Giants*

*The Valley of the Grizzlies*

*Loons*

*The Grizzly Almanac*

*Salmon Country*

# CONTENTS

# ACKNOWLEDGMENTS

Thanks are due to the numerous individuals who provided information for this almanac: Renée Askins, The Wolf Fund; Norman Bishop, U.S. National Park Service; Dave Burke, U.S. Fish and Wildlife Service (USFWS); Lu Carbyn, Canadian Wildlife Service (CWS); Nancy Checko, Algonquin Provincial Park; Colleen Clark, Wolf Haven International; Lou Feiring, The Living Desert; Pattie Fowler, Arizona-Sonora Desert Museum; Steven Fritts, USFWS; Nancy Gray, Great Smoky Mountains National Park; Dan Groebner, Arizona Game and Fish Department; Bobbie Holaday, Preserve Arizona's Wolves (PAWS); Minette Johnson, Defenders of Wildlife; Bud Lensing, Mexican Wolf Coalition; Susan Lyndaker Lindsey, Wild Canal Survival and Research Center; Björn Ljunggren, Föreningen Varggruppen; Byron Mason, Trophy Wildlife Records Club of British Columbia; Pat McGary, Defenders of Wildlife; Mike Phillips, USFWS; Christoph Promberger, Euronatur; Will Waddell, Point Defiance Zoo and Aquarium; Deborah Warrick, Wildlife Rehabilitation Center Sanctuary; Laura Wasson, Humane Society of the United States; and the dozens of provincial, state, and federal wildlife agencies that kindly provided statistics from their files. Hannah Barron of Earthroots and Sadie Parr of Wolf Awareness, Inc. provided extensive help in compiling hunting, trapping, and wolf control data for the Canada provinces.

And to Peter Burford, my thanks for his conception of this project and for his faith in my work.

# FOREWORD

ONE OF THE STRANGE AND perhaps wonderful things about history is the fact that we are often unaware that we are living deeply in the midst of it.

This is frequently the case with human histories, and it can likewise be the case with what we term *natural history*—as if such separation, rather than mere estrangement, exists between humans and the rest of nature.

We tend to look at most images and to experience the world as snapshots in time—fixed points of reference. A forest burns, and we think of it as dying rather than being born or rejuvenated. A wave of beetles attacks a stand of pine or fir, and we see only gray spars. We fail to perceive the underlying and necessary increase in soil nutrition that will be aided by the coming disintegration of those burned trees; fail to imagine the bright blue blazes of songbirds that will be sustained by the beetles. To perceive nature as static—or, for that matter, "catastrophic" or "tragic"—is to fail not just our ability to imagine, but our ability to learn and make larger connections.

Such reference points—our perceptions of nature—are not fixed, of course (with the possible exception of species extinction), but are always part of a greater and dynamic narrative: a pulse, a breath, a contraction and expansion of energy, desire, and the graceful, measured utilization of energy across the landscape itself.

In nature, geology equals destiny, and in this fast-forward, remotely controlled culture, hitting the FF button might quickly surf us from pre-Cambrian lakebed bedrock into a time of glaciers into the glaciers' retreat and the erosion of mountains yielding a thin curtain of soil, which then summoned the grazing animals and their inseparable compatriots, the carnivores and omnivores, such as wolves. Against such a vast and dramatic canvas of time and space, the wolves seem to me to be as integral as anything—as much a part of the canvas as stone or sky or the forests, ice, rivers, grass, sunlight—and to erase them from the equation would be in some regard like erasing the sky overhead or the soil and stone beneath our feet.

And yet erase them we did. Then, repentant or like little gods or both, we brought them back; we "allowed" them to return.

So now that the wolves are back—nearly 2,000 wolves currently inhabit the West where twenty years ago there were thought to be none—the important question is: How do we cohabit/manage big landscapes of wilderness of which wolves are but one component? They are a very important component it's true, but like any of us, they are but a part of the whole.

This has always been one of the great things about wolves—the way they can elicit not just our raw emotions, but, over time, deeper questions and considerations.

One of the great values of *The Wolf Almanac* is that it's a resource for examining and learning the narrative of wolves not only in the West, but wherever they may be (or may not yet be or once were) found: Arizona, Italy, New York, Texas, Minnesota. Everywhere, the story is nearly the same: wolves inhabited the landscape with adaptability, grace, and purpose; people killed them; and, with a few notable exceptions, people failed to protect big chunks of wilderness in which the wolves could continue to fit the greater world—a world in which a multitude of connections, rather than fragmentation, existed.

So our species is responsible for eradicating wolves in this country and others, but now we are changed. We have become witnesses to and, to some extent, partners in their return.

Whether humans now desire wolves or not is a much-disputed topic, and it may be neither the right question to ask nor have a correct answer. A more interesting question from a natural historian's perspective might be: Does the world desire wolves?

Examining the facts contained in this almanac, the answer undeniably seems to be *Yes*. In this country, as in many others, wolves were like a fire upon the land that was extinguished, tamped down, snuffed out.

And yet from somewhere—from the text of the rock itself it would seem, as well as from some deeper desire, deeper yearning, in the world—they returned. Surely such a dynamic process reflects the presence of a larger spirit and of individual spirits.

We would do well to remember the provenance of such spirit as we continue, given the wolves' second coming, to "manage" them, to accommodate them, to reexamine them, and, we hope, to learn from them. Wolves possess an amazing society and ecology: but this time around, they can act as a lens through which we can be more attentive to the larger lessons of landscape.

People understood, at a macro level, that when wolves returned to Yellowstone, for instance, the dynamics and interactions between wolves and elk and wolves and coyotes would change. In retrospect, we were not prepared—not imaginative enough, perhaps, and not experienced or educated enough—to realize the seemingly obvious: that aspen groves would begin recovering, or that nesting brilliant neotropical songbirds would recolonize the riparian habitat that had previously been suppressed by large nonmobile herds of elk.

There is no end to all the things we do not know. The redistribution of energy—of nutrients gotten by the elk from the grass grown from the sun and consumed by the wolves and carried vast distances across the landscape—is a new chemical and ecological narrative, one that might take us decades to understand or measure.

It is all a round river, or, in healthy nature, that which possesses a full component of wilderness, in which death becomes life and a wolf becomes a lazuli bunting. We are beyond fortunate, even blessed, to have animals as powerful and dramatic as wolves to help illustrate such connections, as we try to move away from fragmentation and back toward wholeness.

*—Rick Bass*

# PREFACE

THE WOLF ALMANAC was first published over two decades ago. In the original preface, I wrote of my hope that the book would serve to fill the gap between wolf myth and wolf reality with facts. I believe the book served its purpose well.

When the executive director of one of the largest wolf organizations in the United States wrote me, stating that he had started volunteering with that organization after reading about it in my book, and he eventually became its executive director. No writer could ask for a greater compliment.

And no writer on wolves could help but feel gratified with the progress that wolf conservation has made in the past decade.

Wolf numbers are rebounding in many areas, and the "howling wilderness" described by 19th-century writers is living up to its name once more.

But that wilderness will never be the way it was, the way my grandfather first saw it when he arrived from Europe at the turn of the 20th century. Since that time, the veneer of wilderness has been systematically peeled back, ploughed up, or paved over. Yes, parks and preserves have been set aside, but they remain scattered islands of hope, a sad mere remnant of what used to be.

It is up to our children and our children's children to continue the fight to preserve wilderness, to recognize the rightful place of predators, and to promote scientifically based wolf conservation initiatives.

We have come a long way in the last decade, and we who have fought for the wolf should be proud of what we have done. We will never return the wolf to all of its historic range, but in the southeastern United States, southern Arizona, the northwestern United States, and parts of Europe, the wolf is back.

I cling desperately to this concept of atonement, of restoring what once was, and of leaving a legacy of what should be in the world of the wild.

It is this legacy of atonement that allows us to move one step closer to Thoreau's dream of achieving "an entire heaven and entire earth."

It is my hope that this new volume will ten years hence have played a tiny role in the fulfillment of that dream.

*—Robert H. Busch*

CHAPTER

1

# THE EVOLUTION OF THE WOLF

THE EVOLUTIONARY HISTORY OF THE WOLF is not totally clear, but many biologists believe that the wolf developed from primitive carnivores known as miacids. Miacids ranged from gopher-sized to dog-sized animals and appeared in the Lower Tertiary about 52 million years ago. Miacids in turn had evolved from Cretaceous insectivores. The direct descendants of miacids today are animals called viverrids, which include the genet of Africa.

Relatively late in the evolutionary history of miacids came the appearance of the first canid. Some authorities believe that canids originated in North America and then spread to Asia and South America, while others ascribe an Asian origin to the group. Still others believe that the dog family originated in North America, migrated to Asia, and then returned.

Wolf ancestors began to develop in the Paleocene, about 60 million years ago. By the Miocene, about 20 million years ago, canines and felines had branched into two separate families. In one ancestor of the wolf, *Tomarctus*, the fifth toe on the hind leg became vestigial and is evidenced today by the dewclaw on both wolves and domestic dogs.

Research by Robert Wayne at the University of California suggests that a number of wolflike canids diverged from a common ancestor about two to three million years ago. The first gray wolf, *Canis lupus*, probably appeared in Eurasia sometime in the early Pleistocene period about a million years ago. Around 750,000 years ago, it is thought to have migrated to North America. The dire wolf, *Canis dirus*, larger and heavier than the gray wolf, evolved earlier and the two coexisted in North America for about 400,000 years.

THE WHITE MAN MUST TREAT THE BEASTS OF THIS LAND AS HIS BROTHERS. WHAT IS MAN WITHOUT THE BEASTS? IF ALL THE BEASTS WERE GONE, MAN WOULD DIE FROM A GREAT LONELINESS OF SPIRIT. FOR WHATEVER HAPPENS TO THE BEASTS, ALSO HAPPENS TO THE MAN.

–Chief Seattle of the Puget Sound Suwamish tribe, 1855

As its prey became extinct around 16,000 years ago due to a climatic change, the dire wolf gradually became extinct itself. Around 7,000 years ago, the gray wolf became the prime canine predator in North America.

It is not known exactly when humans first encountered the gray wolf in North America, but one of the oldest archeological sites that contains both human and wolf remains is the Sandia Cave in Las Huertas Canyon, New Mexico. The wolf bones there have been dated at about 10,000 years old.



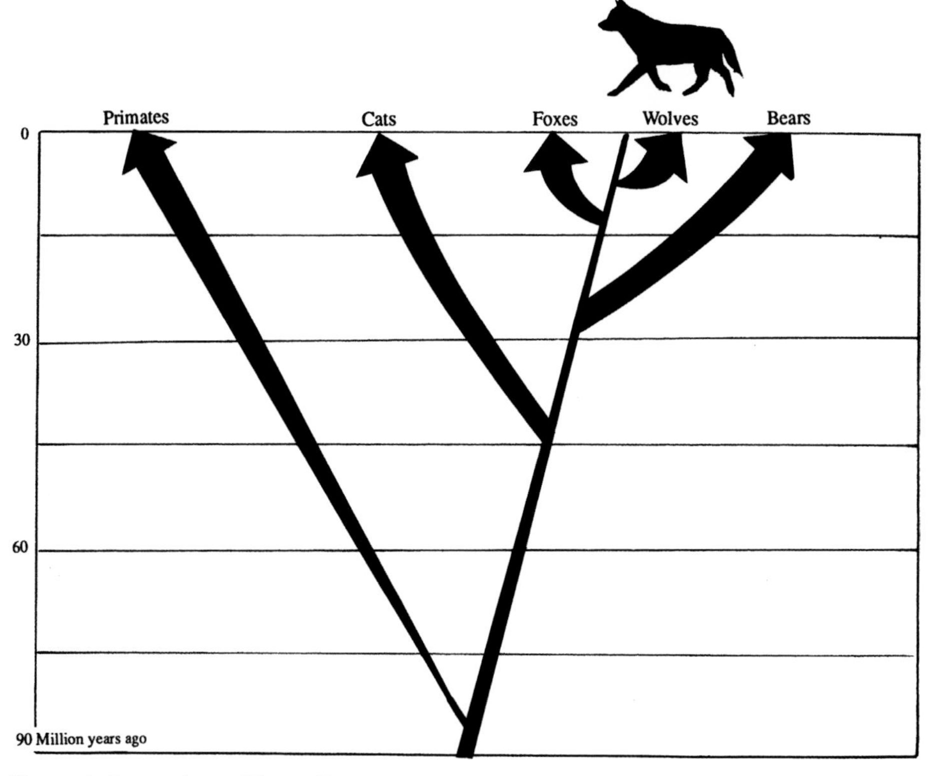


The evolutionary tree of the wolf.

The evolution of the domestic dog is still a matter of much debate. Past genetic research indicates that humans domesticated dogs from wolves in Asia about 14,000 years ago. However, domestic dog remains found in Europe may be 16,000 years old suggesting that wolves may have been domesticated by humans twice, once in Europe and once in Asia. A prevailing hypothesis is that wolves began hanging around human settlements to feed on garbage, and the bolder wolves that were less fearful of humans eventually became dependent on humans for food and were domesticated over time. The scientific name for domestic dogs is *Canis lupus familiaris*, indicating they are a wolf subspecies.

The domestic dog has been reclassified by some taxonomists as *Canis lupus familiaris*, a subspecies of wolf. © Robert H. Busch

In most of North America, the predominant wolf coat color is gray. Julie Lawrence photo, © Wolf Haven International

## Scientific Classification of Wolves

The gray wolf was classified as *Canis lupus* by the Swedish scientist Carl von Linné (also known by the Latin name Carolus Linnaeus) in 1758.

| | |
|---|---|
| Kingdom Animalia | (all animals) |
| Phylum Chordata | (animals with notochords) |
| Subphylum Vertebrata | (animals with a skeleton of bone or cartilage) |
| Class Mammalia | (mammals) |
| Subclass Eutheria | (placental mammals) |
| Order *Carnivora* | (carnivores) |
| Family *Canidae* | (dog family) |
| Genus *Canis* | (dogs) |
| Species *lupus* | (gray wolf) |



### GRAY WOLF TAXONOMY—NORTH AMERICA

The determination of subspecies is a topic much in debate among modern biologists. A subspecies is a group of individuals within a species that share a unique geographic area or habitat, unique physical characteristics, or a unique natural history. For decades, some biologists recognized twenty-four subspecies of gray wolves in North America.

*Canis lupus:*

* *alces* the Kenai Peninsula wolf; one of the largest of North American wolves, extinct by 1925

*arctos* the white wolf of the high Arctic, found from Melville Island to Ellesmere Island

*baileyi* the smallest North American gray wolf, originally found from Mexico to the southwest United States; according to many authorities, indistinguishable from *C.i. mogollonensis*

* *beothucus* the Newfoundland wolf, now extinct; reported as almost pure white

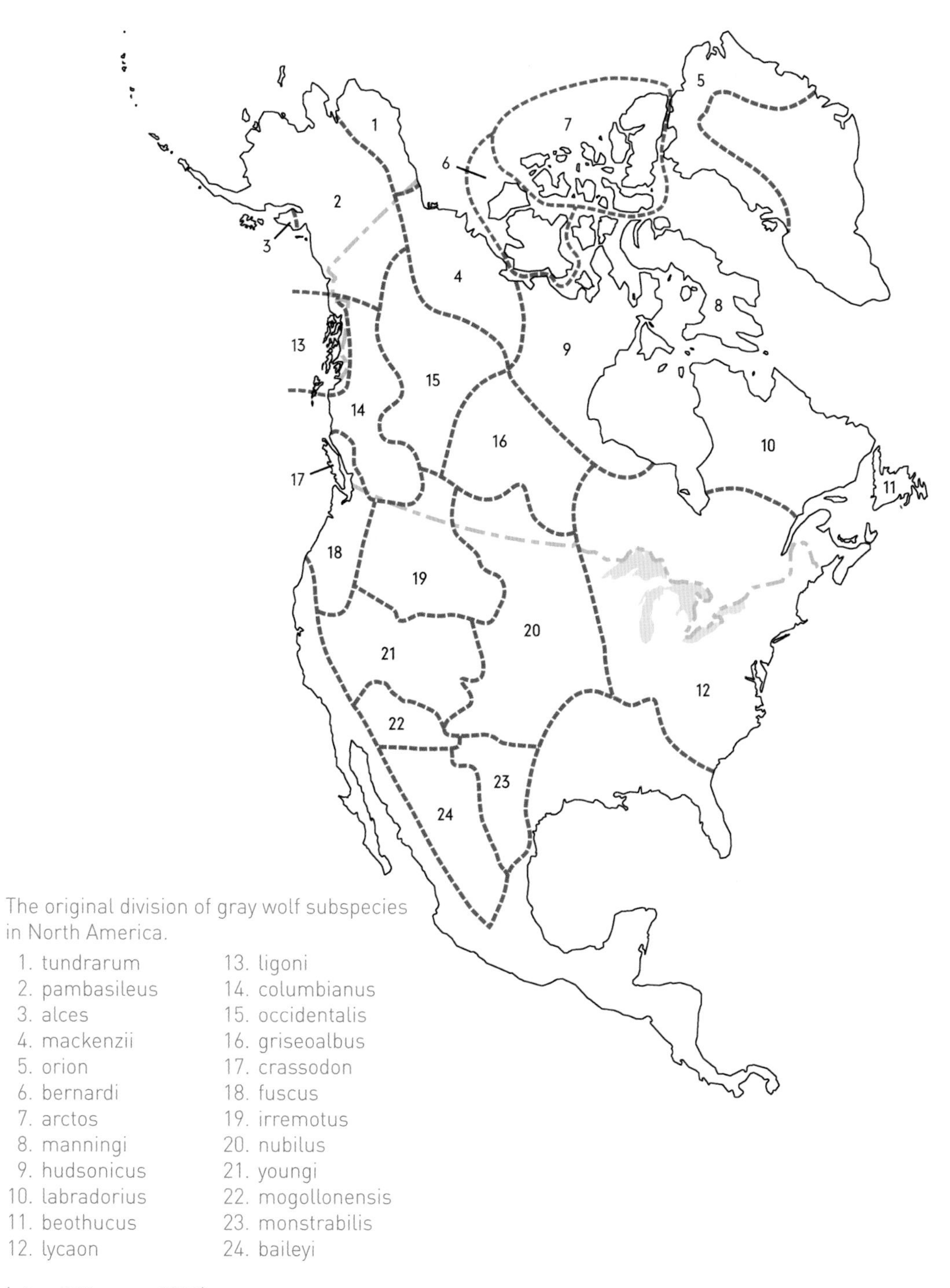


The original division of gray wolf subspecies in North America.

1. tundrarum
2. pambasileus
3. alces
4. mackenzii
5. orion
6. bernardi
7. arctos
8. manningi
9. hudsonicus
10. labradorius
11. beothucus
12. lycaon
13. ligoni
14. columbianus
15. occidentalis
16. griseoalbus
17. crassodon
18. fuscus
19. irremotus
20. nubilus
21. youngi
22. mogollonensis
23. monstrabilis
24. baileyi

(after O'Connor, 1961)

* *bernardi* limited to Banks and Victoria Islands in the Arctic, described as white with black-tipped hair along the spinal ridge; not recognized as a subspecies until 1943; extinct sometime between 1918 and 1952

*columbianus* a large wolf found in the Yukon, British Columbia, and Alberta

*crassodon* a medium-size, grayish wolf found on Vancouver Island

* *fuscus* a brownish-colored wolf from the Cascade Mountains; extinct by 1940

*griseoalbus* a large wolf found in northern Alberta, Saskatchewan, and Manitoba

*hudsonicus* a light-colored wolf found in northern Manitoba and the Northwest Territories

*irremotus* a medium-size, light-colored wolf from the northern Rocky Mountains

*labradorius* the wolf of Labrador and northern Quebec

*ligoni* a small, dark-colored wolf from the Alexander Archipelago in the Arctic islands

*lycaon* the eastern timber wolf of Canada and the United States; it originally had the largest range of all the North American subspecies; the first subspecies to be recognized in North America (1775)

*mackenzii* the Northwest Territories wolf; not recognized as a subspecies until 1943

*manningi* the smallest arctic wolf, found on Baffin Island; either white or light colored; not recognized as a subspecies until 1943

* *mogollonensis* a medium-size wolf found in Arizona and New Mexico; extinct by 1935

* *monstrabilis* a wolf found in Texas and New Mexico; extinct by 1942

*nubilus* the Great Plains or "buffalo" wolf; extinct by 1926; usually light in color

*occidentalis* a large wolf from western Canada, also called the Mackenzie Valley wolf

*orion* a white or very light-colored wolf from Greenland

*pambasileus* a dark-colored wolf from Alaska and the Yukon

*tundrarum* the Arctic tundra wolf; light in color

*youngi* the southern Rocky Mountain wolf; extinct by 1935; light buff color

*indicates an extinct subspecies.

OTHER ANIMALS NAMED AFTER WOLVES INCLUDE THE WOLF EEL, WOLF FISH, WOLF SPIDER, WOLF SNAKE, WOLF MOTH, AND WOLF WASP. THE HAIDA INDIANS CALL THE KILLER WHALE THE SEA WOLF.



The above list is still useful to give an idea of the characteristics of wolves in the different parts of their range, as well as to provide information on time of extinction of some of the populations. However, for the last few decades, as more specimens have been examined and as a better understanding of wolf genetics and behavior has been gained, zoologists have tended to recognize fewer populations as being subspecifically or racially distinct. At the 1992 North American Symposium on Wolves, based largely on statistical analysis of skulls, taxonomist Ron Nowak suggested that North American *Canis lupus* be reclassified into the following five groups:

1. *occidentalis* of most Alaska and western Canada (including *alces, columbianus, griseoalbus, mackenzii, occidentalis, pambasileus, tundrarum*)
2. *nubilus* of most of the western United States, southeastern Alaska, and central and northeastern Canada (including *beothucus, crassodon, fuscus, hudsonicus, irremotus, labradorius, lycaon* of Minnesota, *ligoni, manningi, mogollonensis, monstrabilis, youngi*)
3. *lycaon* of southeastern Canada and the northeastern United States
4. *arctos* of most of the Canadian Arctic islands and Greenland (including *arctos, bernardi, orion*)
5. *baileyi* of Mexico and the extreme southwestern United States

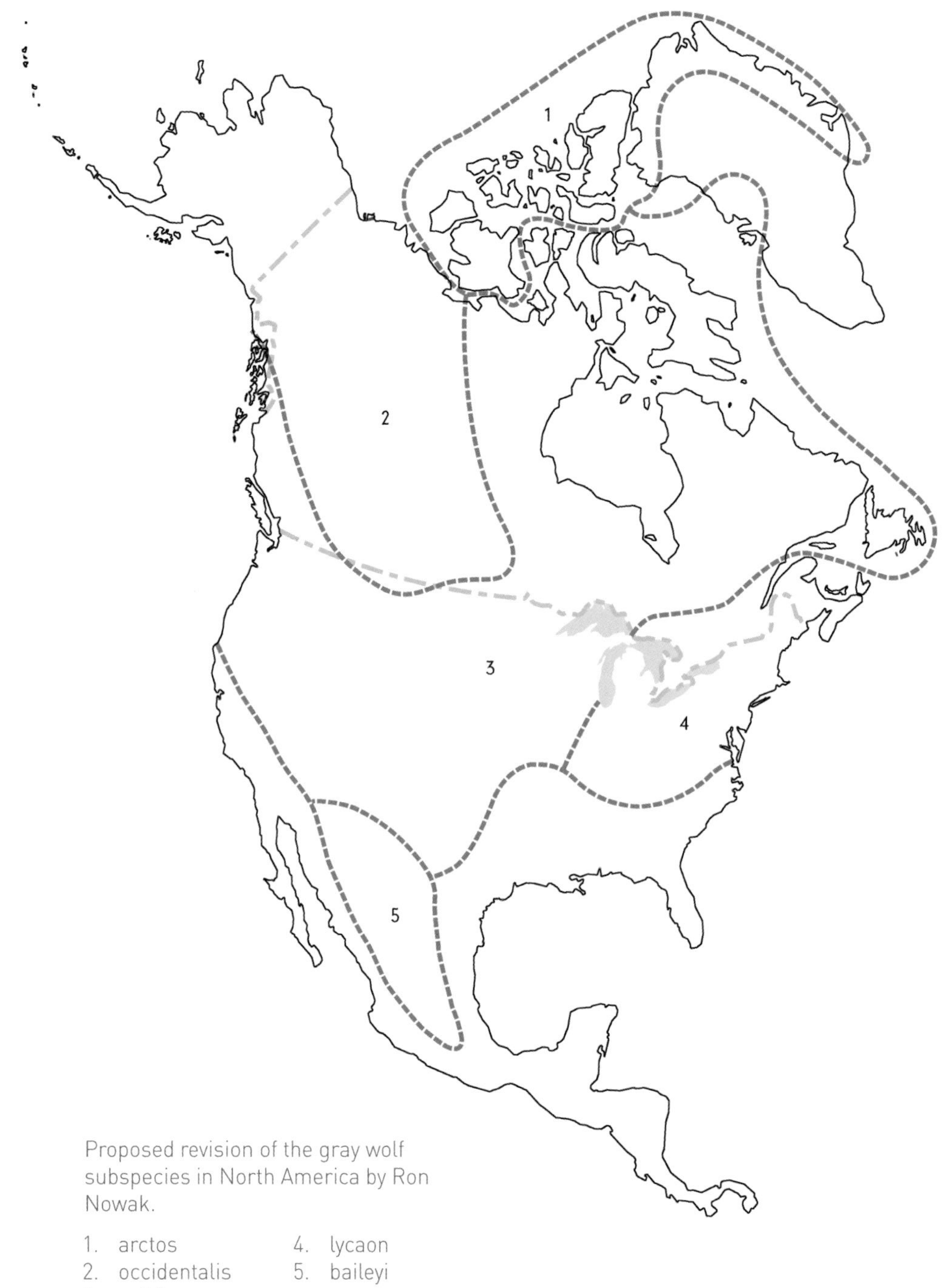


Proposed revision of the gray wolf subspecies in North America by Ron Nowak.

1. arctos
2. occidentalis
3. nubilus
4. lycaon
5. baileyi

(after Carbyn et al.)

Mexican wolves once ranged over northern Mexico and the southern portions of Arizona, New Mexico, and Texas, but were extinct in the wild by the late 1980s. Julie Lawrence photo, © Wolf Haven International



## GRAY WOLF TAXONOMY—EURASIA

In Eurasia, over a dozen subspecies of wolf have been recognized, most of which survive today.

*albus* a large, light-colored wolf from the northern Russian Federation and northern Finland

*arabs* a small, buff-colored wolf from the Arabian Peninsula; not recognized as a subspecies until 1934

*campestris* the central Asian wolf, or steppe wolf

*chanco* (= *laniger*) the wolf of Mongolia and China

*communus* – a gray wolf subspecies with a range in northern Russia

*cubanensis* found between the Caspian Sea and the Black Sea; not recognized by some taxonomists

* *deitanus* a small wolf once found in Spain, now extinct; not recognized as a subspecies by some authorities

Gray wolf subspecies of Eurasia.

1. albus
2. lupus
3. campestris
4. hattai
5. hodophilax
6. laniger/chanco
7. pallipes
8. arabs
9. cubanensis
10. desertorum
11. signatus
12. italicus
13. communis

(after Mech, 1970, IWC 2013)

*desertorum* (= *palies*) Asian desert wolf, found in the arid areas east of the Black Sea; not recognized by some taxonomists

* *hattai* (= *rex*) a wolf once found in Hokkaido, Japan; probably now extinct, although some taxonomists believe that it still survives on Sakhalin Island

*_hodophilax_ a wolf once found in Honshu, Japan; extinct by 1935; much smaller than _C.l. hattai_

_Italicus_ – a subspecies native to the Italian Peninsula, this subspecies has been rebounding after years of population decline

_laniger_ (see _chanco_)

_lupus_ the most common species throughout Eurasia, and the first named of all wolf subspecies, designated by Linnaeus in 1758

*_minor_ a wolf once found in Hungary and Austria; extinct by the early 1900s

_palies_ (see _desertorum_)

_pallipes_ a small wolf of India and southern Asia; synonymous with _arabs_, according to some taxonomists

_rex_ (see _hattai_)

_signatus_ the Iberian wolf of Spain and Portugal

*indicates an extinct subspecies

The distinctive reddish hue of a red wolf's coat is evident in this photo of a captive red wolf. Julie Lawrence photo, © Wolf Haven International

**FALSE WOLVES**

A NUMBER OF OTHER ANIMALS COMMONLY REFERRED TO AS WOLVES ARE NOT TRUE WOLVES. BRUSH WOLF, PRAIRIE WOLF, MEDICINE WOLF, AND LITTLE WOLF ARE ALL COMMON NAMES FOR THE COYOTE (*CANIS LATRANS*). THE AARDWOLF (*PROTELES CRISTATUS*), MANED WOLF (*CHYSOCYON BRACHYURUS*), TASMANIAN WOLF (*THYLACINUS CYNOCEPHALUS*), AND ANDEAN WOLF (*DASYCYON HAGENBECKI*) ARE ALL FALSELY LABELED AS WOLVES.



Nowak has suggested that the subspecies *campestris*, *chanco*, and *desertorum* are synonymous with *lupus*, and distinguished a new subspecies *communis* for a race of large wolves found in the central northern Russian Federation.

Two other canids are classified as separate wolf species:

*Canis rufus*, the red wolf, is a small canid that formerly inhabited the southeast corner of the United States. Some biologists believe that it is not a true species but a hybrid caused by the interbreeding of coyotes and gray wolves. Others assign it true species status, and believe that it may represent the descendant of a primitive wolf that was forced into the southeast corner of the continent by the larger gray wolf. Still others theorize that the red wolf is the descendant of a Pleistocene wolf isolated by glaciation that no longer exists elsewhere.

A genetic study by Robert Wayne of the University of California Los Angeles, published in 2016, found that there is only one species of gray wolf in North America and eastern timber wolves and red wolves are essentially gray wolf–coyote hybrids. In Ontario, these are called Algonquin wolves. However, not all wolf researchers agree with this finding, and it will probably be debated in scientific circles for some time.

The exact status is a crucial one politically, for if the red wolf is not a separate species, it would not qualify for legal protection under the Endangered Species Act, which makes no provision for hybrid animals. In fact, after a study that suggested a hybrid origin was released in 1992, ranchers in Texas and North Carolina tried to have the red wolf removed from the endangered species list. The most prevalent view today is that the red wolf is a discrete species, but that a large degree of interbreeding with coyotes created a "hybrid swarm" that moved slowly eastward, reducing the genetic purity of the species. This might also hold true for eastern wolves, *Canis lupus lycaon*, which has been proposed by some scientists as a distinct species of wolf.

The red wolf is a small canid that was extinct in the wild by 1980.
Julie Lawrence Photo, © Wolf Haven International

Three subspecies of red wolves are usually recognized: *Canis rufus floridanus* (extinct by 1930), *Canis rufus rufus* (extinct by 1970), and *Canis rufus gregoryi* (extinct in the wild by 1980).

All red wolves today are the progeny of 14 "pure" red wolves taken into captivity and bred in a bid to save the species (see chapter 11, "Wolf Reintroduction Programs").

The Ethiopian wolf is the rarest canid in the world. (M Harvey/ABPL)

*Canis simensis*, the Ethiopian wolf, is another debated species that inhabits the highlands of Ethiopia. The plethora of alternate names for the animal reflects its questionable taxonomy: Abyssinian jackal, simien jackal, red jackal, simien fox, Abyssinian wolf, Ethiopian wolf. A recent genetic study found them to be more closely related to gray wolves than to golden jackals.

Although the Canid Specialist Group of the International Union for the Conservation of Nature and Natural Resources (IUCN) has reclassified it as a new species of wolf, its behavior and ecology cause some behavioral biologists to question the classification.

The Ethiopian wolf preys almost exclusively on rodents, which is unique among wolves. Its reddish hide is splotched with white patches on the throat, neck, and chest. It rarely weighs over 40 pounds.

The total population has been reduced to only about 450 individuals, about half of which live in Bale National Park in southern Ethiopia. Much of the park lies above the 13,000-foot level, representing part of the largest alpine habitat on the entire continent of Africa.

One of the main threats to the species' survival is overgrazing by local farmers, which destroys the vegetation necessary to sustain a healthy rodent population. Other threats to the survival of the Ethiopian wolf include loss of habitat, hybridization with domestic dogs, and diseases spread by dogs.

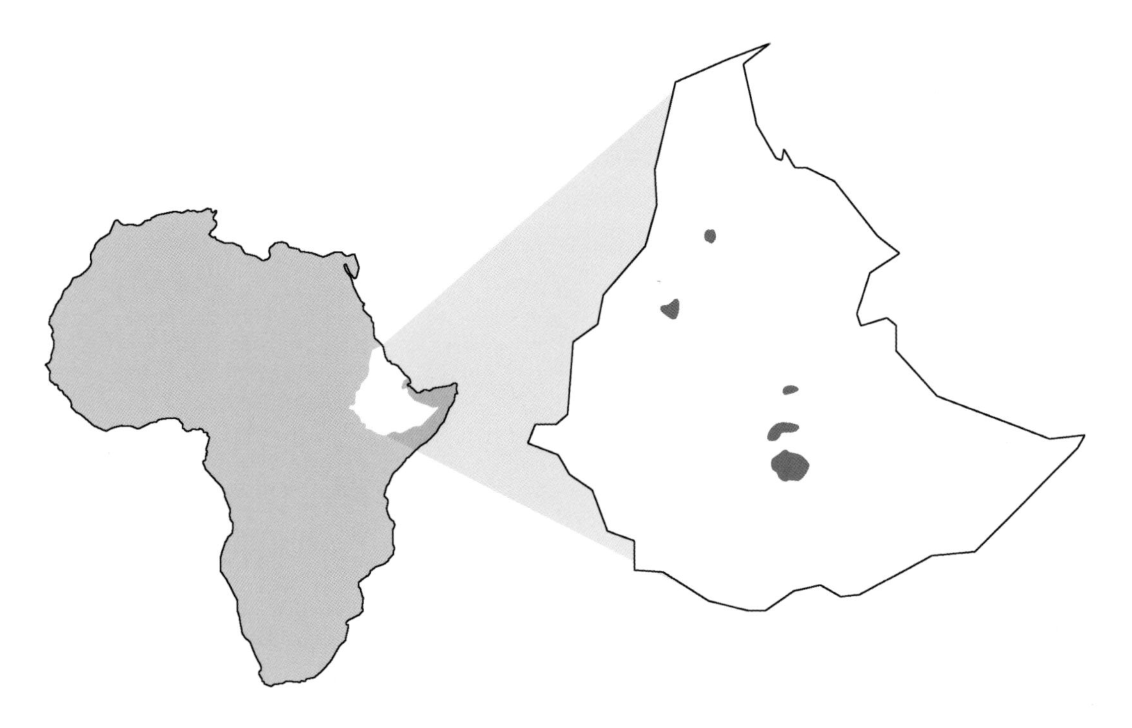

Current range of the Ethiopian wolf. (after Ginsberg and Macdonald, 1990)

To aid in the preservation of this species, Wildlife Conservation International has underwritten a project since 1988 headed by Argentinean biologists Dada Gottelli and Claudio Sillero-Zubiri. Although captive breeding was described as essential to the survival of the Ethiopian wolf in 1990, no breeding efforts have yet begun as they have been opposed by the Ethiopian government. As Gottelli and Sillero-Zubiri have noted, "socio-political issues of greater short-term importance in Ethiopia have prevented the conservation of wildlife from making steady progress."

CHAPTER

2

# THE DISTRIBUTION OF WOLVES

## Range and Habitat

IN *THE WAY OF THE WOLF,* eminent wolf biologist L. David Mech described the wolf as originally "the most widely distributed mammal in the world."

Historically, the wolf once occupied a Holarctic distribution across North America, Europe, and Asia. Its habitats included the high Arctic, tundra, taiga, forests, plains, deserts, and virtually every ecological niche that provided sufficient food for its existence. Tropical jungles appear to be the only ecological niche not inhabited by wolves.

Black wolves are less common in the southern parts of their range. Julie Lawrence photo, © Wolf Haven International

The northernmost limit of wolf habitat is currently Cape Morris Jessup in Greenland, at 83°30' N. The southernmost limit is in Ethiopia at 5° N.

Although biologically the wolf does not require pure wilderness, in practical terms only wilderness provides the absence of human interference that will ensure its survival today.

Paul Paquet, a Canadian wolf biologist with the Southern Rockies Canine Project describes surviving wolf populations as a barometer of wildness: "If you see wolves there, that wilderness is intact."

A large Canadian female wolf; wolves in the northern reaches of their territories tend to be larger than their southern counterparts. Photo courtesy of Scott Ian Barry

Currently, the majority of wolves inhabit the most forested, rugged, and remote regions of the Northern Hemisphere, pushed there by the spread of their most deadly enemy, man.

## NORTH AMERICA

In North America, the wolf once ranged from the Arctic islands beyond the far northern tip of the continent to central Mexico. In 1754, explorer Anthony Henday reported seeing "wolves without numbers" along his epic trek from Hudson Bay west through the Canadian prairies. Along the western coast of the continent, the wolf never penetrated west of the Sierra Nevada range into California and never existed in Baja, California.

It populated Vancouver Island, but was never present on the Queen Charlotte Islands nor on Kodiak Island farther north. On the east coast, the wolf was once present on the island of Newfoundland, but never reached Anticosti Island or Prince Edward Island. In the southeasternmost corner of the United States, the red wolf occupied the greater part of the territory, having very little overlap with that of the gray wolf.

Today, the wolf has been exterminated from 95 percent of its range in the United States and from 15 percent of its range in Canada. A small number have been reintroduced into parts of Mexico where they were formerly extinct. Within the United States, the largest concentration of wolves

Wolves were reintroduced to the central Idaho wilderness In 1995 and 1996. © Jim Yuskavitch

Forest and meadows make up typical wolf habitat in the Northern Rockies. © Jim Yuskavitch

survives in Alaska. However, since the reintroduction of wolves by the federal government to central Idaho and Yellowstone National Park in 1995, they have reestablished themselves in former habitat in the northern Rocky Mountains and have dispersed and established packs in Washington State, Oregon, and California. Wolf populations in the Upper Midwest have also increased their populations.

The northern portions of Canada still support a large number of wolves.



### THE GRAY WOLF IN NORTH AMERICA

| UNITED STATES | Current gray wolf population (in the wild) | | Percentage of historical range occupied |
|---|---|---|---|
| Alaska | 7,000–11,000 | stable-increasing | 95% |
| Idaho | 786 | stable | 30 |
| Michigan | 618 | stable | 15 |
| Minnesota | 2,278 | stable | 30 |
| Montana | 700 | stable | 30 |
| Washington | 115 | increasing | 5 |
| Wisconsin | 866 | increasing | 15 |
| Wyoming | 382 | increasing | 15 |
| Oregon | 112 | increasing | 5 |
| **CANADA** | | | |
| Alberta | 7,000 | increasing | 80 |
| British Columbia | 8,000 | increasing | 80 |
| Labrador | 1,000–1,500 | stable | 95 |
| Manitoba | 4,000–6,000 | stable | 70 |
| Northwest Territories | 4,000 | stable | 95 |
| Ontario | 9,600 | stable | 80 |
| Quebec | 7,000 | unknown | 80 |
| Saskatchewan | 3,000 | stable | 70 |
| Yukon | 4,500–5,000 | stable | 80 |
| Nunavut | 5,000–6,000 | stable | 80 |

(updated 2006 from Ginsberg and Macdonald, 1990, Updated 2017 US and Canadian Federal and State Wildlife Agencies)

THE WHOLE CONTINENT WAS ONE CONTINUED DISMAL WILDERNESS, THE HAUNT OF WOLVES.

—John Adams, 1756

Current range of the gray wolf in North America.

## EURASIA

In Eurasia, the wolf once occupied almost all of the continent north of the 20th degree of latitude. It never populated Iceland, but did survive on the coastal regions of Greenland.

While they are still extinct in England, Ireland, Scotland, Wales, and the Netherlands, wolves have been making a remarkable comeback in much of western and eastern Europe over the past decade.

The largest concentration of Eurasian wolves remains in Russia, where it is widely hunted and persecuted. The historic southeast Asian distribution was never clearly delineated, but reports today indicate that the wolf is now populating portions of China and spreading south.



### THE GRAY WOLF IN EUROPE AND ASIA

| | Current gray wolf population (in the wild) | Percentage of historical range occupied |
|---|---|---|
| Afghanistan | 1,000 | 90% |
| Albania | 250 | 50% |
| Saudi Arabia | 300–6,500 | 70 |
| Bangladesh | unknown | unknown |
| Bhutan | unknown | unknown |
| Bulgaria | 1,000 | 40 |
| China | 12,000 | 20 |
| Czech Republic | 20 | 5 |
| Egypt/Sinai | unknown | unknown |
| Ethiopia | 420 | unknown |
| Finland | 150–180 | 20 |
| France | 250–300 | 5 |
| Germany | 150 | 5 |
| Greece | 300–600 | 50 |
| Greenland | 50 | 60 |
| Hungary | 50 | 5 |
| India | 1,200 | 20 |
| Iran | 3,000 | 80 |
| Iraq | unknown | unknown |
| Israel | 150 | 60 |

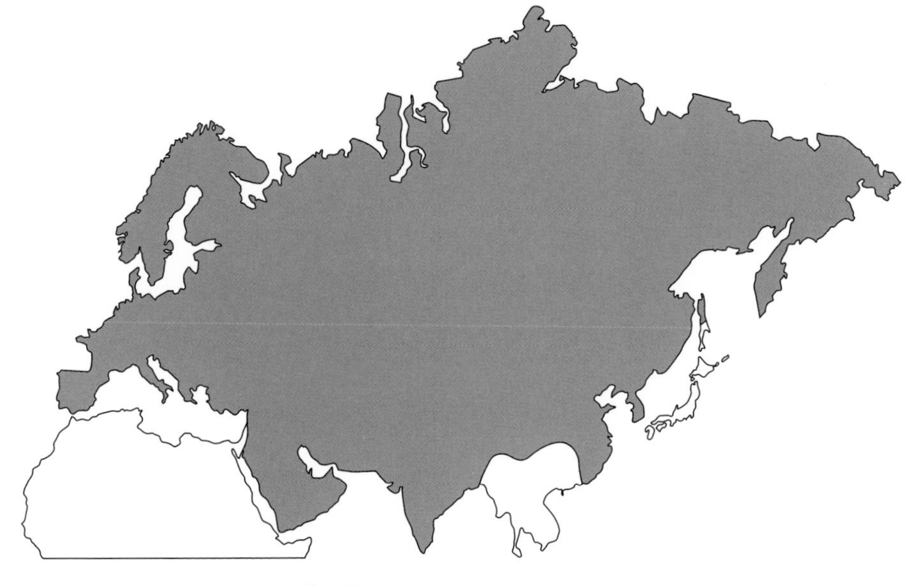

Current range of the gray wolf in Eurasia.

| | Current gray wolf population (in the wild) | Percentage of historical range occupied |
|---|---|---|
| Italy | 1,000 | 25 |
| Jordan | 200 | 90 |
| Lebanon | 10 | unknown |
| Mongolia | 10,000–20,000 | 100 |
| Nepal | unknown | unknown |
| Norway | 38 | 5 |
| Pakistan | 200 | 10 |
| Poland | 950 | 3,090 |
| Portugal | 200–300 | 20 |
| Romania | 2,000 | 80 |
| Slovak Republic | 350–400 | 50 |
| Spain | 1,500–2,000 | 15 |
| Sweden | 342 | 20 |
| Switzerland | 30–35 | 60 |
| Syria | 200 | 10 |
| Turkey | 7,000 | 75 |
| Russia | 50,000 | 75 |
| Slovenia-Croatia-Bosnia-Herzegovina | 700 | 90 |

(Updated from International Wolf Center 2013)

CHAPTER

3

# ANATOMY AND PHYSIOLOGY

## Physical Description

THE GRAY WOLF IS THE LARGEST member of the canid family. The adult male gray wolf stands 26 to 38 inches high at the shoulder and has a head-and-body length of 40 to 58 inches. The tail is 13 to 20 inches long. Males are 15 percent to 20 percent larger than females.

The weight of North American wolves varies between 40 and 175 pounds, with average weights in the 60- to 100-pound range. The coyote, with which the wolf is often confused, is much smaller, at only 20 to 30 pounds.

Despite legends of 200-pound wolves, the heaviest wild wolf weighed only 175 pounds. Photo courtesy of Scott Ian Barry

Despite the many trappers' legends of 200-pound wolves, the heaviest wolf on record in the United States weighed 175 pounds and was shot near 70 Mile River in east-central Alaska in 1939. The heaviest Canadian wolf weighed 172 pounds and was shot in Jasper National Park by a park warden in 1945. The heaviest recent wolf on record is a 122-pound male captured for radio-collaring in Montana in 1994. In January 2007, a 176-pound wolf was reported shot in Bulgaria, but the weight was not confirmed by biologists.

Of 169 nuisance wolves (those causing damage to human property or livestock) killed in Alberta between 1972 and 1979, the average wolf weighed 99 pounds.

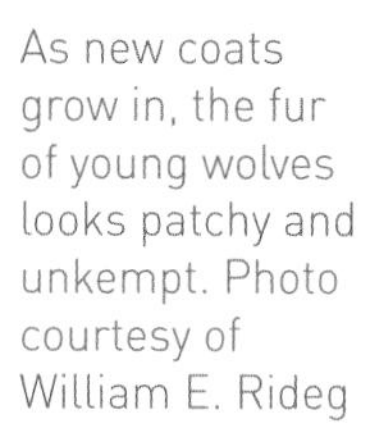

As new coats grow in, the fur of young wolves looks patchy and unkempt. Photo courtesy of William E. Rideg

The average weight of 28 wolves killed in the 1970s in Mexico was only 70 pounds. The little red wolf of the southeastern United States rarely exceeds 65 pounds. Few statistical studies of wolves have been carried out in Europe, but in one study of 25 wolves in Bosnia-Herzegovina, the average weight for

Wolves are perfectly adapted to surviving in deep snow and bitter cold. Photo courtesy of Oregon Department of Fish and Wildlife

male wolves was 95 pounds. The wolves of Saudi Arabia, Israel, and India often weigh only 40 pounds.

Generally, the wolf looks like a large dog with extra long legs and oversized feet. One significant anatomical difference is the presence of a precaudal gland on the upper surface of a wolf's tail, a feature absent in all domestic dogs. The exact function of this gland is a mystery.

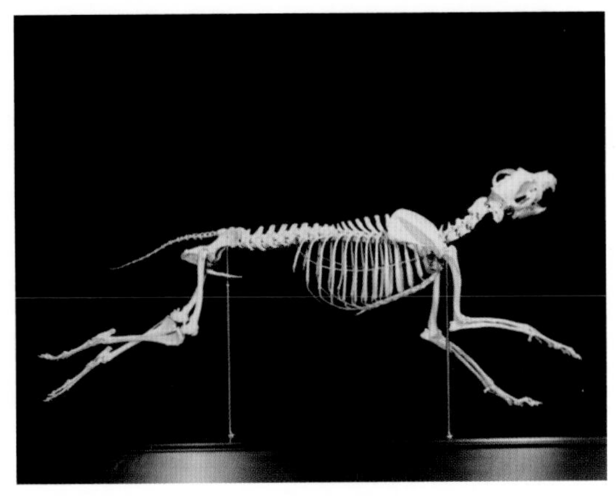

Wolf skeleton. (Neg. no. 318730, courtesy Department Library Services, American Museum of Natural History)



The gray wolf has a broad face, which often appears larger due to the ruff of fur below the ears. Its eyes are usually a golden yellow color, and shine greenish orange at night. (The Bella Coola Indians of coastal British Columbia believed that the gods once attempted to change all animals into men, but succeed in making only the eyes of the wolf human.) Its ears are about 2 inches long, and its black nose can be 1.5 inches wide.

A wolf's body is built for travel. Its chest is narrow, allowing it to push more easily through deep winter snows.

THE BRAINS OF A WOLF DO DECREASE AND INCREASE WITH THE MOON.

—Edward Topsell, *A Historie of Foure-Footed Beastes*, 16th century

The coat is thick and fluffy, especially in the northern regions. It is composed of long guard hairs that repel moisture and a thick wooly undercoat for insulation. Across the shoulders of many wolves, the long guard hairs may grow to four or five inches in length. Thick winter coats are grown in the fall, which according to R. D. Lawrence, writing in *In Praise of Wolves*, "add about a third to their bulk." The bulky winter coats are slowly shed in the spring, and females tend to lose their coats more slowly than males.

Most wolves in North America are a grizzled gray color. © Robert H. Busch

Wolves in the southern portions of North America and Eurasia tend to have thinner coats than their northern cousins. Both the red wolf and the Ethiopian wolf have very short, sparse coats.

In one Alaskan study, 32 percent of the wolves were black. Photo courtesy of Scott Ian Barry

Wolves are built for long-distance travel in all kinds of terrain and weather. Photo courtesy of Dan Stahler/National Park Service

## COLOR

Wolves range from all shades of gray, tan, and brown to pure white or solid black. In 1944, Stanley Young wrote, "The color of North American wolves . . . varies greatly, so much so that it is relatively unimportant for scientific description of the animals." Both the red wolf and the Ethiopian wolf have reddish coats. (Hybridization with domestic dogs has added yellowish hues and mottled white patches to the coat of today's Ethiopian wolf.)

*Arctic Evening-White Wolf* by Robert Bateman, 1978 (© 1978 Boshkung, Inc. Reproduction rights courtesy of Boshkung, Inc., and Mill Pond Press, Inc.)

Wolves with very light-colored coats are often found in the Canadian Arctic. © Monty Sloan

Some wolves have a saddle-shaped patch of color on their back that contrasts with the rest of their coat. Others have splotches of dark markings on their faces. (The Koyukon Indians believe that these were produced in the Distant Time, when Raven tricked a wolf by throwing caribou guts in its face.) The tip of a wolf's tail is often colored black. Most wolves tend to be a grizzled gray-brown color, and it is not unusual to have a variation of

Although most wolves are gray, black-phase wolves are not uncommon. Photo courtesy of Oregon Department of Fish and Wildlife

colors within a litter. One litter born at St. Paul's Como Zoo in Minnesota had five reddish male pups and one gray female. Variations in color within a pack are also common. L. David Mech has reported seeing "a pack with three gray wolves, one black, and one white."

In Alberta, of 498 nuisance wolves captured between 1972 and 1979, 68 percent were gray, 31 percent were black, and 1 percent was white. Similar statistics have been reported from northern British Columbia, where 33 percent of the 481 wolves in one study were black, and from the Kenai region of Alaska, where 32 percent of 254 wolves studied were black. Black wolves are less common in the southern parts of their range. Of 136 wolves killed in Yellowstone National Park between 1914 and 1926, only one was black, one was white, and the rest were gray.

Many of the wolves in Canada's high Arctic are a creamy white color. White hair shafts have more air pockets than coloration pigment and therefore provide better insulation. The explorer Samuel Hearne reported in his chronicles published in 1785 that "the greatest part of those that are killed by the Esquimaux are perfectly white." Today, white wolves have been reported as far south as Minnesota, but in the past they appear to have been quite common in the plains. The Lewis and Clark expedition reported large numbers of almost white wolves on the plains in the 1800s. James O. Pattie confirmed this in his *Pattie's Personal Narrative, 1824–1830,* observing that most of the plains wolves were "large and white as sheep." Painter George Catlin wrote in 1841 of his travels across the American plains "where the wolves are white."

The eerie sight of a pure black wolf, his golden eyes glowing like hot embers. Photo courtesy of William E. Rideg

It is not unusual to see a wide range of coat colors within one wolf pack. Photo courtesy of William E. Rideg

### DESCRIPTIVE SUMMARY AND COMPARISON

| | Wolf | Coyote |
|---|---|---|
| General build | large | medium-sized |
| Legs | very long legged | legs of normal length |
| Height | 26–38" | 23–26" |
| Weight | 40–175 lbs. | 20–40 lbs. |
| Color | gray, tan, brown<br>black relatively common<br>white uncommon | gray, tan, brown<br>black very rare<br>white very rare |
| Muzzle | squared | pointed |
| Ears | rounded<br>relatively short | pointed<br>relatively long |
| Feet | very large | normal size |

There appear to be no documented cases of true albino wolves, although Barry Lopez in *Of Wolves and Men* reported one anecdotal instance of a white wolf with pink eyes shot by an aerial hunter in Alaska in 1957.

## TEETH

The wolf has extremely strong jaws. According to Barry Lopez *in Of Wolves and Men,* the jaws of a wolf have a "crushing pressure of perhaps 1,500 $lbs/in^2$ compared to 750 $lbs/in^2$ for a German shepherd." The upper jaw is equipped with six incisors, two canine teeth, eight premolars, and four molars. The lower jaw has six incisors, two canines, eight premolars, and six molars. The dental formula for animals is expressed in the following ratio:

upper teeth, each side: incisors-canines-premolars-molars

lower teeth, each side: incisors-canines-premolars-molars

Wolves thus have a dental formula of $\frac{3\text{-}1\text{-}4\text{-}2}{3\text{-}1\text{-}4\text{-}3}$ for a total of 42 teeth,

compared with the human formula of $\frac{2\text{-}1\text{-}2\text{-}3}{2\text{-}1\text{-}2\text{-}3}$, which adds up to 32 teeth.

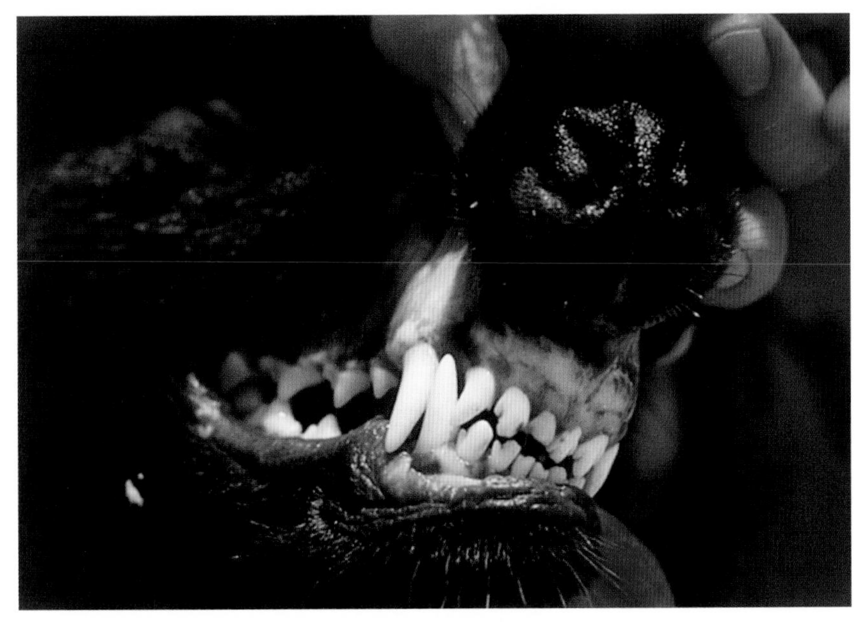

The impressive dentition of an adult wolf. © Robert H. Busch

The incisors at the front of the jaw are used to cut flesh from prey. The long canines, which may reach two inches in length, pierce into flesh to hold prey. Premolars and molars are slicing and grinding teeth. The carnassial teeth, the last premolars in the upper jaw and the first molars in the lower jaw are especially designed to slice and shear flesh. The last molars are used to grind and pulverize food prior to digestion.

Wolves have a total of forty-two teeth, ten more than humans. © Monty Sloan

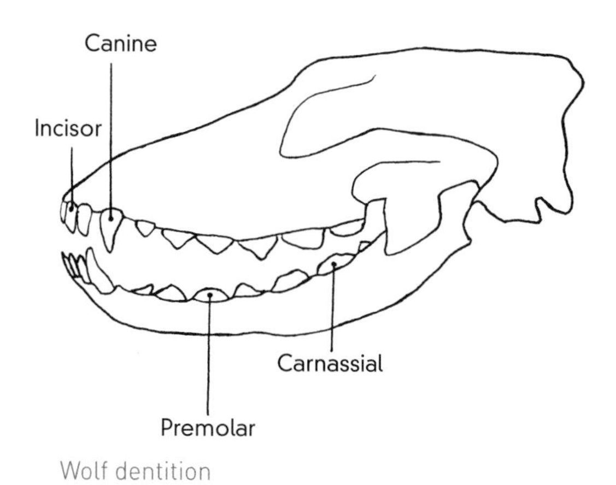

Wolf dentition



Stanley Young wrote that "a wolf can snap off the tail of a yearling, a full-grown cow, or steer with the cleanness of cut as that of a scythe on maturing hay." In fact, tailless adult bison have been seen in Alberta's Wood Buffalo National Park, which supports this statement.

## Wolf Senses

Zoologist Bernhard Grzimek, of the Justus Liebig University of Giessen, Germany, once stated that the wolf possesses sharper vision, hearing, and smell than the domestic dog. Most wolf biologists agree that the most acute of these senses is that of smell.

### SMELL

Grzimek once performed an experiment with covered trays of food to test the relative senses of smell in wolves and domestic dogs. He found that his

The wolf's keen sense of smell allows it to track many types of game. © Robert H. Busch

A wolf's sense of smell may be a hundred times more acute than a human's. Photo courtesy of William E. Rideg



test wolves required five minutes to determine which tray contained food, whereas the dogs in his experiment took an hour to do so.

The surface area receptive to smell in the wolf nose is 14 times that of a human nose, although the degree of sensitivity to smell is not directly correlative to surface area. In *The Wolf: The Ecology and Behavior of an Endangered Species*, L. David Mech wrote, "Researchers estimate that this ability is up to one hundred times more sensitive than that of man."

Many examples of the wolf's excellent sense of smell exist in the voluminous wolf literature.

- Roger Peters, writing in *Dance of the Wolves,* described a wolf's ability to detect a long-dead chipmunk, and found that it "must have been able to smell it ten yards away, buried under almost a yard of snow."
- David E. Brown, in *The Wolf in the Southwest: The Making of an Endangered Species,* wrote about trapper Roy T. McBride's efforts to trap wolves near Sonora, Mexico, using urine and scats from a captive wolf as bait. A full five months after the baited traps were removed, a wolf began visiting the area. "This wolf had visited three of the old trap sites and apparently had smelled the bait even though wind, rain, and sun had ample time to erase the scent."
- R. D. Lawrence, in *Wolves,* wrote that a "five-month old [wolf pup] was able to pick up the smell of a porcupine eating grass in a meadow a mile from the cub."
- L. David Mech reported in *The Wolf: The Ecology and Behavior of an Endangered Species* that a cow moose with twin calves was scented by wolves over four miles away.



## HEARING

Next to smell, the sense of hearing is the most acute of the wolf senses. In fact, one Russian biologist believed that it is the most highly developed

Wolves may be able to hear as far as ten miles away in open tundra. © Monty Sloan

Next to smell, the sense of hearing is the most important sense to a wolf. Photo courtesy of California Wolf Center



wolf sense. A wolf's hearing certainly ranges beyond that of human ears. Barry Lopez in *Of Wolves and Men*, states that "wolves can hear well up to a frequency of 25 kHz." Some researchers believe that the actual maximum frequency detected by wolves is much higher, perhaps even up to 80 kHz (the upper auditory limit for humans is only 20 kHz).

According to Canadian naturalists Miller and Margaret Stewart, "a dog's hearing is about sixteen times as good as ours." Wolves' hearing is even more acute than that. In "Meet the Wolf," a 1991 article in *Defenders* magazine, L. David Mech stated that "wolves can hear as far as six miles away in the forest and ten miles away on the open tundra." And in R. D. Lawrence's *Trail of the Wolf*, he notes that wolves have been known to respond to human imitations of wolf howls from three miles away.

## SIGHT

Compared with smell and hearing, the sense of sight in wolves is relatively poorly developed. Both aerial and ground observations of wolves have, however, shown that their sight is at least as acute as that of humans.

> THE GAZE OF THE WOLF REACHES INTO OUR SOULS.
>
> —Barry Lopez, *Of Wolves and Men*, 1978

Naturalist R. D. Lawrence believes that wolves are quite nearsighted, and has stated in *In Praise of Wolves* that "they can see details clearly up to a distance of about 75 feet."

The eyes of wolves lack a foveal pit, a depression at the back of the eyeball that allows for sharp focusing at great distances. In *Secret Go the Wolves*, Lawrence wrote: "I have actually seen a groundhog sitting still as a statue outside its burrow only 100 yards away while the wolves walked right past it." He believes that wolves are unable to distinguish packmates beyond about 100 to 150 feet.

On the other hand, a wolf's peripheral vision and ability to detect moving objects is excellent. The outer perimeter of a wolf's retina is extremely sensitive to movement, a decided advantage in any nocturnal predator.

The piercing alert gaze of an adult wolf. Julie Lawrence photo, © Wolf Haven International

A wolf's night vision is far superior to a man's. A high proportion of rods to cones in the retina is one measurement of strong night vision; canines have almost 95 percent rods.

Although canid behaviorist Michael W. Fox believes that a wolf's ability to perceive colors is inferior to that of humans, very little research has been performed in this area. Biologists at the University of California at Santa Barbara have performed extensive experiments on domestic dogs and have determined that they lack full color vision. Their experiments showed that dogs could distinguish red from blue but were unable to distinguish yellow from green or orange from red. They found that there were photo receptors for only blue and red in dog retinas, as opposed to receptors for blue, red, and green in humans, making domestic dogs, in human terms, partially color blind.

Few such tests have been given to wolves. Cheryl Asa has found that when red, green, blue, and yellow dyes were placed on a base of clean snow in a captive wolf enclosure, the wolves most frequently detected the red and yellow stains. It has been suggested that this may equate to biologically relevant markings such as blood (red) and urine (yellow).

According to R. D. Lawrence, "wolves become interested in those colors that have red as a base," suggesting some degree of color sensitivity in that particular photo receptor in wolves. L. David Mech has also reported that wolves have a strong ability to detect red from other colors.



## TASTE

Investigations of taste are made difficult by the fact that the influence of smell often plays a major role in the way a food "tastes." It is known that canines possess taste receptors for the four taste categories: salty, bitter, sweet, and acidic. Felines, on the other hand, do not respond to sweetness. The sweetness receptivity would be of adaptive use to wolves, as sweet berries and other fruits do play a minor role in their diet.

## Tracks

Wolf tracks. Photo by Jim Yuskavitch.

Wolf tracks are very similar to those of the domestic dog, consisting of four pad prints plus claw marks.

The foreprint of a wolf varies from $4\frac{1}{2}$ to 5 inches in length and $3\frac{3}{4}$ to $4\frac{1}{2}$ inches in width. The back feet are smaller, leaving prints about $3\frac{3}{4}$ inches long and $3\frac{1}{4}$ inches wide. Tracks in soft media, such as sand or mud, often appear larger and tracks in snow melted by the sun often appear huge. Tales of wolf tracks "the size of pie plates" are pure fantasy. The small "thumbs" on the front feet do not leave a mark, since they are elevated by the level of the remaining claws.

Depending on the gait, the distance between the tracks of the hind feet and those of the front feet varies from 25 to 38 inches.

Wolf footprint. © Robert H. Busch

The only wild canid with a similar track is the coyote, whose tracks seldom exceed 2½ inches in length. A cougar track is larger and looks similar but lacks the claw marks (cougars have retractile claws; wolves do not). A large domestic dog has a very similar track, but experienced trackers use two clues to distinguish them from wild prints. In dogs, the two outside toes often point slightly outward from the heel, but in wolves, the outer toes point straight ahead. In addition, the tracks of a wolf often lie more in a straight line than those of a dog, since dogs tend to wander more to each side of a straight line.



## Wolf Scat

Wolf scat is very similar to that of a large domestic dog, but frequently is filled with hair and bone chips from consumed prey. The feces are brownish, ½ to 6 inches in length, 1 to 1½ inches in diameter, roughly cylindrical, and may have tapering ends. Coyote scat is comparable but is rarely over an inch in diameter.

Wolf scat. Photo by Jim Yuskavitch.

Wolves suffer from many ectoparasites, including fleas. Photo courtesy of Scott Ian Barry

After a wolf eats fresh meat, its feces are often loose and watery. A meal of berries results in mushy feces.

## Diseases

Wolves are susceptible to more than one hundred diseases and parasites, including various protozoa, roundworms, tapeworms, flatworms, mange, mites, ticks, fleas, distemper, cataracts, oral papillomatosis, tularemia, trichinosis, bovine tuberculosis, encephalitis, arthritis, brucellosis, cancers, rickets, pneumonia, Lyme disease, and many other ailments.

External parasites such as flies, ticks, fleas, and mites tend to be less of a problem in cold northern regions. The most common wolf afflictions are mange and tapeworms. Distemper is sometimes seen in wolves that have been in contact with domestic dogs.



### MANGE

Mange is caused by tiny mites that attach themselves to a wolf's coat or skin. In sarcoptic mange, intense itching is caused by the female mites' burrowing under the skin to lay eggs. In demodectic mange, the mites live in the pores of the skin and cause little or no itching. The symptoms of mange include skin lesions, crusting, and fur loss. Wolves that suffer the loss of fur in severe winter are in danger of freezing to death.

In 1909, wolves experimentally infected with sarcoptic mange were released in Montana as a wolf-control measure. It is thought by some researchers that mange was introduced to the Canadian prairies through this draconian route.

In the mid-1980s, mange was a serious problem in Saskatchewan's wolf population, and the province's wolf numbers decreased as a result. According to Francesco Francisci and Vittorio Guberti, writing in *Wolves in Europe: Status and Perspectives*, sarcoptic mange is "possibly the sole relevant disease to wolf demography in Italy."

Mange has caused problems for wolves in Yellowstone National Park and the Druid pack was severely affected at the end of the winter of 2010, losing a number of its members.

## TAPEWORMS

Tapeworm. © Robert H. Busch

Wolves can suffer from infestations of a variety of worms, including at least twenty-four species of roundworms, twenty-one species of tapeworms, nine species of flukes, and three species of spiny-headed worms. By far the most common culprit is the tapeworm.

Two genuses of tapeworm are commonly encountered in wolves: *Taenia* and *Echinococcus*. In a 1955 study of 18 Minnesota wolves, 83 percent had *Taenia* worms. Of 200 wolves studied in Alaska in 1959, 30 percent were plagued by *Echinococcus* tapeworms. Tapeworm larvae are often ingested by wolves from their ungulate (hoofed animals including deer, moose, elk, and caribou) prey. They live in the wolf's intestine, fastening themselves to the intestinal wall by tiny hooks and suckers. The body segments often are observed in the feces of the host wolf. Heavy infestations of tapeworms can cause loss of appetite, reduced weight, and mild diarrhea, which for any wild predator can severely affect its ability to hunt and survive winter conditions.



## DISTEMPER

Canine distemper is a very contagious disease caused by a microscopic virus. The disease often centers on the skin, eye membranes, and intestinal tract, and occasionally on the brain. Symptoms include fever, loss of appetite, and a watery discharge from the nose or eyes. Diarrhea and dehydration may follow, and eventually seizures or spasmodic movements may occur. If the disease reaches this stage, death often results. Distemper is sometimes found in wolves when they have been in contact with domestic dogs. It is not common in the wild. L. David Mech wrote in 1970 in *The Wolf: The Ecology and Behavior of an Endangered Species* that he knows of "no reliable report of the occurrence of distemper in wild wolves." Since then, documented cases have come to light, such as in Manitoba's Riding Mountain National Park, Jasper National Park, and in the Northwest Territories. Although 48 percent of 71 wolves tested for distemper from 1977 to 1984 in northern Minnesota showed positive, distemper is usually not fatal to adult wolves, but pups may be vulnerable.

Wolves in Yellowstone National Park had three major outbreaks of canine distemper—in 1999, 2005, and 2008. During outbreak years, only 23 percent of wolf pups survived in the northern region of the park compared to the more typical 77 percent survival rate.

### HEARTWORM



Heartworm is a southern disease that has slowly spread northward across North America. It is spread by the common mosquito and named for the worms that live inside the right side of the heart and in the larger blood vessels. In serious infestations, more than 200 worms can live in the host animal. Severe cases can result in blocked blood flow, coughing, weight loss, and general loss of condition. Extreme cases can result in heart failure. In the red wolf of the southeastern United States, heartworm has proven to be a serious problem. In the gray wolf population, heartworm has slowly spread north to Minnesota. It has yet to be reported in Canadian or European wolves.

### PARVOVIRUS

Canine parvovirus was first discovered in domestic dogs in 1978, and has since spread to wild canids. It is a viral infection that attacks the gastrointestinal system, causing dehydration, vomiting, and diarrhea. Recently, four red wolf pups born in the Great Smoky Mountains National Park died from parvovirus. L. David Mech and S. M. Goyal have also found that over half of the variance in pup production and a third of the variance in the wolf population in the Superior National Forest of Minnesota are the result of canine parvovirus.

### RABIES

Contrary to popular myth, rabies is very rare in the modern wolf. This was not the case a century ago, when Indians and explorers often reported encountering rabid wolves. According to the Centers for Disease Control in

Atlanta, Georgia, 98 percent of rabies today in North America is found in skunks, raccoons, bats, or foxes.

Wolves are not a primary vector of rabies in North America, usually contracting the disease from foxes or skunks.

Over the past two decades, only a handful of confirmed rabies cases in North American wolves have been documented. The last verified death of a human from a rabid wolf bite appears to have been in Alaska in 1943. Today in Alaska, despite a population of over 6,000 wolves, only four cases of rabies have been verified since 1987. In 1990, a rabies outbreak among arctic and red foxes in Alaska spread to wolves and caused eight suspected wolf deaths. In 1992, the last year of complete statistics available to the Centers for Disease Control, there was not one case of rabies reported in wolves anywhere in North America.

Rabies used to be very common in Europe during the Middle Ages, the period that spawned many of the myths surrounding the wolf. In fact, C. H. D. Clarke, former head of the Fish and Wildlife Division of the Ontario Ministry of Natural Resources, has studied much of the European wolf literature and concluded, "The famous wolves of medieval song and story were all rabid." In the 12th-century Swedish Ynglinga Saga warriors were described as "mad as . . . wolves," and their crazy actions were called *berserkgangr*, giving us our modern word "berserk."

Russian records from 1763 to 1891 document 75 cases of rabid wolves.

Rabies in wolves still occurs sporadically in Europe and Asia. According to British author Liz Bomford, writing in *The Complete Wolf,* "the wolf is the principal virus-carrier mainly in the Asiatic regions of the former USSR." In one study in Kazakhstan from 1972 to 1978, 17 of 54 wolves studied carried the rabies virus. In 1980, Bomford recounts that "ten peasants were attacked by a male rabid wolf near Soleny village in the Voronezh Region of Russia. The victims were airlifted to Voronezh Hospital where they received intensive antirabies treatment. Although they were badly mauled and considered to be in serious condition, all survived." In 1991, 11 people were bitten by a rabid wolf near L'vov. Russian investigators have found that higher densities of wolves tend to support a higher incidence of rabies. According to leading Russian wolf biologist Dimitry Bibikov, today very few wolves in Russia are rabid.

Despite the relative scarcity of the disease in modern times, our knee-jerk reaction to rabies is often severe. As a result of one rabid wolf discovered in northern Alberta in 1952, over 4,200 wolves were exterminated by poisoning in that province in a four-year period. In addition, 50,000 red foxes, 35,000 coyotes, 7,500 lynx, 1,850 bears, 500 skunks, and 164 cougars lost their lives as a result of paranoia.

## Injuries

Wolves are known to suffer from a variety of injuries primarily resulting from scuffles with intended prey. Veteran Yellowstone wolf biologist Douglas W. Smith states that he has "seen wolves that were hanging on [to] a prey animal [being] stepped on, kicked, flung into the air, and slammed into logs." Artist George Catlin reported an 1844 attack upon a lone male buffalo by a pack of wolves in which two of the wolves "less lucky, had been crushed to death by the feet or the horns of the bull."



In 1905, R. R. MacFarlane found a wolf whose hind leg had been shattered by a kick from a moose.

Naturalist John Stanwell-Fletcher, who traveled through northern British Columbia in the 1940s, reported a large, black male wolf "found alive with terrific wounds, broken ribs, and two shattered legs" surrounded by moose tracks. He went on to state that "similar cases were frequently reported by Indians and apparently usually occurred when the wolf had attacked the moose alone."

Minor infections from porcupine quills plague many wolf pups. © Robert H. Busch

E. C. Cross examined one old wolf in Ontario that had two broken ribs on one side, one on the other, a broken left leg, and a fractured pelvis.

Barry Lopez, in *Of Wolves and Men*, states, "Of 110 wolves killed mostly along the Tanana River in Alaska in 1976 . . . fifty-six had survived one or more traumatic injuries . . . fractured skulls, broken ribs, broken legs, and so on." Of 151 wolf carcasses studied in the Yukon, 24 showed rib injuries probably caused by the sharp hooves of prey.

More recently, photographer Jim Brandenburg, on Ellesmere Island in the Canadian Arctic, found a wolf skull with the tip of a musk ox horn broken off in the lower jawbone. L. David Mech similarly once found a skull of a male wolf with a deer-hoof-shaped hole in it. The wolf also had two healed broken ribs, attesting to the rigors of a predator's life in the wild.

Other wolf injuries reported by field biologists have resulted from falls from rock ledges and from drownings in swiftly flowing rivers and deep ponds, and wounds and even deaths have resulted from fights with other wolves. In *The Way of the Wolf*, L. David Mech states, "Most such killings result from territorial disputes, involve adult wolves, and occur a few months before and after breeding season." Wolves have also been found with major wounds inflicted by grizzly bears and with minor infections caused by porcupine quills.

One of the most unusual fatal injuries suffered by a wild wolf was the poisoning of a red wolf in October 1993, caused by its drinking automobile antifreeze that had spilled onto a road. Two other odd deaths occurred in Denali National Park in Alaska, where two radio-collared wolves were killed in an avalanche. A female Yellowstone wolf and her pup suffered the same fate, and biologists were unable to retrieve their bodies until spring.

## Longevity

While disease, parasites, and injuries take a heavy toll, and hard winters and food shortages shorten the lives of many wolves, especially pups and subordinate pack members, the only true enemy of the wolf is man.

In Algonquin Provincial Park in Ontario, up to 60 percent of the wolf mortality has been through human causes. In Riding Mountain National Park in Manitoba, prior to 1980 up to 78 percent of the individual packs were lost each year as a result of human activities. Most losses occurred through both legal and illegal hunting, collisions with vehicles, trapping, or predator control. Diane Boyd and Paul Paquet found that from 1984 to

This captive wolf is a pampered resident of one of North America's many wolf parks. Photo courtesy of Deborah Warrick, Founder, St. Augustine Wild Reserve

The average wolf in the wild likely lives less than 5 years; in captivity, they can live up to 18 years. Photo courtesy of California Wolf Center

1991, 91 percent of the wolf mortality in Banff and Glacier National Parks was caused by humans. Of 60 wolf carcasses collected in Italy from 1984 to 1990, 78 percent had been killed by humans, with the majority shot or poisoned.

In *The Way of the Wolf*, L. David Mech stated, "Probably most wild wolves die before they reach five years of age." This is borne out by numerous field studies. In one Minnesota study of 165 wolves, only 10 lived beyond 9 years of age. Another study of 55 wolves in the same state determined that 6 lived beyond 9 years, one reached 13, and the rest all died before 8 years of age. In Alberta, of over 100 problem wolves killed and examined by provincial biologists, the oldest wolf according to dental records was 9 years old. (Tooth structure is the primary means of calculating the age of a wolf.

Canine and premolar teeth are horizontally sectioned and stained, and the cementum annuli are counted just as with tree rings.) The average life expectancy of a Yellowstone wolf, not including pup mortality, is a mere 3.4 years.

In captivity, wolves often live to 13 or 14 years of age, and occasionally older. Wolf Haven, near Tenino, Washington, had one wolf that lived to be over the age of 18. In 2017 the oldest gray wolves at Wolf Haven International, six total, were at least 14.

CHAPTER

4

# BEHAVIOR AND ACTIVITIES

## The Wolf Pack

THE MAIN UNIT OF the wolf social system is the wolf pack, which is primarily an extended family unit. The bond of the pack is extremely close; wolf biologist John Theberge has stated, "Their social bonding and care-giving behavior are second only to those of humans and other social primates."

A pack usually consists of a pair of breeding wolves, known as the alpha pair, their current offspring, and a few yearlings or other young wolves. There may also be a few adult subordinate wolves in the pack, sometimes including brothers or sisters of the alpha pair. The alpha pair may not necessarily be the largest wolves in the pack, and the leader of the pack may be the alpha female, not the alpha male. The term "alpha" was coined by Swiss

Wolf packs may range in size from under ten to over fifty wolves. Photo courtesy of Scott Ian Barry

The alpha male and female in a wolf pack head the social hierarchy of a wolf pack, but may not be the only pair in the pack that mates. © Monty Sloan

animal behaviorist Rudolf Schenkel, and has since been applied to dominant individuals in a number of other animal social systems. At the opposite end of the pack hierarchy from the alpha pair is the omega wolf, the lowest individual on the wolf totem pole and the subject of much harassment.

Play in wild animals helps enforce social bonds and can act as practice for hunting behaviors. Photo courtesy of William E. Rideg

Almost half a wolf's time is spent sleeping or resting. Photo courtesy of Bert Buxbaum

Most wolf packs are composed of four to seven individuals. The largest documented true pack appears to be the now defunct Druid pack in Yellowstone National Park, which counted thirty-seven members in 2000. John Stanwell-Fletcher reported a pack of thirty-one wolves in northern British Columbia in 1942. A twenty-nine-member wolf pack was reported in Denali National Park in Alaska in 1992. There are undocumented reports of packs of over fifty wolves in Alaska in the 1940s and 1950s.

Extra-large packs have never been reported for the red wolf or the Abyssinian wolf. Large packs may provide improved hunting efficiency when game is scarce or may alternatively be a response to abundant prey. Some studies have found that larger packs tend to choose larger prey species such as moose over smaller species such as deer.

> THE STRENGTH OF THE PACK IS THE WOLF, AND THE STRENGTH OF THE WOLF IS THE PACK.
>
> —Rudyard Kipling, *The Jungle Book*, 1894

European wolf packs tend to number only three to four wolves, and lone wolves are very common. Apparently there is a lesser need for large packs in Europe since the current prey are animals such as rodents and hares. In Poland, Boguslaw

## AVERAGE PACK SIZES IN NORTH AMERICA

| Area | Year of study | Average number of members |
|---|---|---|
| Northeast Alberta | 1980 | 7.2 |
| Manitoba | 1981 | 12.5 |
| Ontario | 1969 | 5.9 |
| Quebec | 1985 | 4.4 |
| South-central Alaska | 1987 | 9.0 |
| Central Alaska | 1983 | 9.3 |
| Kenai Peninsula, Alaska | 1984 | 9.8 |
| Alaska | 1977 | 11.6 |
| Minnesota | 1955 | 4.2 |
| Minnesota | 1975 | 8.0 |
| Minnesota | 1981 | 4.3 |
| Minnesota | 1977 | 5.8 |
| Minnesota | 1973 | 6.5 |
| Idaho | 2015 | 6.4 |
| Montana | 2016 | 6–8 |
| Yellowstone National Park | 2016 | 10 |

(Source: USFWS , 1988, National park service 2017, Idaho Department of Fish and Game 2017, Montana Fish, Wildlfie and Parks, 2017)



Bobek studied 397 packs in four different populations and found an average of 2.24 to 2.95 animals per pack. In one of his studied populations, 40 percent of the animals were lone wolves. In Hungary, Sándor Faragó observed 87 wolves and determined that 58 percent were lone wolves. Francisco Fonseca of the University of Lisbon has stated that in Portugal, "wolves now travel alone most of the time."

The wolf pack is one of the most cohesive social organizations in the animal world. And according to Steven B. Young, director of the Center for Northern Studies, "Wolves are considered by many to have the most complex social behavior of any nonprimate animal."

Fights between packs can be deadly and often occur in times of decreased numbers of prey animals.

The social rank of the individual wolves in the pack is enforced by a fascinating set of body positions and movements, by intimidation, and by harassment. This social structure is one of the most intensely studied facets of wolf behavior. Although most observations have been of captive wolves, most reported behavior has been confirmed by field biologists.

These studies have resulted in a lengthy list of dominance/subordination postures used by wolves.

## DOMINANT POSTURES

These include walking with head held high, tail partly erect, eyes directed straight toward other wolves. Dominant animals may show raised hackles, may growl, and may sideswipe or body-slam subordinate animals, sometimes pinning them to the ground. They may show bared teeth, upright ears, or a wrinkled forehead. They may seize the muzzle of subordinates and nip or bite them. Dominant animals tend to be the first to eat at kills, the first to attack in aggressive encounters with other packs, and tend to have breeding rights not enjoyed by lower-ranked individuals. They usually urinate in a standing position, with raised hind leg.

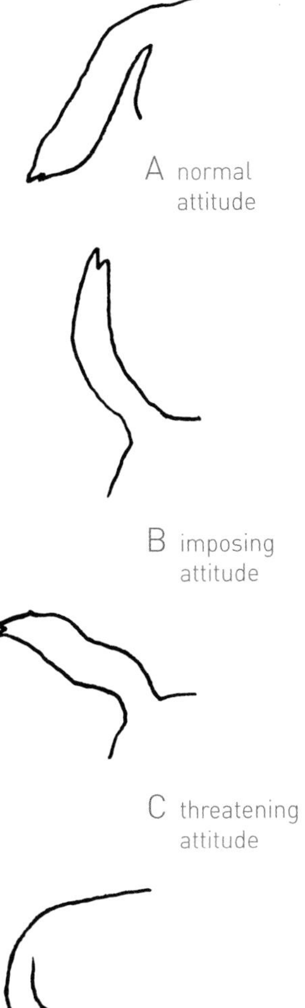

Positions of tail (after Schenkel, 1947)

Two wolves establishing dominance; note the lowered tail and submissive body stance of the wolf on the bottom. © Monty Sloan

Observers may note a "riding up" posture in which a dominant animal places its forelegs across the shoulders of a subordinate in a posture similar to that of two mating animals.

## SUBORINATE POSTURES

These include lowered tails (in extreme submission, curled right under the body), ears folded back, the peeling back of lips to form a submissive "grin," crouching or lowered body position, and urinating in a squat position. A subordinate animal may lick a superior wolf's muzzle, or lie on its side, raising a hind leg to expose the groin area to the superior. It may bend its head back to expose the throat area, and in extreme submission may urinate on itself. Subordinate animals may also whine or squeal in

The social structure of wolf packs has been one of the most intensive areas of study for wolf researchers. Photo courtesy of William E. Rideg

A subordinate wolf adopts a posture of submission at the approach of the pack's alpha male. Photo courtesy of Jim Peaco/National Park Service

Even in captivity, this wolf enforces its social status through peeled-back lips and exposed fangs. Julie Lawrence photo, © Wolf Haven International



submission to superior wolves, making timid small steps toward superiors with one forepaw lifted up.

Rudolf Schenkel of the University of Basel further divided submissive gestures into either active or passive submission. Active submission is a friendly display toward a dominant animal, while passive submission is the response of a lower-ranked animal when approached by a more dominant animal. Subordinate animals often actively solicit responses from more dominant pack members in order to reaffirm their status and pack position. Though many of these ritual gestures appear vicious, they actually serve to preserve pack cohesion without bloodshed.

The social ranking of pack members is not fixed; as wolves sexually mature, reach old age, become wounded or ill, or alter alliances with other pack members, the social ranking of each individual moves up or down the lupine social ladder.

If one of the alpha pair dies or becomes weakened, the next dominant wolf, known as the beta wolf, will take its place.

Lois Crisler, who reported on wolf observations in Alaska in *Arctic Wild*, concluded, "The strongest impression remaining with me after watching the wolves on numerous occasions was their friendliness." Pack members will

The yawn of a wolf sometimes indicates tension in the animal. Photo courtesy of California Wolf Center

often greet each other nose to nose, with wagging tails and whole bodies wriggling with joy. Rick McIntyre, who has observed a number of wolves in Denali National Park in Alaska, has written about the "joy of companionship that wolves experience by belonging to a pack."

The bond of the pack is so close that many observers have reported evidence of a wolf's sense of loss at the death of a pack member. Jim Brandenburg, in *White Wolf: Living with an Arctic Legend,* wrote of arctic wolves visiting the body of a dead yearling wolf: "One by one they would sniff his body then curl up beside him."

The wolf literature is also filled with a number of reports of charitable gestures among pack members. In *Dance of the Wolves,* Roger Peters wrote of a 16-year-old wolf in the Chicago Zoo that, crippled by arthritis, "remain[ed] inside at mealtime" and "another wolf would bring him food." Roberta Walker, writing about a wolf pack in Canada's Banff National Park, wrote, "An old, crippled wolf that could no longer hunt was brought food by other pack members and fed like a pup." Rick McIntyre observed a male wolf with a damaged front leg holding up the progress of a hunt, but "the other pack members halted and patiently waited for him to reach them." John A. Murray wrote about an alpha female giving birth out on the tundra in Alaska, where the rest of the pack members brought her food and protected her until she could move her pups to the den site.

Pack members have also been reported to be solicitous of other animals in distress. Lois Crisler wrote of a dog with porcupine quills in its nose whose wolf friend "hovered anxious-eyed around his face, whimpering when the dog cried."

The strong pack ties and friendly nature of pack members led Crisler to conclude, "Wolves have what it takes to live together in peace." But there is also aggression.

The strict social hierarchy, or "pecking order," in a wolf pack is strictly enforced. Photo courtesy of William E. Rideg



Aggression between pack members seems to be most common between female members of the pack, especially in captivity. Studies at the Burger's Zoo in Arnhem, the Netherlands, determined that captive females, especially alpha females, tend to be very intolerant of other females, not only during courtship, but in such situations as feeding and howling. Low-ranking females may even be killed if they are unable to escape their tormentors.

There may also be aggression when one pack enters another pack's territory. The reaction between the two packs depends on the availability of food and territory, and the existence of genetic ties between the packs.

Aggression is customarily directed toward the omega wolf, the lowest-ranked animal in the pack. This unfortunate individual often becomes the pack scapegoat, suffering so much physical and mental stress that it may leave the pack.

## Lone Wolves

When subordinate animals leave the pack as a result of physical and mental harassment, intimidation, hunger from inadequate food supplies, or a need to mate, they often become lone wolves. Studies by L. David Mech and E. M. Gase in northeast Minnesota from 1969 to 1989 showed that most of the wolves that left the security of the pack did so before the age of two years. Deposed alpha animals may also become lone wolves. Abyssinian wolves have such strong pack bonds that males either stay with the pack or become lone wolves. Researchers Dada Gottelli and Claudio Sillero-Zubiri "never recorded any instance of a male leaving his natal pack to join a different one."

Loners may live on the edge of the pack or move away to join existing packs or form new ones. A lone wolf haunting the fringes of a pack may be chased off, killed, or accepted by the pack. Lone wolves make up "less than 15 percent of an established wolf population," according to John Gunson, a biologist with the Alberta Fish and Wildlife Division.

Lone wolves usually comprise less than 15 percent of a total wolf population. © Robert H. Busch

When individual pack members die, lone wolves sometimes move in to fill the gap.

Lone wolves tend to cover a larger territory in their search for food or a mate and travel the longest distances when they are cast out (see the section on travel in this chapter, 77–80). In captive situations, where dispersal is not possible, loners must often be removed and sent to other zoos or wildlife parks.

Loners have a high mortality rate because they are often unable to catch sufficient prey, and they lack the protective support of a pack. In one study of eighteen dispersing wolves on Isle Royale, Michigan, at least ten (56 percent) died within the one-year period that they were studied.

## Communication

In addition to body gestures and facial expressions, wolves use both vocal expressions and scent marks as means of communication.

Wolf howls help maintain contact among wolves in thick woods. Photo courtesy of William E. Rideg

To many, the howl of a wolf is the voice of the wilderness. Julie Lawrence photo, © Wolf Haven International

## VOCAL EXPRESSIONS

Wolves express themselves vocally through a variety of howls, yips, squeals, growls, chirps, and barks. R. D. Lawrence has described a "howl-bark," which he defines as an "alarm call that starts with a high-pitched bark that almost immediately turns into a short howl." The best studied of all wolf vocalizations is the howl.

Wolves howl for many reasons, including the following:

- to notify other pack members or other packs of their whereabouts, or to reassemble a scattered pack
- to attract a mate
- to stimulate and rally the pack before a hunt
- to startle prey and cause it to come out of hiding (Although this is disputed by Dan Strickland, who wrote in *Wolf Howling in Algonquin Provincial Park* that "prey animals simply fail to make a connection between howling and its source.")
- when disturbed, but not sufficiently alarmed to run away
- upon awaking

- after intense sessions of play or other social interactions
- to announce alarm at the presence of an intruder
- when stressed; lonesome wolf pups often howl their distress

Young wolf pups learn to howl by imitating adult members of the pack. (Photo of captive wolves from Wildlife Science Center in Forest Lake, MN. Courtesy of Jenni Bidner)

Other reasons for howls have been reported in the wolf literature. Canadian biologist Lu Carbyn reports a wolf frustrated in his efforts at bringing down a bison calf sitting down and howling perhaps "to call for help." And Adolph Murie reported a lone wolf howling while hunting mice, perhaps in frustration.

It is likely that wolves often howl just for the fun of it. R. D. Lawrence, in *Trail of the Wolf*, states, "somewhat like humans, they enjoy a singsong." He has also stated, "Wolves probably howl for a variety of reasons, one of which, I am convinced, is that they enjoy doing so." Lois Crisler, in *Arctic Wild*, wrote that some wolves "will run from any distance . . . hardly able to wait to sing." She believed that "a howl is . . . a happy social occasion. Wolves love a howl."

Crisler went on: "There are many howls—the happy social howl, the mourning howl, the wild deep hunting howl, the call howl."

A howl may range from a half second in duration to about 11 seconds. Communal howls often begin with a few sharp barks by a few pack members, followed by a low howl that builds to a louder group howl.

Fred Harrington found that larger wolves tend to have deeper voices than small, young wolves. He also found that when adults were away hunting, pups used low-pitched adultlike howls that may aid in protecting them from other packs.

Wolf howls may carry for as much as 10 miles in the winter. Photo courtesy of William E. Rideg

A number of observers have noted that wolves seldom stay on the same note while howling, but rather shift pitch to achieve almost harmonic effects. In *Beasts in My Belfry*, Gerald Durrell described these as "one of the most beautiful animal noises." Lois Crisler, in *Arctic Wild*, wrote that "wolves avoid unison singing; they like chords." Jim Brandenburg, in *White Wolf: Living with an Arctic Legend*, writes that "when two packmates hit the same note, they change pitch until discord is re-established." He postulated that "perhaps a discordant pack sounds larger and more formidable."

A chorus of howls can indeed confuse an untrained listener. In his memoirs, General Ulysses S. Grant wrote of traveling through the American Midwest on horseback and hearing wolf howls ahead. His guide asked the general how many wolves he thought there were. Grant answered, "Oh, about twenty." However, "there were just two of them," he wrote. "Seated upon their haunches, with their mouths close together, they had made all the noise we had been hearing for the past ten minutes." Dan Strickland, writing about public wolf howls in Algonquin Provincial Park, Ontario, states that "we have heard listeners guess twenty-five or thirty wolves when there were fewer than ten."

[THE HOWL OF A WOLF] IS INDEED A HORRIBLE NOISE, THE MOST HATEFUL A MAN ALONE IN THE WILDERNESS AT NIGHT CAN BEAR.

—John Capen Adams, California mountaineer and grizzly hunter

Roger Peters, who wrote his doctorate on wolf communication, believes that after a howling session, "wolves enter a fifteen-minute refractory period, during which nothing in the world can get them to howl again." He theorizes that this allows time for packs to hear each other howl.

Wolf howls may be audible as far away as 10 miles under ideal weather conditions. Fred Harrington and L. David Mech found a high response to tape recordings of howls near kill sites. They also found that the alpha male was the pack member that most often responded to the playbacks.

Contrary to popular belief, wolves do not "howl at the moon." Many studies have shown that the phase of the moon plays no role in stimulating howls.



A number of observers have reported that the wolves found in southern Asia howl only on rare occasions. The reasons for this are unknown, but it has been suggested that long-standing persecution by humans has resulted in the evolution of a quieter wolf.

Wolves can howl while lying down, standing up, sitting upon their haunches, or in almost any other position. Barry Lopez, in *Of Wolves and Men*, writes, "I've even seen a wolf, with an air of not wanting to miss out, howl while defecating."

Howls constitute a long-distance form of communication. The immediate, short-range form of wolf communication is scent marking.

## SCENT MARKING

Researchers have described four different types of scent marks:

- raised-leg urination
- squat-position urination
- defecation
- scratching

Raised-leg urination is performed primarily by the alpha male of the pack. Females squat and, in general, tend to scent mark less than males.

The urine is usually directed toward some raised object such as a rock, post, stump, or tree. Roger Peters and L. David Mech found that of 583 raised-leg urinations they studied in Michigan, 99.3 percent were directed at a particular object.

Scent marking helps delineate margins of wolf territories. © Monty Sloan

Squat-position urination is performed by subordinate male members of the pack and not usually directed at any particular object.

During the mating season, a double urination mark may be made by the breeding female, who urinates first, and the breeding male, who follows with a raised-leg urination on or beside the female's mark. The double mark likely serves to help bond the pair through hormonal secretions contained in the urine marks.

As early as 1947, the biologist Rudolf Schenkel believed that scent marks helped to maintain "contact between neighbors." Roger Peters and L. David Mech discovered that raised-leg urinations are more common on the perimeters of territories than in the centers. This suggests that these marks are used either to mark territorial boundaries or to advertise the presence of a particular pack. In the world of the wolf, a series of scent marks along a territory boundary constitutes an olfactory "no-trespassing" sign. Scent marks may also act as a location system for wolves within their territory—a set of sensory "street signs" to aid the wolves in finding their way. It has also been found that packs increase the rate of scent marking when signs of other packs are encountered.

The piercing gaze of a curious wolf. Photo courtesy of William E. Rideg



R. J. Rothman and L. David Mech discovered that lone wolves rarely perform raised-leg urinations. This is probably a survival tactic to prevent packs from discovering their presence. Similarly, subordinate captive wolves have been observed urinating repeatedly in ponds, apparently to minimize the signs of their presence within the enclosure.

Wolves will also urinate on empty food caches, perhaps to indicate that they have already been used, and on food that they are not interested in eating. Biologists Dada Gottelli and Claudio Sillero-Zubiri have observed Ethiopian wolves urinating with a raised leg on the site of a kill, perhaps establishing possession of the site through scent marking.

Defecations may stimulate anal glands and release hormonal secretions, in addition to constituting an obvious visual signal. According to Liz Bomford, writing in *The Complete Wolf*, "wolves leave a scat about every 250 yards along well-used routes." L. David Mech and Cheryl Asa reported in 1985, "Our captive alpha and beta males deposited scats significantly more toward the end of their enclosure closest to human approach and where they were fed and drugged." It is not clear exactly what message these wolves were trying to leave.

Scratching, or aggressively pawing the ground with both front and back legs, may also serve to release odors from glands in the paws and leaves visual evidence of the wolf's presence. Scratching is usually done after urinating.

## Curiosity

Lois Crisler, in *Arctic Wild,* wrote how a "black wolf stood by her first patch of newly-opened dark-pink daisies, acquainting herself with them. She brushed her nose across them, raised her paw and touched them. . . . A wolf's curiosity is impersonal. It goes beyond food and fear."

Bradford Angier, in *How to Stay Alive in the Woods,* states that the wolf's curiosity "will sometimes lead to close investigations especially during protective darkness, and this has stimulated some of the tales about wolves trailing individuals with the alleged motive of eventually attacking."



A report from northern British Columbia is typical. Two hunters in the winter of 1993 found themselves being trailed by a small lone wolf. The animal showed no aggressive tendencies, but the men panicked and shot it. The body was taken to the local conservation officer, who did not charge the two hunters. One week later, a provincial news magazine described the incident under the headline "Wolf Attack Near Chetwynd."

## Intelligence

Part of the reason for the wolf's curiosity is its high level of intelligence.

In *The Soul of the Wolf,* animal behaviorist Michael W. Fox states that "the domestic dog has a brain one-sixth or so smaller than a wolf of comparable size." Biologist V. Goerttler claims an even greater difference, stating, "Domestic dogs have a brain thirty-one percent smaller than wolves."

Harry Frank, of Michigan State University, found in experiments that wolves learned very quickly how to open a door by turning a doorknob after watching humans. The dogs in his experiments never learned.

L. David Mech, in *The Way of the Wolf,* described a captive wolf that "learned to raise a drop door in its pen by jumping to the top of the eight-foot-high pen, and grabbing with its teeth the door handle."

Michael W. Fox has written in the *Journal of Mammalogy* of a captive wolf that moved its cubs indoors when the keeper hosed down the outside pen, and then shut the door behind the cubs by pulling on a pulley rope.

It is often safer to explore the world when you are not alone! Photo courtesy of William E. Rideg

In the classic *The Wolves of Mount McKinley,* Adolph Murie described a wolf that "wandered about in several loops" and "walked in shallow puddles of water apparently by choice to destroy his scent."

In *Arctic Wild,* Lois Crisler tells of trying to pull a wolf with a rope around its neck into a traveling crate. The wolf "did the wisest thing he could think of: he dug a hole, gathered the rope into it and buried it." She also wrote of a wolf that watched her husband operate a door bolt: "As soon as he left, she took the bolt in her mouth and tried to open it."

## Interaction with Other Species

### COYOTES

Over much of North America, the former range occupied by the wolf is now populated by the coyote, one of the most adaptable of predators. Where wolf-coyote encounters do occur, they usually are of an aggressive nature, a fairly normal situation for two competing predators. Most observations of wolf-coyote interactions have involved the defense of den, food, or territory.

- In Canada, A. W. F. Banfield discovered signs in Saskatchewan's Prince Albert Park of a pack of wolves that "caught and ate a coyote on a frozen pond."
- In the literature of the wolf there are numerous references to coyotes following wolves to scavenge at kill sites.
- In Minnesota, one study showed that coyotes purposefully avoided wolves, and that coyote ranges tended to exist where wolves were absent or rare.
- A number of biologists have observed aggressive behavior between red wolves and coyotes in Great Smoky Mountains National Park in Tennessee. In August 1993, a coyote killed a red wolf pup in that park.
- Since the reintroduction of wolves to Yellowstone National Park beginning in 1995, the resident coyote population has declined by 50 percent, mostly because wolves kill coyotes. Most coyotes are killed by wolves at prey kill sites.

In contrast to these aggressive encounters, the interbreeding of wolves and coyotes that has played some role in the evolution of the red wolf shows that under some circumstances, very friendly relations between the two species can occur. There is also evidence of interbreeding between the two species in Minnesota, Ontario, and the eastern United States. The so-called Tweed wolf of Ontario and the coydog of the eastern United States may, in fact, be wolf-coyote hybrids.

## GRIZZLY BEARS

Grizzly bears have been known to kill and eat wolf pups, and a number of observers have described wolves attempting to chase bears away from den sites.

- In 1976, two Yukon Territory biologists observed a fight between three grizzlies (a sow and two large yearlings) and seven wolves. The bears, which were digging at the entrance of an occupied wolf den, were driven off by the wolf pack.

Grizzlies will kill and eat wolf pups given the opportunity. © Robert H. Busch



- In 1989, biologists in the same area found evidence that grizzlies had dug up and eaten four wolf pups.
- Frank Glaser, an employee of Denali National Park in Alaska, once observed a female grizzly and three cubs approach a wolf den and be driven off by the pack of five wolves. When the grizzlies retreated into a river and stood their ground, the wolves gave up the chase.
- In 1990, a twelve-wolf pack in Denali "hunted down" a female grizzly and three yearlings that had come too close to the wolf den the previous day. Two of the young grizzlies were killed by the wolves, and the other two bears were both wounded.
- Grizzly biologist Chris Seventeen observed in 1993 a pack of seventeen to eighteen wolves chasing a grizzly sow and cub west of Glacier National Park in Montana.
- Since the reintroduction of the wolf to Yellowstone National Park, wolves have occasionally killed grizzly bear cubs.
- There are a few documented cases of wolves and bears coexisting in peace:

Wolves and grizzly bears interact in many ways wherever their habitats overlap. © Jim Yuskavitch



- Adolph Murie observed wolves and grizzlies feeding within 25 feet of each other at a garbage dump in Alaska in the 1940s.
- In 1964, a grizzly and a lone wolf were observed feeding side by side on a caribou carcass in Alaska.
- John A. Murray described a 1989 encounter between a wolf and a family of three grizzlies. "The wolf stopped dead in his tracks when he saw the bears—about fifty feet away—and then altered his course by forty-five degrees to avoid any further contact."

### BLACK BEARS

Most black bear–wolf interactions are also of an aggressive nature:

- L. David Mech has observed a black bear chasing wolves near a tree where her cubs were hiding.
- In Ontario's Algonquin Park one incident is on record of a black bear killing a lone wolf at her den.
- Minnesota biologists have at least one documented instance of a wolf pack killing and eating an adult female black bear and her newborn cubs.

- In Great Smoky Mountains National Park a pack of red wolves successfully attacked and killed a small black bear cub.

One of the few nonaggressive interactions between black bears and wolves is the description by L. David Mech of a black bear constructing her den within 330 yards of a wolf rendezvous site in Minnesota.

## COUGARS

The relative scarcity of the North American cougar has led to a paucity of wolf-cougar observations, but most reports have documented the animosity between the two large predators. As a solitary hunter, the cougar is severely disadvantaged in a fight with a wolf pack.

- Maurice Hornocker, perhaps America's foremost authority on the cougar, has stated that there are at least eighteen documented accounts of wolves stealing food from cougar kills. In some cases, the wolves did not get away alive.
- In 1985, an Alberta biologist found one of his radio-collared wolves killed by a cougar, apparently after it had attempted to scavenge at a cougar kill site.
- In 1990, there was a rare kill of a cougar by wolves near Glacier National Park, followed by two more kills in 1993.

A pack of wolves were confirmed to be the cause of death of three cougar kittens at their den in northeastern Oregon in fall 2014.

## FOXES

Foxes have been observed stealing from wolf kills and robbing wolf food caches. Wolves, in turn, have in many cases appropriated fox dens for their own use and will steal from fox food caches.

- On Michigan's Isle Royale, wolves have been observed to occasionally kill and eat red foxes, but more often they ignore these tiny predators.
- In Denali National Park, Adolph Murie, in *The Wolves of Mount McKinley*, wrote that "no evidence was found in Mount McKinley to show that wolves are harmful to foxes."

- Observers in Canada's high Arctic, where food is less plentiful, have observed wolves killing arctic foxes on sight.

## RAVENS

One of the most fascinating relationships between animals is the one that seems to exist between wolves and ravens. The raven, scavenger of food of all types, will often follow wolf packs in hopes of morsels of food. And wolves have learned to watch for circling ravens as a sign of possible food below. But there seems to be more than just a symbiosis based on food between the two species; many observations have been made that can only be described as a friendship between the big predator and the wily bird.

- In *Arctic Wild*, Lois Crisler states her belief that "ravens and wolves just liked each other's company." She described one play session between the two species, with the raven diving at the wolves and jumping around just out of reach. "He played this raven tag for ten minutes at a time. If the wolves ever tired of it, he sat squawking till they came over to him again."
- L. David Mech, in *The Wolves of Isle Royale*, described the "peculiar relationship" between a flock of ravens and a large wolf pack and wrote that wolves and ravens "often seem to play together."

Many observers have noted the unusual relationship between the raven and the wolf. © Robert H. Busch

- When wolves were reintroduced to Yellowstone National Park (see p. 203), park ranger and wolf researcher Rick McIntyre reported, "The ravens watched the wolves and learned to show up immediately after they made a kill or tore open a carcass."
- Biologists Dan Stahler and Bernd Heinrich have studied wolf-raven interactions in Yellowstone National Park and determined that the average wolf kill there attracts an astonishing twenty-nine ravens.

### LYNX

Studies by Erkki Pulliainen of the University of Helsinki have shown that in Finland, wolves and lynx do not coexist in the same territory. He found that as wolves decreased in population, lynx numbers increased. According to one authority quoted by Pulliainen, the wolf is the most important natural enemy of the lynx in Finland.

A similar relationship was found to exist in Hungary. Sándor Faragó, in *Wolves in Europe: Status and Perspectives,* wrote, "If wolves suffer losses of range, expansion of lynx may increase. . . . With increasing numbers of wolf observations, those of the lynx gradually diminished."

### TIGERS

Arjan Singh, one of India's most famous conservationists, has written in *Tiger! Tiger!* that before the decimation of that country's tiger population, tigers used to prey on wolves.

More recently, at a safari park in Ontario, when a tiger got loose and entered the wolf compound, the 130-pound alpha male wolf attacked the 500-pound cat immediately before workers gained control of the situation.

### WOLVERINES

Lois Crisler, in *Arctic Wild,* once observed a female wolf chasing a wolverine away from the wolf's den. Alaska biologist B. L. Burkholder has found tracks in the snow where a pack of wolves killed a female wolverine that was feeding on a carcass. Adolph Murie observed three incidents when wolverines were chased by wolves.

## ALLIGATORS

At least three of the reintroduced red wolves in the Cape Romain National Wildlife Refuge in South Carolina have been killed by alligators.

## OTHER WILD SPECIES

Wolf kills provide a buffet for many wild species, including magpies, eagles, and hosts of invertebrates such as beetles, which have an amazing ability to detect carcasses. In addition, nutrients from carcasses gradually leech into the soil under the carcass, potentially allowing a more luxuriant growth of grasses and other vegetation.

## DOGS

Although wolves are physiologically capable of breeding with domestic dogs, such crosses usually happen only in captive situations. Trappers' tales of wild wolves mating with domestic dogs are usually little more than campfire myth. Despite this, in the 1947 book *Trapping: The Craft and Science of Catching Fur-Bearing Animals*, authors Harold McCracken and Harry Van Cleve stated, "Any person who has handled a dog team knows the value of having wolf blood in his animals . . . the dogs owned by Eskimos and Indians . . . occasionally fall heir to a litter of half-breed wolf pups by natural course of events. It is also possible to tie out a domestic bitch when in heat."

Statistical evidence for such breedings are lacking. M. A. Bogan and P. Mehlhop examined over 250 skulls of southwest wolves, and found only two specimens that may have been true hybrids.

Most encounters between wild wolves and their domestic cousins are aggressive in nature, and it would seem natural for the dog to be deemed a competitor and trespasser in a wolf's territory. Small, yapping dogs may also simply be attacked by wolves as noisy nuisances. Steven Fritts and Bill Paul, after one study in Minnesota, concluded that "small- to medium-sized dogs, which may be particularly excitable and vocal, are more likely to provoke attack by wolves." (See "Wolf-Dog Hybrids," p. 191.)

## Travel

According to an old Russian proverb, the wolf is kept fed by his feet, and indeed very few predators are better adapted to running. William O. Pruitt Jr., wrote in *Wild Harmony*, "Creeping and bellying are for ambushers such as the lynx; the wolf is a chaser, a runner."

The wolf is made for running. Its long legs and narrow chest facilitate plunging ahead through deep snow, and its huge paws act as snowshoes in winter, allowing the wolf to overtake prey foundering in deep snow.

The wolf in winter travels where the going is easiest, following frozen lakes, moose trails, or one another in single file through deep snows. Unfortunately, wolves also use man-made paths; in February 1994, a wolf was struck and killed by a train north of Prince George, British Columbia, as the animal traveled along the train tracks in winter.

In Denali National Park, the park highway, according to Adolph Murie, "gives them an easy trail along the entire winter range." One American wolf

The large feet of the wolf act as snowshoes in winter. © Robert H. Busch

The usual pace of a wolf is a slow trot at about four to six miles per hour. Photo courtesy of William E. Rideg

Wolves are built to run, with narrow chests and long legs. © Monty Sloan

researcher once reported that the wolves he was following on snowmobile had doubled back and were using his well-packed trail.

The usual pace of a wolf is a slow trot at about four to six miles per hour. In *The Wolves of Isle Royale,* L. David Mech recounts the movements of one wolf pack on Isle Royale that traveled at an average pace of "about 5 mph." Much greater speeds, have, of course, been recorded.

M. H. Stenlund reported that Minnesota wardens once chased a wolf across a frozen lake at thirty-five to forty miles per hour. Desmond Morris, in *Animal Watching: A Field Guide to Animal Behavior,* writes, "the speed of one wolf was recorded at between 15 and 30 mph for a distance of 12 miles." And Darryl Stewart, in *The Canadian Wildlife Almanac,* states that the speed record for a Mongolian wolf is thirty-six miles per hour.

Wolves are also capable of great feats of endurance. One wolf in Scandinavia was found to have traveled 125 miles in one day and night, pursued by dogs and hunters. In *Of Wolves and Men,* Barry Lopez tells of an Eskimo hunter chasing down a wolf with a snowmobile: "the wolf had run for 12 miles at speeds between 15 and 30

IN MOTION, THEY RIPPLE, THEY FLOW.

—Lois Crisler, *Arctic Wild,* 1958

mph before slowing to a trot, which he kept up for another 4 miles, at which point he began walking." John Stanwell-Fletcher once tracked two wolves that traveled for 22 miles nonstop in 6 feet of powder snow in northern British Columbia.

It is not unusual for a wolf to travel 20 miles or more each day in search of food. Adolph Murie's famous East Fork pack traveled 20 miles each way to prey on caribou in their calving grounds. In *The Way of the Wolf*, L. David Mech notes that a "pack of 15 wolves covered an average of 31 miles a day to hunt moose." Robert Burton, in *Carnivores of Europe*, wrote that the wolf in Europe, where prey is scarce, "ranges up to 200 km (120 miles) per day in search of food."

Naturalist Franklin Russell wrote in *The Hunting Animal* that "the feet of the wolf drive the animal along as if on rails, mile upon mile." Great distances have, in fact, been traversed by wolves, primarily by lone wolves dispersing from the pack. Biologists believe that no other modern terrestrial mammal travels as far.

According to Rick Bass, writing in *The Ninemile Wolves*, "the farthest overall dispersal is . . . over 829 miles" by a wolf in Canada.

The large surface area of a wolf paw allows it to readily travel over loose snow in search of prey. Photo courtesy of William E. Rideg

Other accounts of long distances traveled by wolves include the following:

- A male wolf trapped in Minnesota was found to have traveled 550 miles in two months into Canada.
- A marked female wolf from the Glacier National Park area of Montana was shot 520 miles north in British Columbia. A wolf radio-collared in the Brooks Range of Alaska in 1986 was shot 434 miles away in 1992 by a Northwest Territories hunter.
- One wolf marked in the Northwest Territories trekked 419 miles south into Alberta.
- One Yellowstone wolf was hit on the road near Denver, a straight-line jaunt of over 400 miles.
- Another Yellowstone wolf ended up in a coyote trap set near Salt Lake City.
- Oregon wolf dubbed OR7 made international headlines when he traveled more than 1,000 miles from his home pack in northeastern Oregon, into Northern California, before establishing a pack in the southern Oregon Cascade Mountains.



## Play

Wolves love to play, shouldering one another, bumping bodies together, flopping tails over each other's backs, and leaping up placing forepaws around others' necks. Play, especially in pups, develops strength and hunting skills, and aids in establishing pack communication and hierarchy.

Pups play with each other, by themselves, with adults, and with a variety of puppy trophies: bits of bone, feathers, plants, and any other prizes they can scrounge.

The intention to play is often signaled by the gesture well known to dog owners of dropping the front quarters into a crouch position, with smiling face and wagging tail.

Adults stage mock fights, play chase, and leap on each other. The ambushing of unwary pack members is a favorite game.

Franklin Russell, in *The Hunting Animal,* wrote that "play, to a wolf, . . . is not merely important as a training and regulatory device; it also exemplifies the sense of humor that makes it possible for there to be an identification with man, and vice versa."

## Swimming

The wolf is very comfortable in the water, and does not hesitate to wade through icy streams or swim across short stretches of lake. In summer, wolves often bathe in streams to keep cool, and they will readily follow prey into water.

In *The Way of the Wolf,* L. David Mech wrote that "a wolf in northeast Minnesota was seen swimming behind a deer until it caught up, killing the deer while both swam." An earlier report from Minnesota documented a wolf treading water while eating a floating moose carcass.

Wolves can easily cross shallow rivers and often follow prey into water. © Monty Sloan

## Grooming

Wolves depend upon their thick coats for warmth in the northern portions of their range, so it is not surprising that they spend part of their leisure time in grooming behavior.

Wolves returning to a pack after hunting are often warmly greeted with head-rubbing or muzzle-rubbing. © Monty Sloan

For example, Jim Brandenburg observed wolves on Ellesmere Island in Canada's Arctic washing mud from their coats in the icy fjords offshore.

It is likely that the grooming of other pack members helps reinforce the social bonds that tie the pack together. Two wolves will lick each other's coats, nibbling gently with their teeth to remove foreign matter. Reciprocal grooming is especially common during courtship. Injured wolves are intensely groomed by other pack members, providing both physical and mental comfort.

## Courtship

During late winter and early spring, a pair of wolves may begin to court. The two will approach each other while making quiet whining sounds, mouth each other's muzzles, touch noses, and bump their bodies together. There may be mutual grooming and nibbling of each other's coats and the two may walk pressed close together. The male may bow to the female, toss and tilt his head, and lay his legs over her neck in what can only be described as a flirting manner. The two may even sleep side by side.

Mutual grooming and nibbling of each other's coats represent the first signs of wolf courtship. Photo courtesy of Scott Ian Barry



As courtship progresses, the male will smell the genital region of the female to determine her readiness to mate, his tongue flicking in and out, testing the air for traces of sex hormones. If she is not sexually receptive, she will repel the male with growls and snaps of her jaws.

Strong social ties bind a wolf pack. © Monty Sloan

The bond between the mated pair is extremely strong; Stanley Young, an early biologist in the southern United States, once trapped an alpha male whose mate returned to the capture site sixteen nights in a row until she too was trapped. If one mate is killed, the other will usually eventually find a new mate.

Courtship is a time of much social tension in the pack, as subordinate animals are often prevented from breeding through physical and mental harassment.

## Reproduction



The female wolf is in estrus only once a year, in late winter. The estrus lasts for about five to seven days, with the most receptive period generally occurring in the latter half of estrus.

A breeding pair will mate anytime from January to April, with most North American breedings taking place in February to March. Wolves in the southern portions of their range tend to breed earlier than those in the far north. There are even a few records from Arizona of wolves breeding in

The social bonds of wolves are second only to those of humans and nonhuman primates. © Monty Sloan

December. The Ethiopian wolf, which lives only a few degrees north of the equator, breeds anytime from August through December.

Female wolves are usually sexually active in their second year, although there are records of wolves breeding at the age of one, and there is one zoo record of a captive female successfully breeding at the age of 10 months. Males are normally fertile by the age of 22 months. In practice, according to L. David Mech in *The Way of the Wolf*, "many . . . do not breed until four or five." Even at that age, the reproductive capacity of the wolf exceeds that of many other predators. The grizzly, for example, often does not breed until eight years of age.



Although it is often stated that only the alpha pair will mate, this is not so. According to L. David Mech in *The Way of the Wolf*, "twenty to forty percent of the packs containing at least two adult females produce two litters." It has been observed that among tundra wolves, a high number of subordinate females become pregnant each year. This might be a survival response to lack of food or to a severe climate. Multiple litters are much more common than previously thought. Thomas Meier and L. David Mech found in Denali National Park from 1988 to 1991 at least nine cases of multiple litters being born to the same pack. The East Fork pack even produced three litters one year. These multiple litters occurred when there was increasing wolf density and adequate food supplies, and following severe winters. Biologists have also noticed that when the social hierarchy of the pack is disturbed, subordinate females may successfully mate. This can lead to short-term increases in wolf populations after artificial wolf culls by humans. (Thus, to be biologically effective, wolf culls, or population control measures, may have to be continued for a long period of time. Canadian wolf biologist John Theberge states, "Periodic killing of wolves . . . is a waste of time.")

The physical sexual act is usually accomplished with the male mounting the female from the rear. A copulatory tie results when a gland on the male's penis swells, and the female's vaginal muscles tighten, resulting in a physical tie that binds the animals together. Wolf copulatory ties can more readily separate than the domestic dog's, an obvious survival advantage in the wild. Ties can last from 5 minutes up to 36 minutes. The female wolf may whine softly during the tie. During the inglorious period of wolf persecution on the American prairies, wolves caught in copulatory ties were often clubbed to death.

Although wolves often have long-lasting attachments to their mates, if one wolf dies, the widowed mate may breed with another wolf. In addition, some males may bond to different females in different years, destroying the long-held "mate-for-life" wolf myth.

The gestation period for wolves has long been known; Aristotle's *Historia animalium* lists it as fifty-nine to sixty-three days. Most documented periods today last sixty to sixty-three days.



False pregnancies are not uncommon among wolves, even to the point of milk production.

Rick Bass, in *The Ninemile Wolves*, reported that a mated pair will often go on a "road trip," one last, long hunting trip together, prior to denning.

## Inbreeding

Inbreeding in wolves has been observed in both wild and captive populations. Both granddaughter-grandfather and mother-son couplings have been reported by biologists studying wild wolves, and numerous close breeding relationships have been documented among zoo animals.

The degree to which wolf inbreeding is harmful is not clear. For years there was no evidence that inbreeding was harmful to wolf populations, but it is now known that under specific circumstances, wolf populations can suffer from inbreeding depression, or the negative physical effects of inbreeding.

On Michigan's Isle Royale, wolves first reached the island traveling over ice from the mainland in about 1949. It is unlikely that any new animals have reached the island since then. Genetic studies in 1988 and 1989 showed a high degree of inbreeding, but after thirty-nine years and numerous generations of offspring, no ill effects from inbreeding were noted. Since then, the population has declined from a high of about 50 wolves in 1980 to two in 2017. Over the years, as the population declined and no new wolves arrived on the island, inbreeding has had a significant effect on the population. Of the two remaining wolves, a male and female, the male is the female's father and half-brother, and wolf researchers did not expect them to mate.

In 1991, a study of wolves kept in Scandinavian zoos suggested that inbreeding had caused loss of genetic variability. Physical effects included blindness, loss of weight in juveniles, reduced reproductive ability, and reduced longevity.

In both of these situations, inbreeding has occurred as a result of circumstance or lack of choice. In most wild situations, the opportunity for input of new genetic material is high enough to prevent much inbreeding.

## The Birthing Den

Shortly before giving birth, a pregnant female will seek out a den. Dens may be a deep riverbank hollow, a cleft between rocks, a hollow log, a space under upturned tree roots, or a space under a rock overhang. A. W. F. Banfield, in *The Mammals of Canada*, reported a temporary den in Banff National Park under an old wapiti (elk) hide. Rick Kunelius, in *Animals of the Rockies*, reported that "one wolf even took over an abandoned beaver dam." Adolph Murie, writing in *The Wolves of Mount McKinley*, stated that "so far as I know, all the wolf dens found in Mount McKinley National Park were renovated fox dens." L. David Mech found four sites on Ellesmere Island where the female gave birth in a shallow depression right on the ground.

A wolf den under a rock overhang. © Robert H. Busch

Wolf pups are preyed upon by a wide variety of predators, including bears, cougars, and other wolves. Photo courtesy of William E. Rideg

By three weeks of age, wolf pups explore the area immediately around their den. Photo courtesy of William E. Rideg

Female wolves are attentive mothers; litters range from one to eleven. © Monty Sloan

Dead trees and log piles are common locations for wolf dens. Photo courtesy of Oregon Department of Fish and Wildlife



Dens are often reused by generations of wolves; one den in Jasper National Park was used by wolves eight times in fifteen years. One on Ellesmere Island may be even older, since it contained bones dated at 783 years old.

In a normal den, the birthing chamber lies at the end of a tunnel that may be up to 15 feet long in soft soils. L. David Mech, in *The Arctic Wolf: Living with the Pack,* wrote of one den dug in a hard medium that "apparently had been dug over a period of years up into a river bank, and still was only three feet deep." The den is often slightly elevated above the rest of the tunnel, and no den-lining material is used. The mother keeps the den clean by eating the fecal matter of her pups. The birthing chamber is usually about three feet in diameter and about two feet high.

The entrance to the den is about 20 to 28 inches wide and 15 to 20 inches high. Dens may have two or more entrances, both of which are usually marked by a large pile of dirt. Den sites are often near a source of water and often elevated so that the wolves can detect approaching enemies.

The alpha male is very protective of the den. He will often act as a decoy, leading predators away from the site. Although wolves will often stand their ground against wild predators at the den site, they will usually run away from the den at the approach of humans.

Occasional cases of more than one female using the same den at a time have been reported.

Wolves may change dens through the year, moving their pups a mile or more. This may occur because of parasitic infestation of the den or because of a disturbance of the den site by humans or other animals. In Yellowstone National Park, it has been found that females reuse the previous year's den 70 percent of the time.



## Litters

Just prior to birth and for a few days after birth, the female will not allow the male into the den. The time of birth is private, for her and her alone.

By four weeks of age, wolf pups are off exploring their wild world. Photo courtesy of William E. Rideg

The blue eyes of wolf pups change to a gold color by 8 to 16 weeks.© Monty Sloan



Most wolf pups are born in late March to early May, with southern wolves giving birth earlier in the season, and arctic wolves sometimes giving birth as late as June. The litter averages five to six, but ranges from one to eleven. (Some reported litters of thirteen may actually be two combined litters in the same den.) In one Montana study of twenty-seven litters, the average litter comprised four to five pups.

Pack stresses can cause increased litters; in Yellowstone National Park, litters of ten to eleven pups followed several years of wolf poisonings, shootings, and trapping. The same response to long-term population threats has been observed in coyotes.

There is much excitement in the pack caused by the birth of pups. Prior to a birth, pack members may gather at the den entrance, whining and scratching the ground. Lois Crisler, in *Arctic Wild,* described how her "male wolf . . . kidnapped a dog pup, not to kill but to care for. Wolves are crazy about puppies."

Pups at birth have large, blunt heads; short, thin tail; small ears; and their eyes are tightly closed. Their little bodies are 8 to 13 inches long, they weigh about 12 to 16 ounces, and they sport a brownish or slate-blue wooly coat.

### STAGES OF PUP DEVELOPMENT

*10 to 13 days:* the eyes open.

*3 weeks:* they can hear, their milk teeth appear, they explore the den area.

*4 weeks:* they leave the den regularly, weigh 5–6 pounds, begin to eat meat, and begin to howl.

*5 weeks:* they may travel up to a mile from the den.

*5–8 weeks:* pups are weaned and then moved to a rendezvous site.

*12 weeks:* they begin to accompany adults on hunting trips.

*16–26 weeks:* the milk teeth are replaced.

*7–8 months*: they actively begin hunting.

Young wolf pups spend much of their day sleeping. (Photo of captive wolf from Wildlife Science Center in Forest Lake, MN. Courtesy of Jenni Bidner)

At first, pups are nursed in the den by their mother. Nursing pups feed four or five times each day for periods of three to five minutes at each feeding. During this time, other wolves bring the nursing mother food.

Most pups are born with blue eyes, which gradually change to a yellow-gold color by eight to sixteen weeks, though sometimes their eyes can change color much later. Occasionally, a mature wolf will be found with blue eyes. (One male wolf at Wolf Haven, near Tenino, Washington, reached the age of fifteen years without his eyes ever changing from a light blue color.)

By around five to eight weeks, the pups are weaned on more solid foods. Most of their fare at this point is food regurgitated by other pack members. According to L. David Mech, in *The Way of the Wolf*, an adult can regurgitate from any one stomachful "at least three times." Pups eagerly await adults returning from hunts with a hot meal, charging the adults and licking their muzzles and wriggling with their entire bodies in anticipation. It is common for other pack members to baby-sit the pups while their mother is off hunting.

In captivity, mother wolves may eat injured pups, a deviant behavior that does not appear to have been documented in the wild. Females both in the wild and in captivity have been seen to bury their dead pups.

At about eight weeks of age, the pups are moved to a so-called rendezvous site, which is really a summer nursery for the pups. These half-acre to one-acre sites are a mile or less from the den site and usually near water. The rendezvous site contains space for the pups to roam around, playing and learning from observing the other pack members. Durward Allen once wrote that they "climb over, chew, and harass the long-suffering elders, who often have to move away."

Wolf pups grow quickly. John Gunson in Alberta found that about 96 percent of the total length and 79 percent of the total weight are achieved in their first year of life. By six months wolf pups are hard to distinguish from adults. By eight months the pups have almost reached their full adult weight.

Pups spend their first year with the pack learning hunting and survival skills and the complex social hierarchy of the pack. All members of the pack aid in training the pups, pushing them with their noses to move them along or pinning them to the ground or giving scruff bites to discipline them.

Less than half of all wolf pups survive to adulthood. (Photo of captive wolf from Wildlife Science Center in Forest Lake, MN. Courtesy of Jenni Bidner)

Wolf pups are usually born in April and early summer and are out of the den and practicing their wolf skills, like howling, four weeks later. Photo courtesy of Oregon Fish and Wildlife

After a year or so of this canine college, the pups either disperse or stay as full-fledged pack members.

Pups represent the future of the pack, and are therefore prized and coddled members of the group. Rick Bass, in *The Ninemile Wolves,* told the moving story of a male wolf in Montana that, after his mate was shot, raised their six pups by himself. R. D. Lawrence, in *In Praise of Wolves,* stated that when pups die, pack members "mourn as deeply as might a human family."

Pup mortality in their first year ranges from 6 percent to 80 percent, according to various studies. Pups die from diseases, malnutrition, and starvation in times of depleted food supplies. Dada Gottelli and Claudio Sillero-Zubiri found the highest mortality in the Abyssinian wolf to occur "between six months and one year of age, when weak juveniles starve to death or succumb to diseases."

Less than half of all pups survive to adulthood.

## Territories

A territory can be defined as the area in which a wolf pack ordinarily feeds and that it is willing to defend.

The size of territories depends on the interdependent factors of prey abundance, climate, presence of other predators, presence of other wolf packs, and the nature of the terrain.

Territories tend to expand in winter, as the prey density decreases. Territories also tend to be larger in tundra areas, where prey is scarce, than in wooded regions, and often are larger in the north, where prey density is low.

The size of territories may thus range from 18 square miles to over 1,000. One of the smallest gray wolf territories on record is the 25 square miles for one pack on northern Vancouver Island. This small territory is possible because of its lack of predators and its high deer population.

A gray wolf travels along a trail on the pack's rendezvous site in the Clearwater National Forest, Idaho. © Jim Yuskavitch

## TERRITORIES OF NORTH AMERICAN WOLVES

| Area | Year of study | Average territory size |
|---|---|---|
| Northeast Alberta | 1980 | 207 (square miles) |
| Northwest Alberta | 1983 | 150 |
| Southeast British Columbia | 1985 | 319 |
| Vancouver Island | 1982 | 27 |
| Ontario | 1967 | 20 |
| Southern Ontario | 1969 | 68 |
| East-central Ontario | 1972 | 88 |
| Quebec | 1985 | 125 |
| Alaska | 1977 | 809 |
| Alaska | 1983 | 260 |
| Northwest Alaska | 1983 | 631 |
| Kenai Peninsula, Alaska | 1984 | 249 |
| South-central Alaska | 1987 | 643 |
| Minnesota | 1975 | 38 |
| Minnesota | 1977 | 87 |
| Minnesota | 1979 | 85 |
| Minnesota | 1981 | 134 |
| Minnesota | 1982 | 90 |
| Yellowstone National Park | 2015 | 106–239 |
| Montana | 2002 | 185 |
| Idaho | 2016 | 265 |

(Source: USFWS, 1988, National Park Service, 2016, Montana Fish, Wildlife and Parks, 2002, Idaho Department of Fish and Game)

One of the largest is the 1,000-square-mile territory described by L. David Mech for a pack on Canada's Ellesmere Island. Adolph Murie reported a territory of over 1,800 square miles in Denali National Park in the 1940s. The average territory in the lower forty-eight states may be less than 100 square miles, while in Alaska, territories may be many times that size. Territories of up to 2,300 square miles have been recorded for lone wolves.

Eurasian wolves often occupy very small territories, as the result of a severe lack of habitat and high densities of people. Dada Gottelli and Claudio

## DENSITIES OF WOLVES IN NORTH AMERICA

| Area | Years of study | Wolf density |
|---|---|---|
| Northwest Alberta | 1978–1980 | 23 (square miles/wolf) |
| Alberta | 1942–1946 | 43 |
| Northeast Alberta | 1975–1978 | 47 |
| Northern British Columbia | 1977–1982 | 44 |
| Manitoba | 1975–1979 | 17 |
| Northwest Territories | 1960–1965 | 7 |
| Northwest Territories | 1968 | 11 |
| Ontario | 1961–1962 | 10 |
| Ontario | 1975–1979 | 26 |
| Northern Saskatchewan | 1946–1951 | 61 |
| Quebec | 1981–1984 | 36 |
| Central Alaska | 1975 | 25 |
| Kenai Peninsula, Alaska | 1976–1982 | 24 |
| Isle Royale, Michigan | 1959–1976 | 9 |
| Minnesota | 1946–1953 | 17 |
| Minnesota | 1971–1972 | 11 |
| Minnesota | 1972–1977 | 23 |
| Minnesota | 1966–1985 | 14 |
| Northern Range, Yellowstone | 2013 | 53 |

(Source: USFWS, 1988)

Sillero-Zubiri found that the territories of Ethiopian wolves ranged from only two and a half to four square miles.

Depending upon the presence of other wolf packs, some territories may be quite flexible, allowing the wolves to follow migrating caribou herds. The Barren Lands wolves of Canada's Northwest Territories do not appear to have fixed territories in winter. Studies in Finland and Russia have also confirmed that to some extent the wolves there follow the migrating prey.

Although wolf densities were often stated in the past as averaging one wolf per 10 square miles, they actually can cover a much larger range. One recent USFWS summary of wolf densities ranged from 7 to 61 square miles

Wolf pups will mouth their mother's muzzle to ask for regurgitated food. © Monty Sloan

per wolf, with the average density being seventeen square miles per wolf. One of the highest wolf densities in the world is in the Peace-Athabasca delta in Alberta's Wood Buffalo National Park in Canada, where there is one wolf per 1.6 square miles.

## Food

Although John A. Murray has described the wolf as an "impartial consumer of anything from mice to moose," most studies have indicated that ungulates

**WOLF PREY IN NORTH AMERICA**

| Area | Primary prey | Secondary prey | Year of study |
|---|---|---|---|
| Southern Alberta | elk 59% | mule deer 18% | 1947 |
| Northern Alberta | buffalo 65% | fox 6% | 1955 |
| Central Alberta | elk 40% | mule deer 29% | 1974 |
| Northeast Alberta | moose 49% | hares 36% | 1980 |
| Central Manitoba | elk 87% | moose 10% | 1983 |

## WOLF PREY IN NORTH AMERICA

| Area | Primary prey | Secondary prey | Year of study |
|---|---|---|---|
| Northwest Territories | caribou 47% | birds 13% | 1972 |
| Ontario | beaver 48% | deer 35% | 1967 |
| Southern Ontario | deer 80% | moose 8% | 1969 |
| Central Ontario | deer 52% | beaver 31% | 1976 |
| Quebec | moose 43% | beaver 36% | 1984 |
| Central Alaska | caribou 43% | Dall sheep 26% | 1944 |
| Alaska | moose 56% | hares 30% | 1976 |
| Alaska | caribou 67% | moose 26% | 1977 |
| Central Alaska | moose 55% | caribou 12% | 1983 |
| Northwest Alaska | caribou 94% | ground squirrel 15% | 1983 |
| Kenai Peninsula, Alaska | moose 67% | hares 12% | 1984 |
| Michigan | deer 38% | deer 38% | 1944 |
| Isle Royale, Minnesota | moose 76% | beaver 11% | 1966 |
| Isle Royale, Minnesota | beaver 51% | moose 49% | 1977 |
| Minnesota | deer 80% | hares 8% | 1955 |
| Minnesota | deer 44% | beaver 16% | 1972 |
| Minnesota | deer 46% | moose 30% | 1975 |
| Minnesota | deer 67% | moose 27% | 1981 |
| Minnesota | deer 78% | hares 23% | 1983 |
| Northwest Montana | deer 60% | elk 30% | 1984 |
| Wisconsin | deer 97% | hares 3% | 1952 |
| Oregon | elk 60% | deer 38% | 2017 |
| Yellowstone National Park | elk 89% | bison 4% | 2005 |
| Yukon Territories | moose 79% | Dall sheep 18% | 1991 |

(Source: USFWS, 1988, National Park Service, Oregon Department of Fish and Wildlife, Yukon Fish and Wildlife Branch, 1991)

A COMPLETE LIST OF WOLF FOOD ITEMS WOULD INCLUDE THE FOLLOWING: MOOSE, DEER, ELK, BUFFALO, CARIBOU, GOAT, SHEEP, SAIGA ANTELOPE, TIBETAN ANTELOPE, YAK, URIAL, ARGALI, TIBETAN GAZELLE, CAMEL, IBEX, CHAMOIS, WILD HORSE, WILD BOAR, BEAVER, PORCUPINE, RABBIT, HARE, MOUSE, GOPHER, SHREW, MOLE, RAT, RACCOON, MUSKRAT, WOODCHUCK, MARMOT, INSECTS, NUTS, BERRIES, FRUITS, SHELLFISH, BIRDS, EARTHWORMS, CARRION, AND HUMAN GARBAGE.

(hoofed animals including deer, moose, elk, and caribou) tend to be predominate in the wolf's diet.

Deer are an important wolf-prey item the world over. © Robert H. Busch

Wolves, like domestic dogs, will also eat grass as an intestinal scour or purgative.

Food sources are flexible and change through the year with availability. Adolph Murie, in *The Wolves of Mount McKinley*, wrote that "when the caribou calves make their appearance they furnish to wolves a large and easily obtainable food supply. At this time wolf predation on sheep practically ceases." In Jasper National Park, wolves often switch from adult mule deer to their calves in the spring. It has also been observed that some tundra wolves turn to mice and ground squirrels when the caribou migrate north for the summer. One study in Denali National Park found that rodents made up 26 percent of the wolf's diet during the summer months.

Beavers are an important alternate food in summer in much of central and northern Canada, when many wolves hunt alone. And in Denali they are important in late winter, when other prey is scarce. According to Canadian wolf biologist Lu Carbyn, "Prey smaller than the beaver rarely form a substantial part of the wolf's diet."

Wolves have been observed fishing in many northern areas of North America. Photo courtesy of William E. Rideg

One of the most unusual food sources for wolves is fish. Though in the Northwest Territories, biologist Bob Bromley once observed a wolf catch 5 fish in 15 minutes in the Talston River.

It is important to realize that wolves are not only hunters, but also scavengers. In one study of thirty moose carcasses in Algonquin Park, only four were killed by wolves; the remainder had all died natural deaths before their carcasses were scavenged by wolves. It is often difficult to determine whether an animal has been killed or its carcass scavenged, and many early wolf researchers completely ignored this point. In Europe, many wolves have learned to scavenge around human garbage dumps, echoing the unfortunate habits of North American black bears.

Wolves eat an average of 5 to 12 pounds of food per day, but often go for days without eating. They will stay at a large kill site for a few days gorging on the food, then lie about with bloated stomachs for days after. In fact, in 1989 and 1990, researchers in Alaska's Gates of the Arctic National Park found that 48.8 percent of their study wolves' time was spent sleeping or resting (walking or running occupied 34.6 percent of the remainder, feeding 9.8 percent, and social behavior 6.8 percent).

In one study at Isle Royale, Michigan, each wolf ate an average of 9.7 to 13.9 pounds of moose per day during winter. A similar study in northeast Alberta found a consumption rate of 10.8 to 13.4 pounds of prey per day, with 2 to 12 days between kills.

In one documented case in Russia, a wounded wolf went seventeen days without eating in winter and was still in relatively good health when it was finally shot.



After such an enforced fast, the wolf's appetite can be truly voracious. Jack O'Connor, in *The Big Game Animals of North America,* stated that "after one such fast, one 110-pound wolf devoured over 19 pounds of meat at one meal." The idiom "wolfing down" was no doubt inspired by such observations.

Morsels of large prey are sometimes cached at sites up to a half mile from the den site. The caches are dug using the front feet, and the dirt is replaced on top of the food using the nose. These caches are often dug up by foxes, weasels, and other scavengers, and are an important food source for these smaller scroungers. Caching seems to be more common in the northern and Arctic areas. Some biologists believe that caching sometimes represents a type of displacement behavior, an activity used to distract the wolf from a stressful situation, noting that captive animals cache food quite regularly.

In captivity, wolves are often maintained on commercial dry dog food mixes, although there are a few reports of stomach torsion from eating these dry foods. In addition to commercial dry dog chow, captive wolves are fed commercial mixes such as ZuPreem and Central Nebraska Feline Diet (carnivore) plus ground red meat or chicken backs and necks.

Some zoos supplement this food with occasional road-killed deer supplied by government wildlife agencies. Captive wolves have a smaller caloric requirement than most wild wolves because of their relative lack of activity. Thus, most zoos feed only two to three and a half pounds of food per day to each wolf in their care.

Wolves require from one to three quarts of water per day, depending on the size of the animal, the climate, and the moisture content of the prey.

## Hunting

Wolves detect prey by three primary means: scent (most common), tracking, and chance encounters.

After prey is detected, wolves may split up to search through brush, travel on ridgetops searching for the prey below, or test herds looking for signs of weakness.

It has long been recognized that wolves often take advantage of weak individuals in a herd. In 1804, Captain William Clark of the famed Lewis and Clark expedition wrote that prairie wolves followed the buffalo and fed "on those that are killed by accident or those that are too pore or fat to keep up with the gangue."

Later researchers reinforced the image of the wolf as a predator of the very young, the very old, the weak, or the diseased. Adolph Murie, in *The Wolves of Mount McKinley*, wrote: "Many bands seem to be chased, given a trial, and if no advantage is gained or weak animals discovered, the wolves

Deer constitute a prime food item for wolves in much of North America. © Monty Sloan

THE CARIBOU FEEDS THE WOLF, BUT IT IS THE WOLF WHO KEEPS THE CARIBOU STRONG.

—Keewatin Eskimo saying

travel on to chase other bands until an advantage can be seized." Lois Crisler notes, in *Arctic Wild*, "In all our time in the arctic, the only healthy caribou we saw or found killed were fawns with big herds." She observed that adult caribou killed had "hoof disease, or lung tapeworm, or nostril clogging . . . botflies." In a 1980 study in northeast Alberta, T. K. Fuller and L. B. Keith found that "wolves killed disproportionately more young, old and probably debilitated moose (*Alces alces*), as well as more female calves." Canadian biologists Lu Carbyn and Tim Trottier found that in Alberta's Wood Buffalo National Park, "wolves selected herds with calves over herds without calves." In a 1992 study in Poland, 61 percent of the red deer and 94 percent of the wild boar killed by wolves were less than one year old. Studies in Yellowstone National Park have shown that the average age of cow elk taken by wolves there is fourteen years, with many older than twenty. A study of moose kills on Michigan's Isle Royale found that most were either very young or very old. None were one- to six-year-old prime animals. In fact, the only animal that habitually preys upon prime, mature animals is man.

*Greedy Wolves Over Dead Buffalo*. Ink wash over graphite on paper by Peter Moran, c. 1879–90. (ACM No. 75.65, Amon Carter Museum, Fort Worth, Texas)

Thus, although it does not prey only on the weak and the ill, the wolf is an opportunist, and it is inevitably the disadvantaged animals that are easiest to catch.

Murie concluded that "through predation the weak and diseased are eliminated, so that in the long run what seems so harmful may be beneficial to the species." This removal of biologically inferior animals has been termed the "sanitation effect" by modern biologists.

Weakened animals may show their condition to predators through body stance, uncoordinated movements, the smell of wounds or infection, or some other tangible signal. The reading and evaluation of these signals compose what Barry Lopez has poetically termed "the conversation of death."

Once a weak individual is selected by a pack, it is brought down after a chase. Usually the chases are short, but L. David Mech has stated, "One wolf I know of chased a deer for 13 miles." Lu Carbyn observed a wolf hunt in Alberta's Wood Buffalo National Park in which a pack intermittently attacked a bison calf for eleven hours.

Prey that runs is usually chased. Prey that stands its ground may be able to bluff off its pursuers. Moose and elk often take to deep water or swift rivers and await the departure of pursuing wolves. But more often than not, the wolves wait. While the majority of the pack rests, one or two members test the prey for signs of fatigue.

David Gray described one such encounter in Canada's high Arctic in *The Muskoxen of Polar Bear Pass*: "the wolves approached to within a hundred meters of the herd . . . one wolf lay down as two others circled the milling herd."

When the attack comes, the prey is usually seized by either the nose or the rump. Rarely, if ever, does a wolf hamstring a prey animal. This is one of the oldest and most pervasive false beliefs held about wolves. As late as 1980, the *Audubon Society Field Guide to North American Mammals* stated that the wolf kills "by slashing tendons in the hindlegs." This is pure myth. In a 1955 study by M. H. Stenlund in Minnesota, "no evidence of hamstringing of deer was found." L. David Mech, in a 1966 study, determined that "no evidence of hamstringing was found during the present study."

All that remains of the prey after a wolf kill are a few bones and bits of fur.
© Robert H. Busch

The actual death of the prey is usually caused by massive blood loss, shock, or both. Sometimes with smaller prey a neck bite will snap a backbone.

Wolves usually begin to feed on the rump if it was exposed during the chase or else on the internal organs. The muscle and flesh is the last portion of the prey that is eaten, in contrast with human eating habits.

After the prey is consumed, little remains at the killing site. Lu Carbyn described a 1980 wolf kill of a bison calf: "Virtually nothing remained of the calf carcass within twenty-four hours except small tufts of hair and small portions of both scapulae, pelvis, and lower jaw."

Contrary to popular belief, most prey chased by wolves actually gets away. In one study on Michigan's Isle Royale, only 3 percent of the moose that were tested ended up being killed and eaten. Another study on the same island found that 8 percent were killed. One study of musk ox on Banks Island in Canada's Arctic determined that only 14 percent of the musk ox chases were successful. A northeast Alberta study found that 13 percent of the attempts on moose succeeded there. In Yellowstone National Park, the hunting success rate for wolves preying on elk is no more than 20 percent and drops to 10 percent when they target adult elk rather than calves. The percentage of prey that is killed is called the "predation efficiency," and in spite of the wolf's prowess as a hunter, the majority of its prey escapes death.

Another myth is that packs are required to bring down large prey; several observers have seen single wolves catch and kill elk and moose. The first wolf to return to Sweden after the extermination of its wolf population regularly brought down large moose by itself.

The choice of prey depends to some degree on terrain and climatic conditions. Rolf Peterson and Durward Allen found that in deep snow conditions, when snow is packed and crusted, wolves are able to maneuver better in hunting. However, animals such as snowshoe hares are difficult prey in winter because of their agility on their huge snowshoelike feet. In times of scarce food, wolves will often return to old kills or to their food caches.

Wolves, especially young ones, can become prey specific; Rick Bass, in *The Ninemile Wolves*, wrote of orphaned pups that became "used to whitetails and wouldn't touch" the offered sheep carcasses brought by concerned USFWS agents. Lu Carbyn found that mule deer were the primary prey of wolves in Jasper National Park despite the fact that elk were three times more abundant.

During the summer, many wolves hunt individually rather than with the pack. On Ellesmere Island, L. David Mech observed one wolf that "left the den to forage individually about eighty percent of the time." At this time, small rodents and birds can become a significant part of a wolf's diet. These animals are caught by the wolf's jumping up and stabbing down with its forelegs onto the prey. Solitary foraging is the norm year-round for the Abyssinian wolf.

One of the most confusing aspects of hunting behavior is that of surplus killing, or the killing of prey beyond the food requirements of the pack. (Technically, the term is to be applied only when the prey is not eaten.) L. David Mech has theorized that this may be more common when wolves are denning, thus ensuring a food supply for the new pups, crucial to the long-term survival of the pack. Another theory is that due to the chaos that ensues during a hunt and individual wolves not always being aware of what the others are doing, more prey animals are inadvertently killed than are needed. Even when surplus killing occurs, the carcasses do not go to waste, as the wolves will return periodically to feed on them. The myth that wolves will go into a killing frenzy and kill other pack members after a successful and particularly gory kill is not true. Again, the human imagination has wrongly tainted the wolf.

Wolf hunting behavior may minimize the chances that they will deplete the prey source in their territories. L. David Mech found one pack in Minnesota that varied its killing by hunting in a different part of its territory each year, allowing prey numbers elsewhere to recover, aiding the long-term survival of the pack.

CHAPTER

5

# THE WOLF IN HUMAN CULTURE

PROBABLY NO OTHER ANIMAL IN history has suffered the amount of misplaced animosity as has the wolf.

For centuries, the wolf was the very symbol of avarice, viciousness, and guile. It has only been in the past two decades that humans have become more accepting of predators and of their rightful place in ecological systems.

## The Wolf as a Nurturer

One of the earliest legends involving wolves is that of Romulus and Remus, which originated around the fourth century BC. Its most popular version

Romulus and Remus being suckled by a she-wolf. Musei Capitolini, Rome, Italy. Photo courtesy of the Italian Tourist Board

was that written by Plutarch, who described in AD 70 the story of the twin sons of a vestal virgin, banished to the wilderness and raised by wolves until rescued. The twins then went on to become heroic figures, the legendary founders of ancient Rome.

The nurturer image was repeated in Turkey, whose legendary founder, Tu Kueh was suckled by a wolf, and in Aztec and Navajo legends. The sixth-century religious reformer Zoroaster was reputed to have been suckled by a she-wolf, and the Teutonic hero Siegfried was supposed to have had a she-wolf for a foster mother. There is also an Irish legend of a young king who was raised by wolves and grew up to reclaim his throne.



All of these legends most likely grew from observations of the close family ties that exist within wolf societies. Sadly this positive early image was soon eclipsed by myth and fear.

## The Big Bad Wolf

The European mythology surrounding wolves is large and complex.

The stories attributed to Aesop (c. 600 BC) are some of the first recorded references to the cunning and deceit of the wolf. Aesop was a slave whose witty fables were in fact responsible for his death.

The gaze of the wolf was once thought to cause blindness. Photo courtesy of William E. Rideg

He was accused of sacrilege, found guilty, and thrown over a cliff. Many of his fables feature wolves as the main characters. These include "The Dog and the Wolf," "The Wolf and the Lamb," "A Shepherd and a Young Wolf," "The Wolf and the Crane," "The Wolf Helps the Dog," "The Wolf and the Shepherds," "The Wolf and the Mouse," and "The Wolf and the Hunter." "The Shepherd Boy and the Wolf" (popularly known as "The Boy Who Cried Wolf") is perhaps the best known of these wolf fables.

THE WOLF DOTH SOMETHING EVERY WEEK THAT KEEPS HIM FROM THE CHURCH ON SUNDAY.

—*Old English proverb*

Around 300 BC, wolves became the object of a devotional cult among the Celts, who saw them as companions of a god. Celtic saints said to have tamed wolves were thought to have incredible powers.

In Greek mythology, Charon, the ferryman, wore wolf's ears. In the *Epic of Gilgamesh*, the goddess Ishtar had the power to turn enemies into wolves. Hecate, the goddess of death, was shown as wearing three wolf heads. In another Greek myth, a king named Lycaon was turned into a wolf by the great god Zeus. (The name Lycaon survives today in the gray wolf subspecies *Canis lupus lycaon*, the eastern timber wolf.) The Athenians had great respect for the wolf and decreed that any man who killed one had to pay for a funeral for the animal.

As soon as humans began to farm lands and protect herds, the wolf's reputation as a symbol of birth and death became that of a voracious killer.

In the Bible (John 10:12), Jesus described himself as a shepherd protecting the sheep from the wolf. Lord Byron wrote of an attacker "coming down like a wolf on the fold." In the 10th century, England's King Edgar the Peaceful (a horrible misnomer) allowed his loyal subjects to pay their

**THE BOY WHO CRIED WOLF**

A SHEPHERD'S BOY KEPT HIS SHEEP UPON A COMMON, AND IN SPORT HAD A ROGUISH TRICK OF CRYING, "A WOLF! A WOLF!" WHEN THERE WAS NO WOLF. HE HAD JESTED THE COUNTRY PEOPLE SO MANY TIMES WITH HIS FALSE ALARMS THAT AT LAST WHEN HIS FLOCK WAS ATTACKED BY WOLVES AND HIS CRIES WERE IN EARNEST, NO ONE WOULD BELIEVE HIM. AND SO THE WOLVES GOT HIS SHEEP.

Little Red Riding Hood and friend. Engraving by Gustave Doré for *French Fairy Tales*

taxes with wolf heads. T. H. White's *The Book of Beasts,* a translation of 12th-century Latin tales, called the wolf "a rapacious beast hankering for gore," and declared "what can we mean by the Wolf but the Devil." And Shakespeare called hunger "the universal wolf."

From such beginnings grew our modern sayings referring to a human as being as "hungry as a wolf" and stocking up to "keep the wolf from the door."

During the Middle Ages, wolves were ascribed magical powers, and wolf parts became an important part of many early pharmacies. Powdered wolf liver was used to ease birth pains. A wolf's right front paw, tied around one's throat, was believed to ease the swelling caused by throat infections. Dried wolf meat was a popular treatment for aches in the shins.

It was widely believed that a horse that stepped in a wolf print would be crippled. Many people refused to eat wolf meat in the belief that it was poisonous. Others believed that the breath of a wolf could cook meat. Naturalists of the day believed that wolves sharpened their teeth before going out on a hunt. Dead wolves were buried at a village entrance to keep out other wolves (a bizarre belief echoed today by farmers who continue to shoot predators and hang them on fence posts to repel other predators).

Travelers were warned about the perils of walking through lonely stretches of woods, and stone shelters were built to protect them from attacks. Our modern word "loophole" is derived from the European term "loup hole," or wolf hole, a spy hole in shelters through which travelers could watch for wolves.

La Fontaine's fables gave the wolf intelligence and a soul. *Le Renard, Le Loup, et Le Cheval*, a French engraving by Oudry for *La Fontaine's Fables*, 1751

In Norse mythology, the god Odin kept two huge wolves at his side that accompanied him into battle along with two ravens, which tore at the corpses of the dead. The name Wolfram, meaning "wolf-raven" became a great warrior's name, and to see a wolf and a raven together on the way to battle was thought to ensure victory. The giantesses of Norse legends flew the skies astride huge gray wolves. (Other wolf names include Rudolph, from *Ruhmwolf*, meaning "victorious wolf," and Wolfgang, meaning "wolf going before," a man whose coming is announced by the appearance of wolves.)



France, Germany, and a number of Slavic countries all shared legends of the "corn-wolf" or "rye-wolf," a benevolent spirit that guarded their crops. When the wind set a field of rye into a wavelike motion, the peasants would whisper that "the wolf is going through the rye." In eastern Prussia, peasants would watch for wolves fleeing through the fields during a harvest. If the wolf carried its tail high, it signaled poor weather for the next year and a poor crop; the tail held low was a sign of fertility and a good crop.

The story of Little Red Riding Hood, which originated in the 1600s, reinforces the purported lupine attributes of cunning and viciousness in a story steeped in sexual overtones. Even today, we refer to a lusting male human as a "real wolf." The other famed children's tale relating to wolves, "The Three Little Pigs," again does nothing to help the wolf's image. And it is on these fictional childhood stories that much of the hate and prejudice directed toward the wolf is built.

The literature of the day perpetuated the negative wolf imagery. Daniel Defoe's *Robinson Crusoe*, published in 1719, described wolves as "ravenous" and "vicious creatures."

Jean de La Fontaine's fables, published in France in 1751, were satirical pieces that echoed those of Aesop. La Fontaine, though, believed that animals had souls and a high degree of intelligence, and the wolves in his fables were painted with a more understanding brush.



In 1894, Rudyard Kipling wrote *The Jungle Book*, one of the first novels to portray the close social ties of the wolf pack. In the book, wolves are described as "the Free People." It was a lupine label that was not to be reused for many decades.

## Werewolves

There are a number of cultures that have were-creatures in their mythology, usually involving large predators that hunt by night. Often the were-creature takes the form of the most dangerous animal found in the area. India has weretigers, Africa has wereleopards, but the most famous of all are the werewolves of medieval Europe.

The term "were" is from the Old English word *wer* meaning man. Thus, werewolves, man wolves, are half human and half animal.

References to wolf men arose in Europe around the time of Christ. In Book 10 of Homer's *Odyssey*, the grandfather of the hero Odysseus is named Autolykos, meaning "he who is a wolf." The people of Arcadia believed that some members of their culture had the ability to turn themselves into wolves. If they tasted human flesh during this transformation, they were doomed to live out their lives as a wild beast unless they abstained from eating human flesh for nine full years. The ancient Greek writer Herodotus wrote in the fifth century BC of a tribe living north of the Black Sea whose members could turn themselves into wolves for a few days each year. The roman poet Virgil wrote in the first century BC about a sorcerer who took poisonous herbs to turn himself into a werewolf. The belief in magical herbs lasted for centuries; in the fourth and fifth centuries, magicians sold herbs that "guaranteed" such transformations. One of the earliest uses of mistletoe was as a werewolf repellent.

However, not all scholars of the day were believers. Pliny wrote: "That men can change into wolves and then back to men once more I shall dismiss absolutely as nonsense."

Werewolves were believed to be voluntary or involuntary.

Many voluntary werewolves were believed to be people who had made a pact with the devil. Most werewolf tales described men who turned into werewolves at night, when they devoured people and animals, and then returned to human form at daybreak. Night was the time of the devil.

Involuntary werewolves were those whose actions had inadvertently caused a horrible transformation. People born on Christmas Eve were often thought to be werewolves. In Sicily, a child conceived during a new moon was thought sure to grow up to be a werewolf. German folktales told of a mountain brook whose waters turned humans into werewolves. Tales in Serbia created werewolves from people who drank water collected in wolf footprints. People with slanting eyebrows were also automatically assumed to be wolf men. In Greece, all epileptics were thought to be werewolves.

Some werewolves were believed to be sinners transformed by God for their actions. Certain saints were thought to have the power to change sinners into werewolves. In Armenia, it was believed that an adulterous woman would be visited by the devil, who would bring her a wolf skin to wear. To pay for her sins, she had to wear the skin for seven years before she could return to human form.

Other involuntary werewolves were those who for one reason or another were hated by their contemporaries. In 1685, a wolf preying on livestock near Ansbach, Germany, was identified as the reincarnation of a despised town official. The wolf was killed and dressed in a suit, complete with wig and beard. Its muzzle was cut off and a mask of the official was placed over the face. The body was then hung.

Voluntary werewolves intentionally took magic potions or wore magic robes to achieve the transformation. In the 17th century, English sorcerers believed that they could transform themselves into werewolves by wearing an enchanted girdle and by anointing their bodies with a magical ointment.

Citizens of Rome believed that werewolves could not be shot, for their skin was thought to be bulletproof. The belief in werewolves was so prevalent that bandits wore wolf skins in order to prevent being shot at by local peasants.

Many tales had the common thread of a werewolf suffering an injury at night and the injury reappearing when the beast assumed human form again at daylight. Peasants learned to hide scars for fear of retribution as a werewolf.

Great Britain had myths describing werewolf families, whose curse was passed on through generations.

Authorities took werewolf tales very seriously. In 1572, near the French city of Dole, the municipal government passed a law permitting out-of-season hunting of werewolves in order to rid their town of this terrible menace. The parliament of Franche-Comté in all good faith passed a law expelling known werewolves.

Werewolf legends reached their peak in France in the 1600s, when hundreds of innocent men and children were put to death for their imagined powers. Often it was the mentally ill or the physically handicapped who paid a terrible price for their infirmities. Many were burned at the stake.

In the 18th century, the wolves that chased livestock in some parts of Russia were thought to be transformed Swedish soldiers who had died in the Swedish war with Russia.

Some writers have theorized that many of the medieval werewolves were humans suffering from lycanthropy (from *lykos*, meaning "wolf," and *anthropos*, meaning "man"), the psychiatric disorder in which the patient sincerely believes that he or she is a wolf or some other nonhuman animal, but this is unlikely. According to most medical authorities, the affliction is extremely rare and unlikely to account for the massive numbers of purported werewolves of old.

The belief in werewolves survived in France into the 19th century, when peasants refused to go out at night for fear of the *loup-garou*, the French name for werewolf.

Surprisingly, even today there are those who still believe in werewolves. One study in 1992 showed that almost 80 percent of Russian farmers surveyed believed in werewolves, proving that the negative imagery associated with wolves still lives.

## Man-Eating Wolves

Tales of man-eating wolves are very common in Europe, especially from the period between 1600 and 1800. Of the many stories of man-eating wolves in Europe, none is better known than that of the wolves of Gévaudan.

Between 1764 and 1767, two large wolves were blamed for the killing of a number of villagers in the area near Gévaudan in central France. The wolves were abnormally large, with unusually colored coats. One had a large, bright white throat patch and the other was reddish in hue, neither of which are color traits of true wolves. Their history was recorded by Father François Fabré, the parish priest of Gévaudan, in 1901. He attributed sixty-four killings, mostly of children, to the two wolves. One of the wolves was finally killed in 1765, and was found to weigh over 130 pounds. The other was killed the next year and weighed 109 pounds. One interesting hypothesis on the identity of the man-eating wolves of Gévaudan put forward by Karl-Hans Taake of the University of Osnabruck is that it was not a wolf or wolves at all but a lion that had escaped from a private zoo, which were popular among French noblemen during that period. Descriptions of the animal, including its "Mohawk haircut," suggest that it may have been a subadult, male African lion.

A few years ago, the killings were investigated by C. H. D. Clarke, former head of the wildlife branch of the Ontario Ministry of Natural Resources, who concluded that the Gévaudan animals were probably not wolves, but "dog-wolf crosses with hybrid vigor." At the time, huge mastiffs were commonly kept as guard dogs, and it is likely that hybrids of these strong and vicious beasts were responsible for many of the killings attributed to wolves. Skull measurements of the animals confirmed that they were more dog than wolf.

## Children Reared by Wolves

One of the strongest cornerstones of wolf mythology is that of wolves raising orphaned children. Although there is no documented evidence to support any of the stories, it is possible that they may have originated from small children crawling into wolf dens and being discovered there later by humans who misinterpreted the circumstances. Many of these stories originated in India, where it was common for poverty-stricken parents to abandon their unwanted children. It is also interesting that most of these stories appeared after 1894, when Rudyard Kipling's *The Jungle Book* introduced the character of Mowgli, an Indian orphan raised by wolves.

However, there are much earlier accounts, many of which are probably related to the wolf's early status as a symbol of fertility. The oldest recorded case appears to be that of the German wolf child of Hesse in 1344. Another early report of children purported to have been raised by wolves was that written in 1758 by Linnaeus.



India is especially rich is such tales; that of the wolf child of Mynepuri in 1872 is one of the first from that country. The most famous of the purported wolf children were Amala and Kamala, two girls supposedly found huddled together with two wolf pups in a wolf den near Calcutta in 1920. The girls reportedly could not walk upright, preferred darkness to light, and ate only red meat. One of the girls died a year later at about two and a half years of age; the other, about eight years old when found, lived to seventeen. Both died of kidney failure. The man who was supposed to have found them, the Reverend J. A. L. Singh, wrote in his diary of his obsession of turning a "creature of the Devil" into a servant of God, and made the poor girls regularly attend religious services that they never understood. He published a book about his experience in 1942 that found wide appeal. Unfortunately, investigation of his claims in 1950 found that the Reverend Singh was not

Mowgli, the wild wolf-child, from Rudyard Kipling's *Jungle Book*. Illustration by Stuart Tresilian for the World Book Society, Toronto

a man of good reputation and likely invented the story to raise funds for his orphanage. Several people also claimed that the two children had been brought to his orphanage and were not found in the wild. It is suspected from their recorded behavior that they were either autistic or mentally handicapped.

One of the most recent reports of feral children was in 1972 near Musafirkhana in India. The four-year-old child involved ended up at Mother Teresa's Home in Lucknow, where he died after seven years of care.

It is notable that very few stories of feral wolf children originate in North America. One of the handful of such tales that do exist is that of a girl supposedly raised by wolves in Texas. The girl was born in 1835 and was soon orphaned and presumed dead after the deaths of her parents. In 1845, a naked girl with long hair was reported seen attacking a herd of goats. She was accompanied by a pack of wolves. The girl was caught and held at the nearest ranch, but quickly escaped. She was reportedly seen again in 1852, but then disappeared. Researchers have been unable to authenticate this unusual story.



## The Wolf and the North American Indian

Early records of American Indian life show that the wolf was revered by the native peoples of North America. The wolf's devotion to its family and its pack parallels the relation between an Indian and his or her tribe, and the hunting skills of the wolf were envied by many Native American tribes. Both native peoples and wolves defended territory, and both had to kill to survive.

The survival skills of the wolf spawned many native legends. The Eskimos had the story of Qisaruatsiaq, "the one who turned into a wolf," an old woman abandoned and forced to survive on her own, who eventually turned into a wolf.

Many tribes most revered the pure white wolves, ascribing to them incredible powers. George Bird Grennell recorded the story of a Cheyenne left to die in a pit and rescued by two wolves, one white, and one rabid. The white wolf guarded the man and ensured that its rabid brother did not attack. The man was adopted by the wolves and later returned to his tribe.

The Sioux called the wolf *shunk manitu tanka,* the "animal that looks like a dog but is a powerful spirit." A number of Native American tribes had medicine men who donned wolf skins in order to duplicate the powers of the wolf.

The two tribes that identified the most strongly with the wolf were the Pawnee and the Cheyenne.

The Pawnee, of present-day Kansas and Nebraska, identified so closely with the wolf that the Plains hand signal for wolf was the same as for Pawnee. Other tribes referred to them as the wolf people. To the Pawnee, the appearance and disappearance of the Wolf Star (Sirius) signified the wolf's coming and going from the spirit world, running down the bright-white trail of the Milky Way, which they called the Wolf Road. It is interesting that Canada's Blackfoot also called the Milky Way the Wolf Trail or Route to Heaven. The Pawnee, Hidatsa, and Oto all had wolf bundles, pouches of wolf skins that guarded treasured bits of feathers and bone used in magic and ceremony.

Cheyenne medicine men rubbed wolf fur on arrows to bring them good fortune in hunting.

*The Earth-Maker Wolf*, from a painting by Cree artist Benjamin Tenaskak. (Courtesy of the artist)

The Cherokee would not kill a wolf. They believed that the brothers of the slain wolf would avenge its death and the weapon used for killing the wolf would not work unless it underwent exorcism by a medicine man. The Cherokee sang a song and walked in imitation of the wolf in order to protect their feet from frostbite.

The Nootka of the Pacific Northwest had a ceremony in which it was pretended that the son of the chief was killed and brought back to life by Indians wearing wolf robes and wolf-head hats. This ceremony served to reinforce the close spiritual ties that the Nootka believed they had with the wolf.



Other Pacific had similar beliefs. The Niska of British Columbia had four principal clans: Raven, Wolf, Eagle, and Bear. Both the Tlingit and Tsimshian of coastal British Columbia used wolves as characters on totem poles, believing wolves to be gods. British Columbia's Bella Coola refused to eat the mighty bear, but they respected the wolf so much that when a bear was killed and its hide removed, a song was sung to the wolves to invite them to eat.

The North American Indian not only revered the wolf, but mentally *became* wolves through animist societies. The Arapaho had a wolf division, the Caddo had a wolf band, and Montana's Crow had a Crow Wolf Society whose members draped themselves in wolf skins prior to hunting. Perhaps

A LIST OF INDIANS HONORED WITH WOLF NAMES INDICATES NOT ONLY THE WIDESPREAD REVERENCE FOR THE WOLF IN NATIVE AMERICAN SOCIETY, BUT IS ALSO AN INDIRECT MEASURE OF THE FORMER DISTRIBUTION OF THE WOLF IN NORTH AMERICA:

**INDIAN WOLF NAMES**

HIGH WOLF—LAKOTA
LITTLE WOLF—CHEYENNE
MAD WOLF—SEMINOLE
SLEEPING WOLF—KIOWA
WOLF EYES—HIDATSA
WOLF FACE—APACHE
WOLF GOES TO DRINK—CROW
WOLF IN THE WATER—BLOOD
WOLF LEG—BLACKFOOT
WOLF NECKLACE—PALOUSE
WOLF ROBE—ACOMA
WOLF TAIL—PEIGAN
WOLF TEETH—STONEY
YELLOW WOLF—NEZ PERCÉ

the Cheyenne Wolf Soldiers were the best known of all Indian wolf societies, fierce fighters dreaded by settlers and U.S. soldiers alike.

The Mandan wore wolf tails on their moccasins as a badge of success in battle. Assiniboin wore white wolf-skin caps into battle for luck. Hidatsa women experiencing difficult childbirths rubbed their bellies with wolf skin. Some tribes believed that killing a wolf would cause the big game to disappear, a view completely opposite to that of some modern hunters.

If a Kwakiutl killed a wolf, he would lay the body on a blanket and cut small strips off it. Each hunter who aided in the kill would eat four strips of wolf meat while expressing regret at killing the wolf. The blanket was then rolled up and buried. Alaska's Ahtena propped up dead wolves, and their tribe's shamans ceremonially fed the wolves meals.



When a wolf was killed by Indians, usually only the pelt was used. Occasionally the internal organs were removed and used in magical ceremonies. Except for the Kwakiutl, Indians almost never ate the flesh.

It was common for Indians to interpret natural history in terms of wolf behavior. For example, the Cree believed that heavenly wolves visited the Earth when the northern lights shone in winter. A number of tribes thought that the wolf howls after eating in order to invite scavengers such as birds and rodents to come and eat. And many tribes believed that wolf howls were the cries of lost spirits trying to return to Earth.

Many Plains Indians expressed the four cardinal points in terms of animals: the bear represented the west, the mountain lion the north, and the wildcat the south. The wolf stood for the east.

Of the hundreds of recorded Indian wolf legends, one of the best known is the Cree story of the Earth-Maker Wolf and the creation of the world:

> When all the land was covered with water, the trickster Wisagatcak pulled up some trees and made a raft. On it, he collected many kinds of animals swimming in the waters. The Raven left the raft, flying for a whole day, and saw no land, so Wisagatcak called Wolf to help. Wolf ran around and around the raft with a ball of moss in his mouth. The

> moss grew, and earth formed on it. It spread on the raft and kept on growing until it made the whole world. This is how the Earth was created.

Almost unique in the North American Indian wolf mythology is the Navajo werewolf myth. The Navajo word for wolf, *mai-coh,* means witch. The Navajo believed (and some still do) that one could become a werewolf by wearing a wolf skin. Werewolves were blamed for raiding Navajo graveyards, and many a Navajo home protected itself against werewolves by keeping gall in the house.



## Wolves versus Settlers

The turning point against the wolf in its relationship with humans came when man turned from being primarily a hunter to being a farmer.

The settlers who slowly spread across the American West brought with them their livestock, slow, easy prey for as efficient a hunter as the wolf. In 1717, the residents of Cape Cod even tried to erect a six-foot-high, eight-mile-long fence to keep wolves from their livestock. The war that other settlers waged upon wolves reached the proportions of a crusade, with the wolf paying the ultimate price.

Guy E. Connolly, a USFWS biologist, wrote in *The Big Game of North America* that "the predominant attitude up to the present century was that predators were vermin to be destroyed by any means." The means used against wolves constitute a list straight out of the stories of Edgar Allan Poe. Wolves were shot, poisoned, trapped, bludgeoned, and tortured. Wolves were infected with mange and then released to spread the deadly disease across the plains. Wolves were staked down and torn apart by dogs. Wolves had their jaws wired shut so they could not eat, ensuring a slow, agonizing death by starvation. Wolves were blown to bits by set guns or poisoned by wolf getters, devices that when bitten fired sodium cyanide into a wolf's mouth. Wolves were poisoned by the

> THE WOLVES THAT HOWLED AT EVENING ABOUT THE TRAVELLER'S CAMPFIRE, HAVE SUCCUMBED TO ARSENIC AND HUSHED THEIR SAVAGE MUSIC.
>
> —Francis Parkman, 1892

thousands by strychnine, strewn carelessly across the prairies. (Stanley Young wrote in *The Wolves of North America*, "There was a sort of unwritten law of the range that no cowman would knowingly pass by a carcass of any kind without inserting in it a goodly dose of strychnine sulfate, in the hope of killing one more wolf.") Wolf pups were dragged from their den and either beaten to death or shot. (In the 1907 Annual Report of the Alberta Department of Agriculture, the chief game warden wrote, "Farmers and ranchers should not allow wolf or coyote pups to grow up on or near their lands. A short time spent in trying to locate them will usually meet with success and it is up to everyone to try to protect himself by destroying them.") And wolves were pursued by hundreds of overeager and undertrained bounty hunters.



## Wolf Bounties

Wolf bounties, which reached their zenith of use (or misuse) in the United States, are nothing new. The ancient Greeks had bounties on wolves as early as 600 BC, and Plutarch (c. AD 46–120) recorded a bounty of five silver drachmas paid by Greek officials for each dead male wolf submitted to the local government.

The first wolf bounty in North America was imposed by the Massachusetts Bay Colony in 1630. Julie Lawrence photo, © Wolf Haven International

In Europe, England had wolf bounties by the 1500s, the first wolf bounty in Sweden was passed in 1647, and Norway's first bounty was legislated in 1730.

The voice of the "howling wilderness" that greeted early settlers. Detail from *Le Renard, Le Loup, et Le Cheval*, a French engraving by Oudry for *La Fontaine's Fables*, 1751

The first wolf bounty in North America was passed by the Massachusetts Bay Colony in 1630. Most bounties provided for straight payment of a cash fee for each dead wolf, but the Act for Destroying Beasts of Prey passed in South Carolina in 1695, required Indian hunters to submit a wolf skin or skin of any other predator annually or be whipped in punishment. The spread of wolf bounties across North America parallels the westward spread of "civilization."





## WOLF BOUNTIES IN NORTH AMERICA

Some of the bounties listed stood for years; the wolf bounty in Ontario was not repealed until 1972.

Although it has been reported that in Montana alone between 1883 and 1918 more than 80,000 wolves were killed by bounty hunters, the accuracy of such a figure is open to question. As Peter Matthiessen noted in *Wildlife in America*, the bounty system was "shot through with fraud—dog, coyote, and even stretched fox and rabbit ears commonly passed as those of wolves . . . animals killed in one state were submitted for bounty in another." In the 1907 Annual Report of the Alberta Department of Agriculture, the chief game warden, B. Lawton, wrote:

> The State of Washington estimates that during the year 1906 over four thousand dollars were fraudulently obtained by parties claiming bounty. The State of Montana also had trouble in this respect. It is also stated that parties have claimed from the Province of Saskatchewan bounty

### WOLF BOUNTIES IN NORTH AMERICA

| Year | Place |
|---|---|
| 1630 | MASSACHUSETTS BAY COLONY |
| 1632 | VIRGINIA BAY COLONY |
| 1695 | SOUTH CAROLINA |
| 1697 | NEW JERSEY |
| 1793 | UPPER CANADA (ONTARIO-QUEBEC) |
| 1839 | NEWFOUNDLAND |
| 1840 | IOWA |
| 1843 | OREGON TERRITORY |
| 1861 | QUEBEC |
| 1871 | WASHINGTON |
| 1878 | MANITOBA |
| 1884 | MONTANA |
| 1893 | ARIZONA–NEW MEXICO TERRITORY |
| 1899 | ALBERTA AND SASKATCHEWAN |
| 1900 | BRITISH COLUMBIA |
| 1915 | ALASKA |



> on coyotes killed in this province. Attempts have also been made by residents of the province to collect bounty on the pelts of timber wolves killed elsewhere.

Many biologists have questioned whether bounties are effective for predator control. L. David Mech, in *The Wolves of Isle Royale*, wrote that "about the only time a bounty might help decrease a predator population is when the species has a low reproductive rate, when the population itself is low and the bounty payment high, and when there are very efficient methods of capture." Frank Miller, a biologist with the Canadian Wildlife Service, says succinctly, "Bounty payments . . . have never proven effective as a means by which predators can be controlled."

In addition to local and state governments, numerous stock organizations also offered bounties, financed by wealthy ranchers anxious to protect their stock. Large ranches were equally generous. The Club Ranch in Colorado offered a $50 bounty per wolf in 1909. Even more lucrative was the

*Habitants Chased by Wolves.* Nineteenth-century lithograph by William Raphael. (National Archives of Canada/C-022095)

$150 bounty offered by the Piceance Creek Stock Growers' Association in north-central Colorado in 1912. Some bounty hunters of the day earned almost $1,000 for a week's work, a huge wage for the time. The money attracted many a man down on his luck and looking for work of any kind. By 1914, the western states were paying over $1 million per year in predator bounties.

In the 1920s, one North Dakota outfit, the Ross Island Meat Packing Company, even went so far as to pay a bounty of $8 dollars per head on German shepherd dogs, which were renowned cattle killers in the early West.

The bounty hunter became a legendary figure in American history, and those wolves wily enough to consistently escape their pursuers became demigods.

It is interesting to note that many of these "outlaw wolves" were injured or crippled animals. It is thought that their injuries forced them to seek slow and easy-to-hunt livestock rather than wild prey. Stanley Young, in *The Wolves of North America,* writes that "entire communities sought the renegades by every means . . . despite which these wolves often carried on for many years." Ernest Thompson Seton in 1898 wrote that "they seemed to possess charmed lives, and defied all manner of devices to kill them."

## LEGENDARY WOLVES

**Old Lefty.** Old Lefty hunted in the Burns Hole, Colorado, area in the early 1900s, after twisting off his left front paw in a leghold trap. Lefty was supposed to have killed 384 head of livestock.

**The Sycan Wolf.** The Sycan Wolf was an old male wolf in southern Oregon that was credited with the killing of numerous horses and cattle. When finally killed, the wolf was found to be extremely old, with incredibly worn teeth.

**Three Toes.** This famous wolf hunted in Harding County, South Dakota, and lost one toe to a wolf trap. He was credited with $50,000 worth of livestock killings. It allegedly took 150 hunters and trappers 13 years to catch him.

**The Queen Wolf.** The Queen Wolf (also known as the Unaweep Wolf) was a legendary wolf of the 1920s. She had a deformed foot caused by a trap injury.

**The Ghost Wolf.** Also known as the White Wolf, this creamy-white wolf appeared in the Judith Basin of Montana in the 1920s. She was supposed to

Wolf caught in a leghold trap near Decker, Wyoming, 1921. (U.S. National Archives #22-WB-21415)

have killed $35,000 worth of stock and was vigorously pursued. Hunters shot her in the hind leg, knocked her down, tried to run her down by car, set traps all over the county, and still were unable to catch her. At one point she even outfought five imported Russian wolfhounds. She was finally shot in 1930 (although one account had her trapped in the Highwood Mountains in 1923).

**Spring Creek Wolf.** The Spring Creek wolf was the curse of Colorado's vast Club Ranch. When the wolf was finally killed by William S. Casto, the ranch owners presented him with a new Winchester rifle.



**Spring Valley Wolf.** This was the name actually given to two wolves that hunted in northern Arizona around 1920. The younger wolf was shot by a rancher, and the older wolf was poisoned by government officials.

**Old Aguila.** Old Aguila was another Arizona wolf credited with the killing of dozens of sheep and cattle between 1916 and 1924. Old Aguila was a whitish-colored female that eluded trappers for many years. A bounty of $500 was finally responsible for her death by poisoning in 1924.

**Old One Toe.** Old One Toe traveled the Sonora Desert and grassland areas north of Wickenburg, Arizona, for eight years. He was poisoned in 1924. He was named for the single scratch mark he consistently left, because the other toes on that paw were missing from a trap injury.

**The White Lobo.** Another wolf with a $500 bounty on its head was the White Lobo, an outlaw wolf in Texas in the 1920s. The White Lobo turned out to be an old, deaf female, a remarkable survivor of the efforts aimed at her destruction. She was finally shot in 1925.

**Old Three Toes.** Another wolf named Old Three Toes was trapped in New Mexico in 1928, after traveling there from Colorado. The wolf was found to weigh 109 pounds, very large for a southern wolf.

**Lobo, The King of Currumpaw.** Lobo and his mate, Blanca, hunted in New Mexico in the 1890s and became famous when their killer, author Ernest Thompson Seton, immortalized them in his writing. Their deaths

The outlaw wolf Snowdrift, the Ghost Wolf, trapped in the Highwood Mountains, 1923. Photo courtesy of the Montana Historical Society, Helena, Montana

changed Seton's attitude toward predators and he spent the rest of his life defending the wolf. Lobo was one of the first wolves with a $1,000 price on his head.

**Las Margaritas.** This wolf was one of the last outlaw wolves, taken in 1970. Las Margaritas was named after the ranch of the same name in northern Mexico, a favorite haunt of the wolf. He had lost two toes on his front left paw, and was leery of efforts to trap him for many years. Veteran trapper Roy T. McBride finally caught the wolf after almost a year of effort.

Other famous outlaw wolves include:

*Big Foot*—Lane Country, Colorado

*The Black Buffalorunner*—Cheyenne, Wyoming

*Cody's Captive*—Cheyenne, Wyoming

*The Custer Wolf*—South Dakota

*The Greenhorn Wolf*—southern Colorado

*Mountain Billy*—Medora, North Dakota

*The Nut Lake Wolf*—Fort Qu'Appelle, Saskatchewan

*Old Whitey*—Bear Springs Mesa, Colorado

*The Pine Ridge Wolf*—southeast South Dakota

*Pryor Creek Wolf*—southeast Montana

*Rags the Digger*—Cathedral Bluffs, Colorado

*Split Rock Wolf*—west-central Wyoming

*Three Toes*—Apishapa, Colorado

*The Traveler*—Arkansas

*The Truxton Wolf*—Arizona

*The White Wolf*—Pine Ridge, South Dakota

*The Virden Wolf*—Virden, Manitoba

Almost as famous as the wolves they pursued were the bounty hunters of the American West.



## FAMOUS WOLF BOUNTY HUNTERS

**Bill Caywood.** Bill Caywood was one of dozens of hunters and trappers hired by the federal government to kill wolves for the Biological Survey. Over the winter of 1912–1913, he killed 140 wolves, earning almost $7,000. Some of the famed outlaw wolves he killed were Rags the Digger, the Cuerno Verde Gray, the Butcher Wolf, and the Keystone pack. Most of his work was

Bounty hunter Dick Brown at his camp near Terry, Montana. Photo courtesy of the Montana Historical Society, Helena, Montana

done in Colorado. A 1939 issue of *Outdoor Life* magazine described him as "so good at his job that there's almost no job left."

**Ben Corbin.** Ben Corbin was a hunter who worked the Dakota Territory and was responsible for the deaths of hundreds of wolves. He was also the author of *Corbin's Advice; or The Wolf Hunter's Guide,* a book published in 1900 that became the bounty hunters' bible. Corbin called the wolf "the enemy of the state."

**Roy T. McBride.** Probably the most famous modern-day trapper is Roy T. McBride, who was responsible for trapping Las Margaritas in Mexico. McBride was the trapper chosen by the USFWS to live-trap the last few wolves in Mexico for the Mexican wolf captive breeding program. He is probably the only bounty hunter to possess a master's degree in biology.



**Montie Wallace.** Montie Wallace was one of the many trappers who worked for the government predator control agency in Texas in the 1900s. He was the foreman of the Downie Ranch in Pecos County for many years and was most famous for shooting the White Lobo. His home was filled with mementos of his many hunts, with wolf skins on the floor, on the walls, and on top of tables.

---

ANY INTERFERENCE WITH NATURE IS DAMNABLE. NOT ONLY NATURE BUT ALSO THE PEOPLE WILL SUFFER.

—Indian Chief Anahareo

---

## The Extinction of the Wolf

In Europe, active efforts to exterminate the wolf date from as early as 300 BC, when the Celts were breeding "wolfhounds" especially for killing wolves. (Centuries later, in 1652, Oliver Cromwell disallowed the export of Irish wolfhounds since they were too badly needed for killing wolves at home.)

The Mexican wolf is a smaller wolf that was often confused with coyotes before its extinction in the wild. Photo courtesy of California Wolf Center



In France, around AD 800, Emperor Charlemagne founded an order for the killing of wolves, called the *louveterie*. In the second century BC, the king of Scots decreed that anyone killing a wolf was to be rewarded with a whole ox. In Anglo-Saxon England, the month of January was devoted to wolf slaughter, and was called *Wolfmonat*, or Wolf Month. In AD 985, King Edgar of England demanded a tribute of three hundred wolf skins per year from the king of Wales. As a result, the small Welsh wolf population was rapidly exterminated. In 1281, King Edward I hired a man named Peter Corbet to "take and destroy all the wolves he can find in . . . Gloucestershire, Worcestershire, Herefordshire, Shropshire, and Staffordshire."

The result of the European war on wolves was that the wolf was extinct in most of Europe by 1900. Denmark lost its last wolf in 1772. By 1821, the wolf was gone from Ireland. The last wolf in Bavaria was shot in 1847. The last wolf in Britain was killed in Scotland in 1848. It was extinct from almost all of France by 1918, with perhaps a few packs hiding in the Pyrenees Mountains.

In eastern Canada, the wolf was very rare by the 1870s. It was extinct in New Brunswick by 1880, in Nova Scotia by 1900, and in Newfoundland by 1913.

The extermination of the wolf in the United States is less well documented; most of the early wildlife agencies in the United States were glad to see it go, and kept no records of its extinction.

By about 1900, the wolf had been removed from all of its ranges in the eastern half of the United States, except for the Great Lakes region. The wolves inhabiting the Kenai Peninsula in Alaska were gone by 1925. The Great Plains wolf, *Canis lupus nubilus,* was wiped out by 1926. In 1928, residents of Arkansas figured that to rid themselves of the last few wolves there, they would destroy its habitat, and they set fire to thousands of acres in the Ouachita National Forest. Two years later, the little red wolf of Florida, *Canis rufus floridanus,* was extinct. Two plains and foothills subspecies, *Canis lupus mogollonensis* and *C.l. youngi,* were extinct by 1935. The last wolf in the state of Washington died in 1940. The last western Texas gray wolf, *Canis lupus monstrabilis,* was shot in 1942. The last wolves in both Colorado and Wyoming were killed in 1943. The Texas red wolf, *Canis rufus rufus,* is thought to have reached extinction in the wild by 1970. The last stronghold of the Mexican wolf was in the 1970s; the last gray wolf in Texas died in 1970, in Arizona in 1975, and in New Mexico in 1976. The Mississippi Valley red wolf, *Canis rufus gregoryi,* is deemed to have reached extinction by 1980. Many biologists believe that the Mexican wolf, *Canis lupus baileyi,* has been extinct in the wild since the late 1980s.

## The Wolf as a Threat to Humans

Captain Meriwether Lewis of the Lewis and Clark expedition, described the thousands of wolves he encountered across the American plains as "extreemly [*sic*] gentle."

L. David Mech, in *The Wolves of Isle Royale,* wrote that "wolves in most areas are known to be afraid of man." In *The Wolf: The Ecology and Behavior of an Endangered Species,* he described the wolf as "one of the . . . shyest of all the animals in the northern wilderness." Canadian wolf biologist François

Messier has stated that wolves "have high fear of humans and they will walk away, even if you approach one of their kills."

In 1900, a large wolf pack moved into the suburbs of Anchorage, Alaska, a city of over a quarter of a million people. Not one of them was harmed by the wolves. In fact, numerous researchers have been unable to document a single attack on humans by a healthy wolf anywhere in North America. Despite such testaments to the wolf's true nature, the myth of the wolf as a man-eater prevails. L. David Mech wrote in *Wolves* that in the recent past, "everybody knew wolves were dangerous to human beings. When as a green, twenty-one-year-old graduate student I began the Isle Royale wolf study under the direction of Durward Allen, the National Park Service insisted I carry a sidearm."



Several investigators have done their best to pierce holes in the myth. Canadian explorer Vilhjalmer Stefansson traced every global report of a wolf killing a human between 1923 and 1936. Not one account could be substantiated.

James Curran, the editor of the Sault Ste. Marie, Ontario, *Daily Star*, offered a $100 reward in 1925 to anyone who could document a wolf attack on a human being. No one ever collected the reward.

Wolf, or werewolf, attacking two men. From *Die Emeis* by Johannes Geiler von Kaiserberg. Photo courtesy of the University of Chicago Library, Special Collections Research Center

In 1926, a rabid wolf entered the wilderness town of Churchill in northern Manitoba. As Barry Lopez recounted in *Of Wolves and Men*, the wolf met a quick end, but the incident underlined the paranoid attitude of the town's citizens: "The wolf was run over by a car and bit no one, but in the confusion six dogs and an Indian were shot."

A widely reported 1927 incident in the Northwest Territories was alleged to have involved an attack on biologists camped beside a wilderness river. Inquiries showed that a female wolf had merely approached their camp, only to be promptly pelted with stones by the men. When one man raised his arm to smash a large stone down upon the wolf, it bit his arm in self-defense and then ran away.



Probably the best-known wolf attack was a 1942 incident in which an Ontario man using a line car on a remote railway line was charged by a wolf. The unusual and erratic behavior of the wolf strongly suggests that it had rabies, but in any case the man was not even scratched.

Theodora Stanwell-Fletcher, who lived in the northern wilderness of British Columbia in the 1940s, wrote in *Driftwood Valley*, "[Indians] can cite no cases of men having been attacked by wolves."

In 1945, the USFWS reviewed all reports of wolf attacks that it had received between 1920 and 1945. It found that none was credible. Lee Smits reviewed the documentary evidence available up to 1963 and concluded that "no wolf, except a wolf with rabies, has ever been known to make a deliberate attack on a human being in North America." L. David Mech concluded in 1970 after a thorough review of the literature that "no scientific evidence is available to support the claim that healthy wild wolves are dangerous to man."

Until recently, the most recent wild "wolf attack" in North America was in 1987, when a sixteen-year-old girl in Algonquin Park in Ontario was merely scratched by a wolf when it was chased by two boys into a campground and tried to push past her.

Then, in 1996, a young woman was killed when she tripped and fell at a private sanctuary near Haliburton, Ontario, and was attacked by five captive wolves. (Many predators will attack prey that appears to be wounded and lying on the ground.)

This was followed by three incidents in Algonquin Park, Ontario, which involved nonfatal incidents with children. In one case, a young girl's arm was grabbed by a wolf; in another, a young boy was bitten on the side; and in the most serious incident, a wolf dragged a little boy in his sleeping bag, biting his nose and face. An investigation showed that in each case, the wolf responsible had lost its fear of humans, in one instance after park workers had habituated it to eating doughnuts.

In 2000, a wolf attacked a sleeping camper on Vargas Island, off the west coast of Vancouver Island, British Columbia. The camper was grabbed in the wolf's jaws, creating a wound that took fifty stitches to close. Two wolves were killed as a result of the incident.

A young man was apparently killed by wolves in November 2005 in northern Saskatchewan. An investigation by biologist Paul Paquet suggested that the attack was by four wolves that "[were] either . . . inadvertently fed or intentionally fed in the area. That is the common thread to most wolf attacks that I've investigated," says Paquet. An open garbage dump near a mine in the area may have been the source of the problem. This incident appears to be the first fatal attack on a human being by a healthy wild wolf in North America.

In late 2006, a wolf in northern Ontario's Lake Superior Provincial Park attacked people in three separate incidents. Tests showed it did not have rabies, but six people were left with cuts, scratches, and minor puncture wounds. The wolf was shot by park authorities.

The second recorded fatal attack on a human by wolves in North America took place in 2010 outside the Alaskan village of Chignik Lake when a schoolteacher who was out running was killed and partially eaten by a pack of wolves. Wildlife officials eventually shot two of the offending wolves but the cause of the attack was never determined.

However rare, wolf attacks on humans do occasionally occur. Wolf biologist L. David Mech calls them "extraordinarily rare events," adding that they should "not warrant widespread alarm."

Although there are numerous reports of wolf attacks in medieval Europe, most of these are thought to have been by hybrid or rabid animals. Many of the Russian tales of attacks have been found to be highly exaggerated. In

1931, I. S. I. Ognev wrote that "cases of attacks on men are much rarer than is believed." And in 1956, G. A. Novikov investigated a number of Russian wolf "attacks" and concluded that "there are less authentic cases of attack on man than is supposed." In a book by Bertil Haglund, superintendent of the Swedish Crown Forests, he stated that he was unable to find a single documented case of a wolf attack on a human in Europe in the past 150 years. (See also chapter 3, "Rabies," p. 44.)

CHAPTER

6

# THE WOLF AS A PREDATOR: WOLF CONTROL

THE WOLF KILLS TO EAT. And it is the wolf's status as a predator that has resulted in the deaths of thousands of wolves at the hands of humans. The two prime areas of conflict are the wolf's status as a predator of big game and as an occasional predator of livestock.

## The Wolf as a Killer of Big Game

In the United States, federal Animal Damage Control guidelines define predator control as "control . . . directed toward less desirable species which are depressing populations of more desirable species." Clearly man has deemed the wolf "less desirable."

It is unfortunate that both *Canis lupus* and *Homo sapiens* sometimes seek the same prey. It is even more unfortunate that the wolf has often been wrongly blamed for depleting ungulate populations, populations equally sought by both subsistence and sport hunters. Canadian conservationist and author Farley Mowat has described "the familiar cry from hunters, outfitters, guides, lodge owners, and other financially interested parties: 'Wolves are destroying the game—*the game that belongs to us*!' "

Large-scale wolf kills by humans assume that wolves are the primary limiting factor to a hooved game population. All too often, the wolf is just a convenient and visible scapegoat, the final product of years of prejudice.

The wolf's predation upon big game has resulted in dozens of wolf kills by wildlife managers. © Robert H. Busch

And all too often insufficient studies have been undertaken to determine the true role of the wolf in controlling the prey population. As L. David Mech has written in *The Wolf: The Ecology and Behavior of an Endangered*

Bison are one of the more dangerous prey wolves pursue and often require large packs to attack successfully. © Jim Yuskavitch

Elk are a major prey item for wolves through much of their range. © Jim Yuskavitch

*Species*, "the simple, unqualified question of whether or not predators control the numbers of their prey, cannot, in my opinion, be covered by any broad generality."

Wolf-prey studies across North America have shown conflicting results, and it has become obvious that few generalities can be given. USFWS biologist Guy E. Connolly dryly notes in *The Big Game of North America* that "a sufficiently selective review of the literature can reinforce any desired view on the subject of predation."

> BRING THEM IN REGARDLESS OF HOW.
>
> —**Official slogan, U.S. Dept. of Agriculture, Bureau of Biological Survey, Livestock Sanitary Board, 1922**

Various studies have shown that in fact wolves may control an ungulate population, extirpate the population, have no effect upon it, increase it, or decrease it.

Wolves may thus be a major prey-mortality factor, a minor factor, or not a factor at all. Other important factors include the prey/predator ratio, habitat loss, overhunting by humans, and the effects of severe winters.

Deep winter snow makes prey species such as mule deer more vulnerable to attack. © Jim Yuskavitch

As wildlife biologist Chris McBride has written in *The White Lions of Timbavati*, "The very fact that any species of predator still exists today is proof that it has evolved in such a way that it cannot seriously limit the numbers of its prey. If it did, it would have become extinct." His comments, of course, refer to the long term. Wildlife managers are sometimes not so farsighted.

Overhunting by humans is often a major factor in ungulate declines. In one study of Alaskan wolves, it was found that humans had killed 44 percent of the Nelchina caribou herd from 1971 to 1972, a decrease that had been previously blamed on wolves. One year when caribou strayed too close to the city of Yellowknife in the Northwest Territories and were slaughtered by its residents by the hundreds, outsiders immediately blamed wolves for the kills.

Wolves were, and still are, regularly blamed for the decline in the elk population in Yellowstone National Park's Northern Range from 17,000 in 1995 when wolves were brought back to the park to about 4,000 by 2013. However, what is rarely mentioned is that hunters had been killing 1,500 to 2,000 breeding-age cow elk each year as the elk migrated into Montana for the winter, which had a significant impact on the herd's breeding population.

The history of wolf kills carried out to preserve prey numbers is voluminous, but even a few selected highlights are shocking in their intensity.

Much of the slaughter was performed by federal agents. At least 136 wolves, including 80 pups, were killed in Yellowstone Park between 1914 and 1926. Between 1937 and 1969, U.S. federal agents killed 51,857 wolves across the Untied States. Between 1954 and 1958, about 2,000 wolves per year were killed in the Northwest Territories in a misguided attempt to stop declines in caribou numbers. It is very likely that the actual number of wolves killed in many of these cases was much higher.

A poster from the Canadian Wolf Defenders opposing a 1983 wolf kill in Alberta.© Robert H. Busch

Guy E. Connolly, writing in *The Big Game of North America,* states that "research in the 1930s and 1940s began to show predator control as ineffective and unnecessary in game management." But few people listened.

In the 1940s, a new poison called compound 1080 (sodium monofluroacetate) was developed by the U.S. Armed Forces for use against rats in the Far East. Very quickly compound 1080 became the poison of choice for wolves. It was so named for being the 1,080th formula tried against predators. The poison is nonspecific and killed thousands of wolves, coyotes, foxes, and domestic dogs. According to David E. Brown, writing in *The Wolf in the Southwest: The Making of an Endangered Species,* it also "is suspected of having killed some of the last grizzlies in Mexico."

OUR FIRST DUTY IS TO GET RID OF ALL THE PREDATORY ANIMALS POSSIBLE.

—Washington State Bureau of Biological Survey, 1924

The poison was widely used against wolves between 1949 and 1972 before it was canceled for use on federal lands by the U.S. Environmental Protection Agency. It is still used on wolves in Alberta.

In the 1960s and 1970s, there were dozens of studies into wolf-prey relationships. Unfortunately, many of these studies were severely biased. As James C. Bednarz, research assistant professor in the Department of Biology at the University of New Mexico, has stated, "studies addressing this subject are decidedly inconclusive, but often close with a rather specific statement relating the biases of the authors or of the sponsoring agencies."



However, these studies did establish that wolf predation can accelerate prey declines caused by other factors such as overhunting or habitat destruction. It was also found that wolf predation can delay the recovery of prey numbers. If prey destiny or diversity is low, wolves may indeed have a controlling effect on prey numbers. One disturbing finding was that wolf kills often just result in increased wolf births and immigration into the area by neighboring packs. Thus, to sufficiently reduce wolf populations in the long term, many wolf kills would have to be continued for years.

It is ironic that many fish and game departments exist to support the hunters and fishermen who fund them through the sale of tags and licenses. The irony turns to tragedy, though, when these departments kill wolves to appease hunters.

## CANADA

In 1983, the British Columbia Fish and Wildlife Branch announced plans to kill 8 percent of the wolves in the northeast Peace and Omineca districts in order "to support moose and deer populations." However, the close ties between the department and the hunting lobby quickly became evident. To fund the wolf kill, the government stated its intention to hold a lottery, the first prize being a hunting trip to Zimbabwe. Despite a government report that the moose and deer numbers had decreased primarily because of loss of habitat, overhunting, and a series of severe winters, the wolf was the one put in the crosshairs.

The Wildlife Society of Canada and the Wildlife Biologists section of the Canadian Society of Biologists reviewed the technical data behind the program and stated their opinion, "There is no biological basis or biological justification for the wolf control program." The public outcry was loud and angry, but over 400 wolves were killed before the program was abandoned.

In 1993, a plan to kill 150 wolves in the Yukon in an area adjacent to Kluane National Park was implemented. The purpose of the kill was to support the Aishihik caribou herd, which was declining in number. The kill was opposed as biologically unjustified by the Canadian Nature Federation, the World Wildlife Fund (WWF) in Canada, and a host of other agencies. The likelihood that the void would be filled by wolves immigrating into the area from the adjacent Kluane park was disregarded by government officials. After much public pressure, the Yukon government admitted that the slaughter was a "scientific experiment" using living animals. In early 1993, about seventy wolves were killed, and it was discovered that the wolf population in the area was about 40 percent smaller than expected. Despite this finding, the Yukon government planned to continue the killing. The cost of the initial year of killing was an incredible $2,500 per wolf.

In October 2006, the British Columbia Department of Agriculture and Lands announced another proposed wolf cull. The department, in response to dwindling numbers of endangered mountain caribou, announced that hundreds of wolves and cougars would be killed in order to let caribou numbers rebound. Although the government declared that it "was a management strategy that has to take place," conservationists immediately announced their opposition, stating that the proposal "was based on politics, not on science."

Despite public outcry, British Columbia wildlife authorities continue to kill wolves in the guise of protecting mountain caribou, even though human encroachment and habitat destruction were the real reason for the population decline. In January 2015 the BC government announced that it had shot more than 180 wolves from aircraft in the South Peace and South Selkirks regions over a two-month period. Despite a fierce public outcry, the BC government moved forward with the multiyear wolf removal plan, killing 84 that year and another 163 in 2017. Conservation groups continue to try to stop the wolf control program.

In Alberta, wildlife officials have killed more than 1,000 wolves since 2012 to protect the Little Smokey caribou herd of fewer than 80 animals, which are falling victim primarily to habitat destruction and human disturbance from logging, and gas and oil development. In 2015 and 2016, 268 wolves were killed in this region. The province plans to continue the wolf culls for the next 50 years. Alberta is also the only Canadian province that still allows wolves to be poisoned with strychnine, compound 1080, and cyanide. In addition, Alberta has a number of public and private bounty programs for wolves. Saskatchewan also offers bounties for wolves as does British Columbia on an "unofficial" basis.



## ALASKA

The jurisdiction with the longest history of wolf control is Alaska.

Although Alaska had wolf bounties established as early as 1915, it was not until statehood was achieved in 1959 that legislators moved to prohibit poisoning of predators. Shortly after this, wolf bounties were finally cancelled.

In the 1960s, the wolf in Alaska was classed as both a big-game animal and a furbearer, and the pressures on its numbers increased. Aerial shooting was common, and conservationists were outraged at the lack of "sport" involved.

The severe winters of 1970–71 and 1971–72 produced a serious decline in moose numbers, and many hunters called for wolf control in order to allow the moose populations to rebound.

In 1975, the state therefore authorized wolf control in Game Management Unit 20A, a move that was swiftly challenged in court. While the case dragged through the courts, wolf control continued in 20A, and after three years the federal court ruled in the state's favor. From this point on, the legal system in Alaska became a battleground between hunters and conservationists.

The state reacted by increasing wolf control measures, adding them to Management Units 19A, 19B, and parts of 21. More legal challenges followed until the state again won in 1980.

Pumped with success, the state added wolf control measures in six units in 1980–81 and five in 1981–82.

More legal wrangling began in 1982, followed by wolf control measures in units 12, 20A, and 20B.

In 1985 a total of five bills were introduced in the Alaska legislature on wolf control. Although none passed, the bills served to heighten public awareness on the issue.

A new governor elected in 1986 prohibited government wolf control during his four-year term. The prohibition was controversial, and resulted in increased land-and-shoot taking of wolves by the public, which was still allowed. (Land-and-shoot killing involves chasing wolves by plane until the animals are exhausted, then landing and shooting them.)

The practice of land-and-shoot was challenged in court in 1986. In 1989 the Supreme Court of Alaska ruled in favor of it.

In 1989, the state moved to adopt a scientifically based wolf management plan, inviting stakeholders from all sides of the wolf issue. The invited group first met in 1990 and filed its first report in 1991. The draft wolf management plan of 1991 called for an end to land-and-shoot killing by requiring hunters to be at least 100 yards from their planes, reducing wholesale land-and-shoot killing by the public.

In 1992, the group endorsed wolf control in many large areas, including units 11, 12, 13, 14, 20E, and 20D. The public was outraged, and over 100,000 letters poured into the governor's office. Governor Walter J. Hickel issued a moratorium on the issue until a summit of interest groups could discuss the issue.

That summit occurred in 1993, a raucous gathering patrolled by plainclothes police who came prepared for the worst. The governor's pro-hunting stance became clear when he bizarrely declared that "nature should not be allowed to run wild." Shortly after the summit, it was revealed that Alaska Department of Fish and Game personnel had begun radio-collaring wolves well before the summit, anticipating a go-ahead for wolf control. (The radio collars ensured that wolves could be easily tracked from the air, then shot on sight.) Conservationists were furious, and demanded that the state begin using a scientific basis for wolf management.

In June 1993 the state issued a Wolf Conservation and Management Policy for Alaska that is still the guiding policy today. In 1993 and 1994 the state allowed a limited wolf control plan in unit 20A.

A new governor was elected in 1994 who quickly vowed to end wolf control for good in Alaska. Studies he commissioned suggested, however, that wolf control could be effective in some circumstances, and a nonlethal wolf control program began in 1997 that resulted in the sterilization of alpha males and females. Since that time, the state has authorized nonlethal wolf control in many areas, primarily to boost caribou numbers.



As Wayne Reglin, director of the Division of Wildlife Conservation, Alaska Department of Fish and Game, has written, the state has "tried to develop a policy that recognizes the importance of the wolf to Alaska, recognizes the widely divergent values people have about wolves, and allows wolf populations to be regulated when necessary to maintain the ability of people to harvest moose and caribou." But he admits, "all such efforts have failed or been inconclusive, and the issue is as controversial as ever."

The IUCN Manifesto on Wolf Conservation states that where wolf kills must be carried out, "the methods must be selective, specific to the problem, highly discriminatory, and have minimal adverse effects on the ecosystem." It concludes that "alternative ecosystem management, including alteration of human activities and attitudes and non-lethal methods of wolf management, should be fully considered before lethal wolf reduction is employed."

According to the WWF-Canada, "the only safe conservation route is to stop large-scale wolf-killing programs altogether."

And as wolf biologist Lu Carbyn has noted, wolf control "has become socially unacceptable," but nevertheless, continues almost everywhere wolves live.

## Livestock Predation by Wolves

According to the USFWS, "Wolf predation of livestock—sheep, poultry, and cattle—does occur, but it is uncommon enough behavior in the species as a whole to be called aberrant."

Many studies have shown that 99 percent of all farmers and ranchers in wolf territory will not be bothered by wolves. Of over 7,000 farmers in northern Minnesota, where over 1,700 wolves inhabit the area, only an average of 25 ranchers per year suffered verified predation from wolves between 1975 and 1989. In Canada, only 1 percent of 1,608 wolf scats collected in Manitoba's Riding Mountain National Park contained remnants of livestock.

In Europe, domestic dogs often do more damage to livestock than do wolves. In one study in Spain, half of all the "wolf kills" that were investigated were found to be caused by feral dogs.

According to William J. Paul of the U.S. Department of Agriculture, where wolf predation on livestock does occur, "most losses occur in summer when livestock are released to graze in open and wooded pastures." In many cases, preventative farming practices would eliminate predation. The Alberta Fish and Wildlife Division recommends the following animal husbandry practices in wolf habitat.

- Cattlemen should check their herds regularly.
- Only healthy and nonpregnant cows should be sent to pasture.

Their tendency to attack and kill livestock makes wolves very controversial in agricultural regions. © Jim Yuskavitch

Fladry is one of the more commonly used nonlethal deterrents to keep wolves away from livestock. Photo courtesy Oregon Department of Fish and Wildlife

- Livestock should be removed from pasture as early as possible in the fall.
- Carrion should be buried or removed as soon as possible. (In one Minnesota study by the USFWS, 63 percent of 111 farmers surveyed either left dead livestock in place or just dragged it to the edge of the woods.)
- Grazing leases on remote public lands should be phased out.
- Ranchers should keep animals out of remote pastures after dusk and pen them in corrals where they can be watched.

There is also a variety of nonlethal wolf deterrents that work with varying degrees of success. Fladry—flags that are draped over fences—can scare wolves away as they flap in the wind. Portable or permanent fences can discourage wolf attacks, especially if livestock is penned up at night. Guard dogs such as Great Pyrenees and Akbas, along with human "range riders," can effectively scare off wolves that are coming around to investigate grazing livestock. Battery-operated flashing highway lights in animal corrals and RAG (radio-activated guard system) boxes that pick up the signal of

Range riders who watch over livestock herds and chase wolves away are another effective deterrent to wolf attacks. Photo courtesy Oregon Department of Fish and Wildlife





radio-collared wolves and set off an alarm can also send marauding wolves packing.

It is politically crucial that compensation be paid to farmers who do suffer wolf predation. The existence of compensation schemes goes a long way toward improving ranchers' attitudes toward wolves. It is also crucial that payment be prompt; in Portugal, when payments were delayed, farmers took to setting poisoned carcasses on the edges of woods to register their complaint.

In the United States, Minnesota, Wisconsin, Michigan, Wyoming, Montana, Idaho, Oregon, and Washington pay compensation to ranchers whose livestock are killed by wolves. In Canada, British Columbia, Alberta, Manitoba, and Saskatchewan also pay compensation for depredations by wolves. Between 2000 and 2010, Alberta paid out $708,000 (Canadian) to ranchers in wolf depredation compensation, along with another $236,000 for compensation damage done by other predatory animals.

The recent statistics are presented in the table on page 152.)

## MINNESOTA LIVESTOCK PREDATION BY WOLVES

| Year | Number of Claims | Compensation Paid |
|---|---|---|
| 2006 | 91 | $72,895 |
| 2007 | 63 | $81,683 |
| 2008 | 75 | $95,526 |
| 2009 | 85 | $88,366 |
| 2010 | 130 | $106,615 |
| 2011 | 109 | $102,230 |
| 2012 | 81 | $119,659 |
| 2013 | 94 | $113,714 |
| | average 91 | average $97,586 |

(Source: International Wolf Center)

## MONTANA LIVESTOCK PREDATION BY WOLVES

| Year | Number of Claims | Compensation Paid |
|---|---|---|
| 2008 | 188 | $83,000 |
| 2009 | 305 | $141,462 |
| 2010 | 161 | $96,077 |
| 2011 | 86 | $85,855 |
| 2012 | 107 | $102,714 |
| 2013 | 78 | $86,740 |
| 2014 | 42 | $72,268 |
| 2015 | 64 | $79,312 |
| 2016 | 57 | $59,578 |
| | average 121 | average $89,667 |

(Source: Montana Department of Fish, Wildlife and Parks)

## Wolf Control Tables

### MONTANA—WOLVES KILLED FOR LIVESTOCK PREDATION CONTROL

| Year | Number of Wolves Killed |
|---|---|
| 2008 | 110 |
| 2009 | 145 |
| 2010 | 141 |
| 2011 | 64 |
| 2012 | 108 |
| 2013 | 75 |
| 2014 | 57 |
| 2015 | 51 |
| 2016 | 61 |

(Montana Department of Fish, Wildlife and Parks)

### IDAHO—WOLVES KILLED FOR LIVESTOCK PREDATION CONTROL

| Year | Number of Wolves Killed |
|---|---|
| 2008 | 108 |
| 2009 | 94 |
| 2010 | 80 |
| 2011 | 63 |
| 2012 | 73 |
| 2013 | 94 |
| 2014 | 67 |
| 2015 | 54 |

(Idaho Department of Fish and Game)

## WOLVES KILLED FOR BOUNTIES—ALBERTA

| Municipality | Time Period | No. of Wolves Killed |
|---|---|---|
| Big Lakes | 2010–2015 | 647 |
| Bonnyville | 2013–2015 | 30 |
| Brazeau | 2010–2015 | --- |
| Cardston | 2012–2015 | 16 |
| Clearwater | 2010–2015 | --- |
| Clear Hills | 2010–2015 | 350 |
| Greenview | 2012–2015 | 90 |
| Minburn | 2011–2015 | --- |
| Mountain View | 2010–2015 | --- |
| Newell | 2010–2015 | --- |
| Northern Lights | 2012–2015 | 185 |
| Saddle Hills | 2011–2015 | 35 |
| Smoky River | 2012–2015 | 12 |
| St Paul | 2010–2015 | 60 |
| Taber | 2010–2015 | --- |
| Two Hills | 2011–2015 | --- |

(Courtesy Wolf Awareness, Inc)

## EXPERIMENTAL KILL PROGRAM FOR CARIBOU, ALBERTA—WOLVES KILLED IN ALBERTA'S LITTLE SMOKY CARIBOU RANGE 2005-2012

| Year | Aerial Gunning | Strychnine |
|---|---|---|
| 2005/2006 | 72 | 28 |
| 2006/2007 | 55 | 19 |
| 2007/2008 | 54 | 28 |
| 2008/2009 | 144 | 16 |
| 2009/2010 | 80 | 0 |
| 2010/2011 | 80 | 34 |
| 2011/2012 | 94 | 29 |
| Total | 579 | 154 |
| Total Wolves Killed | | 733 |

(Courtesy Wolf Awareness, Inc)

# THE WOLF AS A FURBEARER

THE EARLIEST FORM OF TRAP used for wolves was the pit trap, an ancient method of trapping that was even mentioned in the Bible. Pits were sometimes lined with smooth rocks to prevent escape or bedded with sharp stakes. Some were filled with water to drown prey. Pit traps were used in North America primarily by native Indians and by the early European settlers.

Deadfall traps (in which a heavy weight is dropped upon the animal when the trap is triggered) were not commonly used for wolves, as they are

Brownish-gray pelts are most in demand by furriers. © Robert H. Busch

TO THE TRAPPER-NATURALIST . . . THE HOWL OF THE WOLF . . . INSPIRES [A] CHALLENGE TO HIS OWN SKILL AS A HUNTER AND TRAPPER.

—**Harold McCracken and Harry Van Cleve,** ***Trapping: The Craft and Science of Catching Fur-Bearing Animals*****, 1947**

usually more effective on smaller animals. However, Lewis and Clark did report their use for wolves by Indians in the early 1800s. Also in occasional use was the palisade trap, a wall of stakes within which animals were driven and then killed.

Although fur-trading giants such as the Hudson's Bay Company were founded much earlier, the trapping of wolves for fur was not significant until the 1800s. In Europe, wolf pelts never achieved much popularity. One 1800s list of pelt values gives the beaver as the most valuable pelt, followed by the otter, muskrat, marten, fox, lynx, fisher, mink, and finally, the wolf. Only the bison pelt had a smaller market.

In North America, wolf trapping took off in the mid-1800s with the development of the steel leghold trap by Sewell Newhouse. The first record of steel traps was in present-day Massachusetts in the 1630s, but Newhouse was the one who perfected the tool. Newhouse first constructed homemade traps in the 1820s using his father's blacksmith shop to make crude traps

Wolves attracted the attention of trappers in the late 1850s. © Robert H. Busch

Biologist sets a steel trap for a wolf for a research project using the same equipment and technique used by the fur trapper. Photo by Jim Yuskavitch

from old scythes and axes. Newhouse joined a religious organization called the Oneida Community in the 1840s and trap making became a sideline of the community. In the early 1850s one member of the community took two trunkfuls of traps to Chicago and found a ready market there among the hardware firms. In 1854, the community brought in a machine shop and began mass manufacturing the traps. A few years later, Newhouses' traps attracted the attention of merchants in New York, and sales increased dramatically.

Fur-trading records document the resultant rapid rise in the sale of wolf pelts. The American Fur Trading Company records for its upper Missouri division show that only twenty wolf pelts were shipped in 1850; three years later, that number had jumped to 3,000. From 1859 to 1867, Newhouse's Oneida Community Limited produced over 750,000 traps.

The special demands of ranch owners in the West caused them to develop a special trap in 1895 for wolves, the famed No. 4½. They also published a booklet, *How to Catch Wolves with the Newhouse Wolf Trap*. The booklet was partly written by Ernest E. Thompson, who was the government naturalist for the province of Manitoba.

Newhouse was extremely proud of his trap and even recommended that it be used on state seals. He described his trap as "the prow with which iron clad civilization is pushing back barbaric solitude, and is replacing the wolf with the wheatfield, the library, and the piano." Most of the early pelt sales were to Europe and Russia, where they were used in coats.

The smooth-jawed No. 4 1/2 trap was replaced about 1900 by the cruel No. 14 trap, which was equipped with jagged steel teeth. The latter trap is still in use today in many remote areas of North America, although many jurisdictions have outlawed its use. Leghold devices are used in three main types of trap:



1. A blind set, in which a trap is placed on a wolf trail and covered with dirt.
2. A bait set, in which a trap is baited or placed near a bait. Bait sets are often placed near fresh wolf kills.
3. A scent set, in which a trap is placed by a rock or bush on which a homemade scent mix is painted. One early recipe consisted of mixing eight coyote or wolf glands, one quarter liver with gall, one kidney, and wolf dung. This appetizing blend was then allowed to stand in a warm place until well rotted. It was then poured over a wolf trap, and was reported to be irresistible to wolves. In the 1907 annual report of Alberta's chief game warden, he wrote:

---

MEAT BAITS ALONE HAVE NOT PROVEN SUCCESSFUL IN CAPTURING THESE SUSPICIOUS AND CUNNING ANIMALS. OF SCENTS AND COMBINATIONS THE FETID BAIT HAS PROVEN THE MOST SUCCESSFUL. THIS IS PREPARED BY PUTTING A PIECE OF RAW MEAT IN A WIDE-MOUTHED BOTTLE OR JAR AND PLACING IT IN A WARM SHADY PLACE. ALLOW IT TO STAND UNTIL THE ODOR THEREFROM HAS BECOME ALMOST UNBEARABLE, WHEN A QUART OF LARD OIL AND 1 OZ. OF TINCTURE OF MUSK MAY BE ADDED.

**THE LARGEST EXPORTERS OF WOLF PELTS, 2000–2005**

CANADA

UNITED STATES

RUSSIAN FEDERATION

MONGOLIA

LITHUANIA

(Source: CITES)

Other scent baits include wolf urine/scat or beaver or castor oil. Today, valerian (a product of the plant genus *Valeriana*) or some other chemical compound is often used as a scent bait.

Neck snares of 3/32-inch- or 3/8-inch-diameter cable, equipped with a locking mechanism, are now used by many trappers throughout Canada. It is not uncommon for snares to catch deer and other animals that use the same trails. For this reason, prior to the wolf's attaining threatened-species status in Minnesota, that state outlawed the use of neck snares. Many conservationists have spoken out against neck snares on humane grounds; at the 1992 North American Symposium on Wolves held in Edmonton, Alberta, Frederick F. Gilbert stated, "Canids have well-muscled necks and reinforced trachea, so no neck snare system is likely to result in a quick death."

Although most jurisdictions stipulate that traps and snares must be checked daily, in practice many trappers do not check each trap for several days. The result is that thousands of animals undergo lingering deaths, slowly freezing to death in winter or chewing off their own limbs in a frantic bid to escape. This is especially common in the winter, when the trapped paw becomes frozen. It is also common for wolves to break teeth in their efforts to chew off the offending trap. Other injuries include skin lacerations and broken legs.

Many trappers no longer pursue the wolf. One of the reasons for this is that the cost of capture, thawing, skinning, and transport often exceeds market value. Other reasons include the high percentage of black coats (for which there is little demand), the occurrence of mange, and the coarseness of wolf fur, especially the long guard hairs, which are quite brittle. Pelt

**THE LARGEST IMPORTERS OF WOLF PELTS, 2000–2005**

UNITED STATES
GERMANY
RUSSIAN FEDERATION
NORWAY
GREENLAND

(Source: CITES)



matching is also a problem; furriers report that it is difficult to find enough perfectly matching pelts to create wolf fur coats.

Wolf fur is primarily used for parka trim (although wolverine fur is a more efficient insulator) and more rarely for rugs and fur coats.

Historic prices for wolf pelts have ranged from less than $1 a pelt in 1830 to $195 in 1990. In 2017, the average price of a wolf pelt was $180, exceeded only by wolverines at $240.

In Canada, the biggest demand for wolf pelts was in the late 1920s; in 1927–28, over 21,000 wolf pelts were taken in Canada. Today, the animal catch is about 3,000 wolves.

Trapping statistics must be taken with caution, for thousands of pelts used locally are simply not reported to authorities. Officially, wolf pelts account for less than 1/2 of 1 percent of all wild canid pelts harvested in North America (the coyote tops the list).

According to statistics from the Convention on International Trade in Endangered Species of Wild Flora and Fauna (CITES), wolf pelts are the most traded of all wolf parts. Between 1980 and 1986, about 50,000 wolf pelts were traded internationally. Canada and the Soviet Union were the largest exporters; the United States and Great Britain were the largest importers.

In 1991, the Council of the European Economic Community adopted a resolution to prohibit the import of pelts taken after January 1, 1995, unless "the trapping methods used meet internationally recognized standards" and "unless sufficient progress is being made in developing humane methods of trapping." Animal welfare groups pointed out that there is, in fact, no form of trap that is humane, since all traps cause some degree of mental and physical

Winter is the peak season for wolf trapping as their pelts are at their most luxurious at that time of year. Photo courtesy of Oregon Department of Fish and Wildlife.



stress. And after years of negotiations, there is still no "internationally recognized standard" that defines either cruelty or humaneness.

## Hunting and Trapping Harvest Tables

**WOLVES KILLED IN RECREATIONAL HUNTING AND TRAPPING SEASONS—MONTANA**

| Year | Trapping Season | Hunting Season |
|---|---|---|
| 2008 | --- | ---- (1) |
| 2009 | --- | 72 |
| 2010 | --- | --- (2) |
| 2011 | --- | 121 |
| 2012 | --- | 175 |
| 2013 | --- | 231 |
| 2014 | --- | 213 (3) |
| 2015 | 76 | 133 |
| 2016 | 83 | 163 |

(1) Wolves were still listed under the Endangered Species Act and recreational hunting was prohibited.
(2) Wolves were temporarily relisted under the ESA on August 5, 2010 and hunting was not allowed for the 2010–11 season.
(3) Includes harvest from both trapping and hunting.
(Montana Fish, Wildlife and Parks)

## WOLVES HARVESTED BY HUNTERS AND TRAPPERS—IDAHO

| Year | Harvest (Includes Hunting and Trapping) |
|---|---|
| 2008 | --- (1) |
| 2009 | 135 |
| 2010 | 46 (2) |
| 2011 | 200 |
| 2012 | 329 |
| 2013 | 356 |
| 2014 | 256 |
| 2015 | 256 |

(1) Wolves were still listed under the Endangered Species Act and recreational hunting was prohibited.
(2) Wolves harvested in 2010 before wolves were relisted under the ESA in August 2010
(Idaho Department of Fish and Game)

## WOLVES SHOT AND TRAPPED FOR PELTS—QUEBEC

| Season | Harvest (includes hunting and trapping) |
|---|---|
| 2000–2001 | 366 |
| 2001–2002 | 357 |
| 2002–2003 | 483 |
| 2003–2004 | 461 |
| 2004–2005 | 448 |
| 2005–2006 | 465 |
| 2006–2007 | 728 |
| 2007–2008 | 471 |
| 2008–2009 | 629 |
| 2009–2010 | 629 |
| 2010–2011 | 618 |
| 2011–2012 | 625 |
| 2012–2013 | 581 |
| 2013–2014 | 659 |
| 2014–2015 | 508 |
| 2015–2016 | 135 |
| Total | 8,163 |

(Quebec Forests, Wildlife and Parks)
Note: Because this chart only reflects the number of wolves killed for the fur trade, it is likely that many more wolves were shot than are included in these figures.

## WOLVES TRAPPED FOR PELTS—ONTARIO

| Trapping Season | No. of Wolves Harvested |
|---|---|
| 2003/2004 | 387 |
| 2004/2005 | 457 |
| 2005/2006 | 474 |
| 2006/2007 | 676 |
| 2007/2008 | 444 |
| 2008/2009 | 439 |
| 2009/2010 | 516 |
| 2010/2011 | 534 |
| 2011/2012 | 602 |
| 2012/2013 | 521 |
| 2013/2014 | 523 |
| 2014/2015 | 624 |

(Courtesy Earthroots)

## WOLVES HUNTED—ONTARIO

| Hunting Season | No. of Wolves Harvested* |
|---|---|
| 2005 | 46 |
| 2006 | 82 |
| 2007 | 160 |
| 2008 | 146 |
| 2009 | 202 |
| 2010 | 233 |
| 2011 | 249 |
| 2012 | 271 |
| 2013 | 233 |
| 2014 | 300 |
| 2015 | 291 |

*Includes gray wolves and wolf-coyote hybrids
(Courtesy Earthroots)

## WOLVES TRAPPED FOR PELTS—BRITISH COLUMBIA

| Trapping Season | No. of Wolves Trapped |
|---|---|
| 1990 | 47 |
| 1991 | 62 |
| 1992 | 105 |
| 1993 | 95 |
| 1994 | 122 |
| 1995 | 117 |
| 1996 | 84 |
| 1997 | 166 |
| 1998 | 88 |
| 1999 | 132 |
| 2000 | 156 |
| 2001 | 138 |
| 2002 | 167 |
| 2003 | 114 |
| 2004 | 138 |
| 2005 | 155 |
| 2006 | 155 |
| 2007 | 81 |
| 2008 | 115 |
| 2009 | 270 |
| 2010 | --- |
| 2011 | --- |
| 2012 | 232 |
| 2013 | 175 |
| 2014 | 212 |

(Courtesy Wolf Awareness, Inc)

## WOLVES HUNTED—BRITISH COLUMBIA

| Hunting Season | No. of Wolves Harvested |
|---|---|
| 1990 | 414 |
| 1991 | 603 |
| 1992 | 555 |
| 1993 | 312 |
| 1994 | 517 |
| 1995 | 571 |
| 1996 | 624 |
| 1997 | 572 |
| 1998 | 610 |
| 1999 | 540 |
| 2000 | 658 |
| 2001 | 491 |
| 2002 | 576 |
| 2003 | 493 |
| 2004 | 388 |
| 2005 | 545 |
| 2006 | 597 |
| 2007 | 827 |
| 2008 | 775 |

(Courtesy Wolf Awareness, Inc)

CHAPTER

8

# THE WOLF AS A BIG-GAME ANIMAL

WOLF HUNTING BECAME A SPORT as early as the 16th century, when leisure time became available to wealthy merchants. In *Tuberville's Book of Hunting*, published in 1577, instruction was given in the luring of wolves to hunting blinds.

The hunting of wolves was popular in Europe in the 18th century, when it evolved into a proper pastime for a gentleman. Dog breeders even worked to establish special "wolfhounds" to aid in the sport.

By the 1800s, North Americans also pursued the wolf for sport. Theodore Roosevelt, the "conservationist president" once went on a wolf hunt with three dozen hunters and over 100 dogs. The use of dogs in wolf hunts was very common at the time. Roosevelt wrote, "The only two requisites were that the dogs be fast and fight gamely; and in consequence they formed as wicked a hard-biting crew as ever throttled a wolf."

However, the Alberta chief game warden wrote in the 1907 annual report of the Alberta Department of Agriculture, "Hunting with dogs has proven more successful with coyotes than with the timber wolf. The large greyhound or wolfhound which runs by sight and hunts in pairs will readily overtake and kill the coyote, but they would be no match for a full grown timber wolf."

One of the most unusual of wolf hunting techniques is the use of eagles. The huge Berkut eagle, largest subspecies of golden eagle, has been used for

> A WOLF KILLED WITH A FIREARM REPRESENTS ONE OF THE MOST PRIZED TROPHIES.
>
> —Clyde Ormond, *The Complete Book of Hunting*, 1962

hunting in central Asia since the days of Genghis Khan. David Bruce, writing in *Bird of Jove*, states that a bird would be "taught to take the wolf through the head after blinding it with blows from its wings." In Kazakhstan, the hunting of wolves with eagles still takes place today.

By the early 1900s, weekend wolf hunts were common events across the American prairies. One participant described them as "the most popular spring enjoyment of the prairie states." He went on to characterize them as "healthful outdoor exercise and fun."



In North America, wolves have been shot from sleighs, trucks, snowmobiles, and airplanes. The big-game hunting of wolves became especially popular in North America after World War II, perhaps representing a delayed-aggression response to the carnage of the war years.

Aerial hunting of wolves was popular from the 1940s to the 1970s. In *The Complete Book of Hunting*, Clyde Ormond wrote, "Wolves also are hunted from planes in winter . . . a choice place to catch a wolf unawares is on the ice"—a sporting proposition indeed.

In the 1960s, the roar of snowmobiles first began to shatter the icy stillness of the northern wilderness. Biologists Douglas Heard and W. George Calef, of the Northwest Territories' Department of Renewable Resources, once described the shooting of wolves after a chase on snowmobiles as "an exciting and desirable sport," and many northerners still agree. Today, most of the wolves shot in the Northwest Territories are shot from snowmobiles.

The end of the line for a northern British Columbia wolf. © Robert H. Busch

Most wolves shot by hunters are used either for meat or for personal trophies. Internationally, there is very little trade in wolf trophies. Between 1980 and 1986, the CITES recorded only 350 wolf trophies sold internationally. In 2005, CITES statistics show that Canada was the largest gross exporter of trophy wolves, with forty-seven trophies exported. Denmark was the largest importer, with twenty-six wolf trophies imported.

## Hunting Statistics—United States

In the lower 48 states, the wolf is classed as endangered or threatened in most of its range and therefore disallowed as a game animal. In Minnesota, where the wolf is officially classed as threatened, state officials for many years attempted to have wolf control return to the state in order to establish a sport hunting season for wolves. However, in 1984, U.S. District Judge Miles Lord ruled that a threatened species could not be hunted unless the secretary of the Department of the Interior establishes that an excess population exists that cannot be otherwise reduced. His decision was upheld by the U.S. Court of Appeals.

Since then, wolves in the northern Rocky Mountain states and portions of the West Coast states have been removed from the Endangered Species Act protection. Now, in addition to Alaska, Montana, Idaho, and Wyoming all allow wolf hunting. A wolf tag in Montana is $19 for residents and $50 for nonresidents. The archery season for wolves runs from September 7 to September 14; the rifle season September 15 to March 15. There is no harvest quota for wolves in Montana, but hunters must report their harvest. Montana also allows wolf trapping.

Idaho wolf tags are $11.50 for residents and $31.50 for nonresidents. Depending on the part of the state, wolf hunting seasons go from August to June or March. The statewide quota is 185 wolves harvested annually. Idaho also allows wolf trapping.

Wolves in Minnesota, Michigan, and Wisconsin were removed from the ESA in 2012, turning management over to the states, but as a result of lawsuits initiated by conservation groups, they were relisted in 2014.

In Alaska, the wolf is classed as both a big-game animal and a furbearer. Although the shooting of wolves from airplanes was outlawed in 1972, in many parts of Alaska aerial shooting still occurs, a function of the vast territory involved and the lack of wildlife agents to adequately patrol the state. In recent years there were even two aerial shooters caught operating within Denali National Park.

Aerial hunting has been replaced in many areas by a land-and-shoot technique that follows an aerial chase. Hunters are supposed to land at least 330 feet from a wolf before shooting, but there have been numerous reports of aircraft pursuing wolves until the animals are too exhausted to escape. And rarely is an observer present to ensure that shooting from the aircraft does not take place. As Frederick F. Gilbert stated at the 1992 North American Symposium on Wolves in Edmonton, Alberta, "problems with enforcement suggest that it may be more of a paper regulation than a real one." Those caught misusing aircraft for the hunting of wolves are subject to maximum fines of $5,000 and six months in jail.



The hunting of wolves from snowmobiles is also very popular in Alaska. According to wolf biologist Gordon Haber, "Snowmobile assisted killing of wolves has become relatively commonplace in open-terrain areas throughout Alaska."

The hunting season for wolves in Alaska is generally August through April, although some game management units permit hunting from December through March. Residents pay a $45 for a hunting license while

Minnesota wolves taken by game wardens as part of a government predator control program. © State of Minnesota, Department Natural Resources

nonresidents need a nonresident hunting license plus a $60 wolf tag. The bag limit depends on the area, varying from 2 to 10 wolves.

Neither the Alaska Department of Fish and Game nor the nonprofit Boone and Crockett Club maintains records of trophy wolves, so there is no record of the largest wolf taken by American hunters.

## Hunting Statistics—Canada

Canada has some of the most liberal hunting laws in the world. As R. D. Hayes and J. R. Gunson reported at the 1992 North American Symposium on Wolves, "The wolf is currently the only big game animal in Canada that is hunted year-round, has no bag limits in most areas, and does not require special seals or licenses to hunt."

**The Northwest Territories:** This area has the largest population of wolves in Canada and predictably simple hunting regulations. Hunting tags for wolves are $20 for residents and $40 for nonresidents. Hunters can kill as many wolves as they have tags for. Season dates vary depending on the area but mainly run from summer though spring.

Because of the huge area of the Northwest Territories—over a million square miles—many wolf kills go unreported.

**British Columbia:** Hunting laws here are almost as lax. No special tag is required for residents to hunt wolves. A wolf tag for a nonresident is $50. The bag limit is three, but may vary regionally. Some areas have no bag limits. Seasons also vary by region, and wolf hunting and trapping rules have been liberalized in some areas where the season may last more than seven months. In some areas there are no closed seasons.

The Trophy Wildlife Records Club of British Columbia keeps records of trophy wolves taken in that province.

**Alberta:** Alberta residents do not need a tag to hunt wolves. The season begins on the opening day of any big-game season of a particular wildlife management unit and ends either May 31 or June 15. A nonresident wolf license is $12.40, which is also good for coyotes.

**Ontario:** To hunt wolves in Ontario, the hunter must have a wolf seal. The cost is $11.14 for residents and $272 for nonresidents. Hunters must also have a small-game license. The bag limit is two wolves per year. The season runs from September 15 to the following March 31. Since 2004, in order to protect the Algonquin wolf, there is no hunting allowed in areas surrounding Algonquin Provincial Park, Killarney Park, and Kawartha Highlands Provincial Park.

**Manitoba:** No special wolf tags are required for either residents or nonresidents, who only need to have a hunting license. The wolf hunting season runs from August 31 to March 31, and the bag limit is one or two wolves depending on the area hunted. Manitoba also allows the use of baits to hunt wolves.

**Quebec:** The hunting season here stretches from October 25 to March 31. There is no bag limit.

**Yukon:** Hunters need a license to hunt wolves, which costs $10 for residents along with a furbearer seal. Hunting seasons vary by region but start on August 1 and go into the following March or April. Bag limits range from one to seven depending on the area hunted.

Throughout Canada, owners who wish to export wolf furs and parts must obtain Convention Export Permits under the CITES agreement, but because the Canadian wolf population is deemed stable, the permits are readily obtainable.

Two wolves vie for the record of the largest trophy wolf taken in Canada. The largest trophy wolf in British Columbia scored 18.2500 (greatest length of the skull, without lower jawbone, in inches, plus greatest width of skull) and was taken near Driscoll Creek in 1984. The current Alberta record is also an 18.2500-score wolf, shot in the Willmore Wilderness Park in 1993.

CHAPTER

9

# THE WOLF AS A ZOO ANIMAL

THE FIRST COLLECTIONS OF LIVING ANIMALS appeared about 4500 BC in Mesopotamia, the site of present-day Iraq. The first large zoo to open in North America was New York's Central Park Zoo, which welcomed the public in 1864.

Gerald Durrell, noted naturalist and founder of the famed Jersey Wildlife Preservation Trust, wrote in *Beasts in My Belfry* that there are three main purposes of modern zoos:

1. To aid in educating people about other forms of life
2. To act as a research center for species that are difficult to observe in the wild
3. To serve as a sanctuary and breeding center for threatened species

Despite these lofty ideals, far too many modern zoos still exist only as amusement centers. The percentage of threatened species exhibited is minimal, and the amount of valid research performed in many zoos is insignificant. In 1991, Barry Lopez referred to zoos as "vestiges of colonialism," and stated that "the primary function of zoos in our culture, however high-minded we insist on being about this, is to entertain."

According to eminent field biologist George Schaller of the New York Zoological Society (NYZS)/Wildlife Conservation Society (WCS), "zoos have no validity nowadays, no purpose, except to help protect and raise endangered animals and to raise public consciousness about the plight of wildlife."

All captive animals require enriched environments to avoid boredom and cage neuroses. Photo courtesy of California Wolf Center

However, it was not until 1981 that the American Association of Zoological Parks and Aquariums (AAZPA) passed a program to implement Species Survival Plans (SSPs) in American zoos. In 1980, when an ad was placed in an issue of the AAZPA newsletter asking for zoological institutions interested in holding male Mexican wolves, only two of the 100-plus member zoos responded. After numerous delays, SSPs are now in place for both the Mexican wolf and the red wolf. In 1992, the IUCN's Species Survival Commission's Canid Specialist Group recommended strongly that "a captive breeding program begin as soon as possible" for the Ethiopian wolf.

The Mexican wolf was declared an endangered species in 1976. Photo courtesy of California Wolf Center

At one time, scientists recognized twenty-four subspecies of North American wolf; today, most accept five. Julie Lawrence photo, © Wolf Haven International

Of the more than 600 zoos that belong to Species 360 (formerly International Species Information System) and that exhibit wolves, over a third have only a single wolf or a pair of the same sex, a sad fate for a species as social as the wolf and a sad commentary on the lack of importance given by zoos to the breeding of threatened species.

According to Anthony D. Marshall, chairman of the Education Committee of the NYZS/WCS, "Being in close proximity to other species brings us to a deeper understanding of the interrelatedness of all living beings." And perhaps this is the true prime justification of zoos today. There is certainly significant educational value in allowing the public the opportunity to see wild animals up close, as opposed to viewing their shadow images on television or their two-dimensional replicas in books. However, the conditions under which they are often kept reinforces the minimal standards that we set for animals.

Captive wolves require space and company to avoid boredom. © Robert H. Busch

Animals as intelligent and as socially ordered as wolves need both mental stimulation and sufficient room for the pack hierarchy to be enforced. A pack of wolves that in the wild may require 300 acres will certainly function abnormally pacing around in a zoo's quarter-acre enclosure. And yet it is very common today for a large wolf pack to be contained within a very small compound, providing no escape or hiding place for the lowest-ranked members of the pack. These individuals must often be removed and sent to other zoos. If they are not removed, they may be seriously wounded or even killed by the other members of the pack. In 1994, the omega female wolf in a captive pack at Wolf Park in Battle Ground, Indiana, had to be removed from the pack after she was attacked by three other pack members. That same year, another female wolf at the Wolf Education and Research Center in Winchester, Idaho, received a broken leg in an aggressive encounter with another captive wolf. The center staff euthanized the unfortunate animal.

Gray wolves breed readily in captivity. According to statistics kept by the IUCN, between 1962 and 1984 there were over 1,000 litters from captive gray wolves. Zoos with outstanding records of wolf births include the National Zoological Park (Washington, DC), Trevor Zoo (Millbrook, NY), The Living Desert (Palm Desert, CA), Arizona-Sonora Desert Museum

(Tucson, AZ), Rio Grande Zoo (Albuquerque, NM), and the Jardin Zoologique du Québec (Charlesbourg, Québec). In Europe, the Whipsnade Wild Animal Park (Dunstable, England), Port Lympne Zoo Park (Hythe, England), Budapest Zoo, El Zoobotánico de Jerez (Jerez de la Frontera, Spain), Leipzig Zoo (Germany), and Tallinn Zoo (Estonia) all have noteworthy records of wolf litters.

OF ALL THE WILD CREATURES OF NORTH AMERICA, NONE ARE MORE DESPICABLE THAN WOLVES.

—William Hornaday, director of the New York Zoological Society, 1896–1926

Unfortunately, it is often difficult to place all the wolf pups produced, and many end up in third-rate game farms and wildlife exhibits. And Bernhard Grzimek, former director of the Frankfurt Zoo, noted in *Grzimek's Animal Life Encyclopedia*, "Many zoos continue to remove pups from the mother at an early age and raise a single pup in the children's zoo for the pleasure of their young, human admirers. As the pups become older, they are then sold and suffer an uncertain fate."

Many responsible zoos now neuter their captive gray wolves to prevent unwanted litters.

## NORTH AMERICAN ZOOS WITH WOLF EXHIBITS

### UNITED STATES

| Alaska | |
|---|---|
| Alaska Zoo<br>Anchorage, AK | gray wolves |
| **Arizona** | |
| Arizona-Sonora Desert Museum<br>Tucson, AZ | Mexican gray wolves |
| Heritage Park Zoological Sanctuary<br>Prescott, AZ | Mexican gray wolves |
| Keepers of the Wild<br>Valentine, AZ | gray wolves |
| Navajo Nation Zoo and Botanical Park<br>Window Rock, AZ | Mexican gray wolves |

| | |
|---|---|
| Phoenix Zoo<br>Phoenix, AZ | Mexican gray wolves |
| **Arkansas** | |
| Little Rock Zoo<br>Little Rock, AR | maned wolf |
| Wild Wilderness Drive Through Safari<br>Gentry, AR | gray wolves |
| **California** | |
| Fresno Chaffee Zoo<br>Fresno, CA | red wolves |
| Folsom Zoo Sanctuary Friends<br>Folsom, CA | gray wolves (rescued) |
| Los Angeles Zoo & Botanical Gardens<br>Los Angeles, CA | maned wolf |
| Big Bear Zoo<br>Big Bear Lake, CA | gray wolves |
| San Diego Zoo<br>San Diego, CA | gray wolves |
| San Francisco Zoo<br>San Fransico, CA | Mexican gray wolves |
| Living Desert Zoo Gardens<br>Palm Desert, CA | Mexican gray wolves |
| Wildlife Waystation<br>Lake View Terrace, CA | gray wolves |
| **Colorado** | |
| Cheyenne Mountain Zoo<br>Colorado Springs, CO | Mexican gray wolves |
| Denver Zoo<br>Denver, CO | maned wolf |
| Pueblo Zoo<br>Pueblo, CO | maned wolf |
| **Connecticut** | |
| Beardsley Zoo<br>Bridgeport, CT | red wolves, Mexican gray wolves |

| Florida | |
|---|---|
| Brevard Zoo<br>Melbourne, FL | red wolves |
| Lowry Park Zoo<br>Tampa, FL | red wolves |
| **Georgia** | |
| North Georgia Zoo<br>Cleveland, GA | gray wolves |
| **Illinois** | |
| Brookfield Zoo<br>Brookfield, IL | Mexican gray wolves |
| Hensen Robinson Zoo<br>Springfield, IL | red wolves |
| Lincoln Park Zoo<br>Chicago, IL | red wolves |
| Miller Park Zoo<br>Bloomington, IL | red wolves |
| Niabi Zoo<br>Coal Valley, IL | red wolves |
| Phillips Park Zoo<br>Aurora, IL | gray wolves |
| Scovill Zoo<br>Decatur, IL | gray wolves |
| Wildlife Prairie State Park<br>Hanna City, IL | gray wolves |
| **Indiana** | |
| Mesker Park Zoo & Botanical Garden<br>Evansville, IN | Mexican gray wolves |
| Washington Park Zoo<br>Michigan City, IN | gray wolves |
| **Kansas** | |
| Sedgwick County Zoo<br>Wichita, KS | Mexican gray wolves, maned wolves |

| | |
|---|---|
| Sunset Zoo<br>Manhattan, KS | maned wolf |
| **Kentucky** | |
| The Zoo<br>Louisville, KY | maned wolves |
| **Louisiana** | |
| Alexandria Zoo<br>Alexandria, LA | red wolves, maned wolves |
| **Maryland** | |
| Plumpton Park Zoo<br>Rising Sun, MD | gray wolves |
| **Massachusetts** | |
| The Zoo in Forest Park and Education Center<br>Springfield, MA | gray wolves (hybrids) |
| **Michigan** | |
| Binder Park Zoo<br>Battle Creek, MI | Mexican gray wolves |
| Garlyn Zoo<br>Naubinway, MI | gray wolves |
| Potter Park Zoo<br>Lansing, MI | gray wolves |
| Detroit Zoo<br>Royal Oak, MI | gray wolves |
| Saginaw Zoo<br>Saginaw, MI | Mexican gray wolves |
| **Minnesota** | |
| Minnesota Zoo<br>Apple Valley, MN | gray wolf |
| Wildlife Science Center<br>Stacey, MN | gray wolves, Mexican gray wolves, red wolves |
| **Mississippi** | |
| The Jackson Wolf<br>Jackson, MS | red wolf |

| Missouri | |
|---|---|
| Dickerson Park Zoo<br>Springfield, MO | Mexican gray wolf, maned wolf |
| **Montana** | |
| Zoo Montana<br>Billings, MT | gray wolves |
| Grizzly & Wolf Discovery Center<br>West Yellowstone, MT | gray wolves |
| **New Mexico** | |
| ABQ BioPark<br>Albuquerque, NM | Mexican gray wolves |
| Wildlife West Nature Park<br>Edgewood, NM | Mexican gray wolves |
| **New York** | |
| Binghamton Zoo<br>Binghamton, NY | red wolf |
| Buffalo Zoo<br>Buffalo, NY | maned wolf |
| New York State Zoo<br>Watertown, NY | gray wolves |
| Rosamund Gifford Zoo<br>Syracuse, NY | gray wolves, red wolves |
| Seneca Park Zoo<br>Rochester, NY | gray wolves |
| Utica Zoo<br>Utica, NY | Mexican wolves |
| **North Carolina** | |
| North Carolina Zoo<br>Asheboro, NC | red wolves |
| **North Dakota** | |
| Dakota Zoo<br>Bismark, ND | Mexican gray wolves |
| Red River Zoo<br>Fargo, ND | gray wolves |

| | |
|---|---|
| Roosevelt Park Zoo<br>Minot, ND | gray wolves |
| **Ohio** | |
| Akron Zoo<br>Akron, OH | red wolves |
| Wolf Timbers<br>Bolivar, OH | gray wolves |
| Cincinnati Zoo & Botanical Garden<br>Cincinnati, OH | Mexican gray wolves |
| Cleveland Metroparks Zoo<br>Cleveland, OH | Mexican gray wolves |
| Columbus Zoo and Aquarium<br>Powell, OH | Mexican gray wolves |
| **Rhode Island** | |
| Roger Williams Park Zoo<br>Providence, RI | Mexican gray wolves |
| **South Dakota** | |
| Bramble Park Zoo<br>Watertown, SD | gray wolves |
| **Tennessee** | |
| Memphis Zoo<br>Memphis, TN | gray wolves |
| **Texas** | |
| Austin Zoo<br>Austin, TX | wolf hybrids |
| El Paso Zoo<br>El Paso, TX | Mexican gray wolf |
| Houston Zoo<br>Houston, TX | maned wolf |
| The Texas Zoo<br>Victoria, TX | red wolves |
| **Utah** | |
| Hogle Zoo<br>Salt Lake City, UT | gray wolves |

| | |
|---|---|
| **Virginia** | |
| Mill Mountain Zoo<br>Roanoke, VA | red wolves |
| **Washington** | |
| Northwest Trek Wildlife Park<br>Eatonville, WA | gray wolves |
| Cougar Mountain Zoo<br>Issaquah, WA | gray wolves |
| Woodland Park Zoo<br>Seattle, WA | gray wolves |
| Point Defiance Zoo & Aquarium<br>Tacoma, WA | red wolves |
| **Washington, DC** | |
| Smithsonian National Zoo &<br>Conservation Biology Institute<br>Washington, DC | gray wolves, maned wolves |
| **Wisconsin** | |
| Lincoln Park Zoo<br>Manitowoc, WI | gray wolves |
| Wildwood Zoo<br>Marshfield, WI | gray wolves |

**CANADA**

| | |
|---|---|
| **Alberta** | |
| Calgary Zoo<br>Calgary, AB | gray wolves |
| Edmonton Valley Zoo<br>Edmonton, AB | gray wolves |
| Wildlife Discovery Park<br>Innisfail, AB | gray wolves |
| Yamnuska Wolfdog Sanctuary<br>Cochrane, AB | wolf hybrids |
| **British Columbia** | |
| British Columbia Wildlife Park<br>Kamloops, BC | gray wolves |

| Manitoba | |
|---|---|
| Assiniboine Park Zoo<br>Winnipeg, MB | gray wolves |
| Thompson Zoo<br>Thompson, MB | gray wolves |
| **New Brunswick** | |
| Magnetic Hill Zoo<br>Moncton, NB | gray wolves |
| **Nova Scotia** | |
| Shubenacadie Wildlife Park<br>Shubenacadie, NS | gray wolves |
| **Ontario** | |
| The Papanack Zoo<br>Wendover, ON | gray wolves |
| Toronto Zoo<br>Toronto, ON | gray wolves |
| Safari Niagara<br>Stevensville, ON | gray wolves |
| Spruce Haven Nature Park<br>Sault Ste. Marie, ON | gray wolves |
| Twin Valley Zoo<br>Brantford, ON | gray wolves |
| **Quebec** | |
| Zoo Sauvage de St-Felicien<br>Saint-Felicien, QC | gray wolves |
| Parc Omega<br>Montebello, QC | gray wolves |
| **Saskatchewan** | |
| Saskatoon Forestry and Farm Park<br>Saskatoon, SK | gray wolves |

## MEXICO

| Mexico (State of) | |
|---|---|
| Zoologico de Chapultepec<br>Chapultepec, Mexico | Mexican gray wolves |

## Wolf Parks

In the past two decades, a number of wolf parks have sprung up across the United States. In some cases these institutions provide homes for unwanted pet wolves and most provide tours and educational facilities to promote wolf conservation in the wild.

### WOLF HAVEN INTERNATIONAL

Wolf Haven was founded in 1982 as a sanctuary for unwanted captive wolves. It has now grown to its position as one of the premier wolf facilities in North America. Wolf Haven currently has forty-seven wolves and four hybrids. It is a participant in both the red wolf and Mexican wolf captive breeding programs (see chapter 11). (These wolves are not available for public viewing.) The sanctuary covers sixty-five acres, with an excellent guided tour of the public portion of Wolf Haven. In 1994, over 25,000 people toured the facility. Wolf Haven actively lobbied against the Alaska wolf kill and was one of the sponsors of biologist Gordon Haber's wolf research in Alaska. It was also one of the sponsors of the 1992 North American Symposium on Wolves in Edmonton, Alberta. The center conducts wolf ecology classes and field howling programs (see chapter 11, "Public Wolf Howls," p. 232). It produces an excellent newsletter and has an adopt-a-wolf program. Wolf Haven is located near Tenino in western Washington. (3111 Offut Lake Rd., Tenino, WA 98589; wolfhaven.org)

Wolf Haven is one of North America's largest and finest wolf parks. Photo courtesy of Wolf Haven International

### CALIFORNIA WOLF CENTER

The California Wolf Center, formerly the Julian Center for Science and Education, has thirty wolves on-site. The center's goals are to provide educational and research opportunities for students, scientists, and the general public. Currently emphasis is placed on studies of wild canid behavior, physiology, genetics, and pathology. A future goal is to breed endangered and threatened wild canids. The center was founded in 1984 and is located just south of Julian, California, in the Cuyamaca Mountains. Facilities include a conference center, a field laboratory, an observation tower, and interpretive nature trails. Members receive a center newsletter. (P.O. Box 1389, Julian, CA 92036; californiawolfcenter.org)

### WOLF HOLLOW

Wolf Hollow (formerly the North American Wolf Foundation, Inc.) is a nonprofit facility dedicated to the preservation of the gray wolf through education and exposure to wolves in a natural setting. It currently exhibits eight wolves in a 1½-acre enclosure that includes a stream-fed pond. The foundation offers memberships, adopt-a-wolf programs, a newsletter, tours, and a gift shop. It is located three miles outside Ipswich, Massachusetts. (114 Essex Rd., Route 133, Ipswich, MA 01938; wolfhollowipswich.org)

### WOLF PARK

Since 1972, Wolf Park (part of the North American Wildlife Park Foundation) has been carrying out behavioral research on captive wolves under the direction of Erich Klinghammer. The park now has sixteen gray wolves and recently opened a new wolf enclosure of 6¾ acres. Wolf Park offers wolf behavior seminars on a regular basis through its Institute of Ethology. The park has an adopt-a-wolf program, a newsletter, and a bookstore/gift shop. It is open daily from May through November, and on Friday evenings only for a public wolf howl from December through April. Wolf Park is located about 80 miles north of Indianapolis. (44004 East 800 North, Battle Ground, IN 47920; wolfpark.org)

### ENDANGERED WOLF CENTER (FORMERLY THE WILD CANID SURVIVAL AND RESEARCH CENTER)

The Endangered Wolf Center was founded in 1971 by zoologist Marlin Perkins and a group of other individuals concerned about the future of wild canids. The center is a private, nonprofit organization located on 50 wooded acres within Washington University's Tyson Research Center near

St. Louis, Missouri. It was the first institution to join the red wolf and the Mexican gray wolf captive breeding programs (see chapter 11). It currently has gray wolves, Mexican wolves, maned wolves, swift foxes, African painted dogs, and fennec foxes. The prime focus of the center is the breeding of endangered wolves for future reintroduction to the wild. The center is open to the public and many tours and programs are available; however, advance reservations are required. (6750 Tyson Valley Rd., Eureka, MO 63025; endangeredwolfcenter.org)

### MISSION WOLF

Mission Wolf, located in the mountains of Colorado near Silver Cliff, currently has 32 wolves, and hosts school field trips, summer camps, and other educational programs and activities. (13388 County Road 634, Westcliffe, CO 81252; missionwolf.org)

### WILD SPIRIT WOLF SANCTUARY

The Wild Spirit Wolf Sanctuary rescues displaced, unwanted, wolf-dog hybrids, and captive-bred wolves that cannot be released into the wild. In addition to offering a place for these animals the sanctuary also offers a variety of educational programs and tours to help people learn more about wolves, ethical treatment of animals, and humans as part of the ecosystem. They currently provide a home for nearly 60 wolves, wolf-dog hybrids, and other canids. (378 Candy Kitchen Rd., Ramah, NM 87321; wildspiritwolf sanctuary.org)

### WOLF PEOPLE

Wolf People, located in the wilds of northern Idaho, was established in 1993 and currently has twenty-seven wolves. (12 miles south of Sandpoint, Idaho on Highway 95; wolfpeople.com)

### INTERNATIONAL WOLF CENTER

The International Wolf Center includes a visitor center that interprets the natural history of wolves and their conservation and offers a variety of programs to educate the public about wolves including adventure programs, tours, school programs, webinars, and scientific symposiums. They also have five ambassador wolves available for viewing by visitors and two "retired" wolves. (1396 Highway 169, Ely, MN 55731; wolf.org)

### LES LOUPS DU GÉVAUDAN (FRANCE)

In 1991, several hundred Mongolian wolf pups were offered for sale to zoos in Europe by an unscrupulous dealer who tried to circumvent international regulations by routing the wolves via Hungary. The wolves were in poor health and were finally rescued by actress Brigitte Bardot and the animal welfare group Friends of Animals. They were taken to France, where they were placed in a new wolf park near Gévaudan, the historic home of a pair of man-eating wolves (likely wolf-dog hybrids) in the 1600s (see chapter 5, "Man-Eating Wolves," p. 117). The park features an educational exhibit describing the natural history of wolves. (Sainte-Lucie, 48100 Marvejols, France)

CHAPTER

10

# THE WOLF AS A PET

ONE OF THE MOST SERIOUS problems faced by humane societies across North America is that of exotic pets. The lure of something different and the social need for status symbols have created a demand for exotic pets of all kinds, including wolves and wolf-dog hybrids. Some even see these animals as tangible symbols of the wilderness, or have misplaced ideas about helping an endangered species by keeping one as a pet. And movies such as *White Fang* and *Dances with Wolves* have unwittingly stimulated interest in wolves as pets.

Many pet wolves end up in backyard pens that are far too small for their needs.
© Robert H. Busch

Wild animals belong in the wild, not in one's home. No domestic situation can fulfill the mental and physical needs of a wild animal, no matter how much that animal is loved by its owner. The American Humane Association (AHA) categorically "opposes the deliberate capture and confinement, or the breeding, or hybrid breeding, of wild or exotic animals as pets."

> MANY PEOPLE ASK ME IF WOLVES MAKE GOOD PETS. I INVARIABLY ANSWER "NO!" AND QUICKLY ADD THAT NO WILD ANIMAL MAKES A GOOD PET.
>
> —R. D. Lawrence, *Trail of the Wolf*, 1993



Considering that millions of unwanted domestic dogs are euthanized by humane societies each year, the demand for pet wolves or wolf-dog hybrids is especially tragic.

Exotic pets often have special nutritional requirements that cannot be met by the average homeowner. Some animals, such as wolves, have territorial needs that cannot be duplicated in the home. The inherent wild nature of the wolf cannot be removed; a Russian proverb states, "You may feed the wolf as much as you like. He will always glance toward the forest."

Most exotic animals kept as pets do not get sufficient exercise and are housed in pens that are far too small for the animal's needs. When they become ill, few veterinarians will treat them. In some jurisdictions, it is illegal for veterinarians to treat wild animals such as wolves.

Wolves in particular need the social support of a pack; lone wolves kept as pets often become stressed and neurotic. They may lose their innate fear of humans and may become difficult or impossible to train. R. D. Lawrence, who has rescued a number of wolves from inhumane owners, states in *In Praise of Wolves* that "a wolf can never be owned; it cannot be mastered."

And wolves are predators; they simply do not understand that the neighbor's poodle is not fair game. If allowed to run with other dogs, pet wolves may attempt to discipline the dogs as if they were wild pack members, sometimes wounding or killing them.

Inevitably many pet wolves become unwanted and their owners decide to place them with a zoo "for their own good." Unfortunately, few zoos can accept such animals, for it is difficult to introduce them into established zoo packs. All too often, the animal ends its short life being humanely euthanized or placed in a third-rate zoo or game farm.

In 1991, a Tennessee man was fined $1,000 for trying to set his two captive-raised wolves free in Glacier National Park. Such animals have little chance of survival in the wild and pose a serious threat to the genetic integrity of wild wolves, increasing the chances of inbreeding by inadvertently introducing wolves into a wolf population they originated from.

## Wolf-Dog Hybrids

According to the Humane Society of the United States (HSUS), there are over 200,000 wolf-dog hybrids kept as pets across the United States. The most common wolf-dog crosses are those resulting from the breeding of wolves with malamutes, huskies, or German shepherds.

Crossing a dog and a wolf undoes 15,000 years of domestication. Julie Lawrence, © Photo Wolf Haven International

The idea behind crossing wolves with dogs is that the mix will dilute the wild nature of the wolf. Nothing could be further from the truth. In fact, hybrids can be more aggressive than pure wolves, a lethal blend of wild predator and domestic animal that has lost its fear of man. Hybrids have a strong hunting instinct and have been known to regard small children as suitable prey. A number of vicious attacks on humans have been documented, including at least six deaths. In September of 1988, a hybrid adopted from a humane society in Florida scaled a four-foot-high enclosure and killed a four-year-old boy. The boy's parents sued, and the humane society had to pay a large settlement.

Hybrids tend to be taller and heavier than most domestic mixed-breed dogs, and much stronger. Their wild nature makes them resistive to both training and confinement. They tend to be timid and fearful of humans, fear-biters that may attack when they feel threatened, teased, or cornered. According to the HSUS, they are "frequently unpredictable, destructive, rarely trainable, and very adept at escaping from confinement."

Their human owners often fail to understand their fear of man and do not understand the reason for an attack. Regardless of the percentage of wild wolf in the cross, hybrids can be unpredictable and dangerous.

Dr. Randall Lockwood, consultant to the HSUS, states, "Wolf hybrids undo 15,000 years of domestication." The HSUS policy on hybrids is that "wolf hybrids are unsuitable as pets."

Unhappy owners of hybrids often have a difficult time disposing of their pets. Often the animal has bonded so strongly with its owner that it cannot be successfully given or sold to a new owner.



Animal shelters are flooded with hybrids, but many now refuse to accept them, fearing lawsuits in case of future attacks and recognizing the animal's unsuitability as a pet.

Steve Kuntz, founder of Wolf Haven in Washington State, says, "We get hundreds of calls from owners who simply do not know what to do with them." During the summer, Wolf Haven often gets over a dozen calls a day.

As with pet wolves, many hybrids' lives are ended by euthanasia, a tragic result of the vanity of man.

## IUCN RESOLUTION ON WOLF-DOG HYBRIDS

(passed April 20 and 24, 1990)

Whereas hybridization between wolves and dogs and the keeping of these hybrids as pets is becoming increasingly common in various countries, and especially in the United States and Canada;

Whereas most wolf-dog hybrids are poorly adapted to be pets, and there have been numerous fatal and non-fatal attacks on people and domestic animals which, in addition to being tragic and unavoidable, detract from the public perception of wild wolves; and

Whereas the perpetuation of these hybrids has no scientific or educational value; and whereas the ease with which escaped or unwanted hybrids can interbreed with wild wolves threatens the genetic integrity of wild populations.

Now therefore it be resolved that the IUCN/SSC Wolf Specialist Group views the existence and expansion of wolf-dog hybrids as a threat to wolf conservation and recommends that governments and appropriate regulatory agencies prohibit or at least strictly regulate interbreeding between wolves and dogs and the keeping of these animals as pets.

## WOLVES AND HYBRIDS AS PETS—UNITED STATES

| State | Wolves as Pets | Classification of Hybrids | Hybrids as Pets |
|---|---|---|---|
| Alabama | not regulated | not regulated | not regulated |
| Alaska | prohibited | undefined | prohibited |
| Arizona | permit required | not regulated | not regulated |
| Arkansas | not regulated | not regulated | regulated |
| California | prohibited | $F_1$ deemed wolves | not permitted |
| Colorado | prohibited | classed as dogs | not regulated |
| Connecticut | prohibited | classed as dogs | prohibited |
| Delaware | permit required | undefined | permit required |
| Florida | permit required | 75%+ deemed wolf | permit required |
| Georgia | prohibited | classed as wolves | prohibited |
| Hawaii | prohibited | classed as wolves | prohibited |
| Idaho | permit required | undefined | permit required |
| Illinois | prohibited | classed as wolves | prohibited |
| Indiana | permit required | not regulated | permit required |
| Iowa | prohibited | classed as dogs | not regulated |
| Kansas | prohibited | classed as dogs | not regulated |
| Kentucky | prohibited | 25%+ deemed wolf | not regulated |
| Louisiana | prohibited | classed as wolf if "appears indistinguishable" from wolf | not regulated |
| Maine | permit required | classed as wolves | permit required |
| Maryland | prohibited | classed as wolves | prohibited |
| Massachusetts | prohibited | classed as wolves | prohibited |
| Michigan | prohibited | classed as wolves | prohibited |
| Minnesota | permit required | not regulated | not regulated |
| Mississippi | permit required | classed as wolves | permit required |

## WOLVES AND HYBRIDS AS PETS—UNITED STATES

| State | Wolves as Pets | Classification of Hybrids | Hybrids as Pets |
|---|---|---|---|
| Missouri | permit required | classed as wolves | permit required |
| Montana | permit required | 50%+ deemed wolf | 50%+ permit required |
| Nebraska | prohibited | 10%+ deemed wolf | not regulated |
| Nevada | not regulated | not regulated | not regulated |
| New Hampshire | prohibited | not regulated | not regulated |
| New Jersey | prohibited | not regulated | not regulated |
| New Mexico | prohibited | not regulated | not regulated |
| New York | prohibited | not regulated | not regulated |
| North Carolina | permit required | classed as dogs | not regulated |
| North Dakota | prohibited | classed as wolves | prohibited |
| Ohio | prohibited | not regulated | not regulated |
| Oklahoma | prohibited | classed as dogs | not regulated |
| Oregon | prohibited | not regulated | not regulated |
| Pennsylvania | permit required | classed as wolves | permit required |
| Rhode Island | permit required | classed as wolves | permit required |
| South Carolina | permit required | classed as dogs | not regulated |
| South Dakota | permit required | classed as wolves | permit required |
| Tennessee | not regulated | not regulated | not regulated |
| Texas | not regulated | not regulated | not regulated |
| Utah | prohibited | classed as dogs | not regulated |
| Vermont | prohibited | classed as dogs | not regulated |
| Virginia | prohibited | not regulated | not regulated |
| Washington | prohibited | classed as dogs | not regulated |
| West Virginia | prohibited | classed as dogs | not regulated |
| Wisconsin | not regulated | not regulated | not regulated |
| Wyoming | prohibited | classed as wolves | prohibited |

$F_1$ refers to first generation hybrids

## WOLVES AND HYBRIDS AS PETS—CANADA

| | Wolves as Pets | Classification of Hybrids as Pets | Hybrids |
|---|---|---|---|
| Alberta | prohibited | considered dogs | not regulated |
| British Columbia | prohibited | not regulated | not regulated |
| Manitoba | prohibited | considered wild | prohibited |
| New Brunswick | prohibited | not regulated | not regulated |
| Newfoundland | prohibited | not regulated | prohibited |
| Northwest Territories | not regulated | not regulated | not regulated |
| Nova Scotia | prohibited | not regulated | not regulated |
| Ontario | not regulated* | not regulated | not regulated* |
| Prince Edward Island | prohibited | not regulated | prohibited |
| Quebec | not regulated | not regulated | not regulated |
| Saskatchewan | prohibited | not regulated | not regulated |
| Yukon | prohibited | not regulated | prohibited |

*Wolves or hybrids bred in Ontario are prohibited.

CHAPTER

11

# CONSERVING THE WOLF

## Wolf Reintroduction Programs

ONE OF THE OLDEST WILDLIFE management techniques known is the reintroduction of extirpated species. In North America, there are wolf reintroduction programs for the Northern Rocky Mountain gray wolf, the red wolf, the Mexican wolf, and the eastern timber wolf.

*Wildlife Management in the National Parks: The Leopold Report*, published by the Advisory Board on Wildlife Management of the U.S. Department of the Interior in 1963, the prime guiding document for park management in the United States, stated that national parks should preserve or re-create "the ecologic scene as viewed by the first European visitors." Wolf reintroductions thus follow this broad guideline, with the proviso that there are very few suitable reintroduction sites left in the United States in which to re-create the original ecological scene.

At a 1975 workshop on wolf reintroduction, L. David Mech recommended a minimum area of 4,000 square miles for establishing "a reasonably viable, well-functioning, well-organized natural population of wolves which would interfere with man minimally." Unfortunately, such blocks of wilderness are few and far between in potential wolf habitat today.

The primary causes of death among reintroduced wolves are car accidents, shooting, and trapping. Thus, sites are required with a low human population. On today's crowded planet, such sites are rare.

It is not unusual for wildlife managers to accept high losses in their reintroduced populations. Many projects in the past have failed altogether. Of 146 international reintroductions tracked by the National Zoo in Washington, DC, only 11 percent have been deemed successful.

In *Wolves in Europe: Status and Perspectives,* Italian wolf biologist Luigi Boitani admitted that wolf reintroductions are highly controversial:

> They should have a set of clearly defined goals; they require a careful management plan of the local people's opinions and attitudes toward the wolves, and a sound technical plan providing for numbers, timing, techniques to obtain, maintain, release and monitor the wolves to be reintroduced. The genetic quality of the released animals is of paramount importance to maintain the local identities of neighboring wolf populations.



## THE RED WOLF RECOVERY PLAN

The reintroduction plan for the red wolf represents a unique milestone in biology: the first attempt to restore a carnivore deemed extinct in its former range.

The red wolf (*Canis rufus*) was formerly found from Texas to Florida, and north to North Carolina, Kentucky, Illinois, and Missouri. It is a small wolf, preying upon small deer, marsh rabbits, raccoons, and groundhogs. It has a thin, reddish coat, and long, thin legs.

In 1962, a biologist first warned that the red wolf was in danger of extinction. The species was listed as endangered by the IUCN in 1967. That same year, the red wolf was declared an endangered species by the USFWS, and a limited recovery plan was put together.

DIRECT REINTRODUCTIONS . . . SHOULD BE SEEN AS A LAST RESORT IN WOLF RECOVERY.

—Wolf Conservation Strategy for Europe, 1992

By 1970, it was estimated that only a few hundred red wolves remained in six counties of southeast Texas and two parishes in southwest Louisiana. Numbers

Historic range of the red wolf.

1. Texas red wolf
2. Mississippi valley red wolf
3. Florida red wolf

(after O'Connor, 1961)

were so low that the wolves may have begun interbreeding with coyotes, as suitable red wolf mates were so rare.

In 1973, the red wolf joined the list of endangered species in the new Endangered Species Act. It is thought to have been extinct in the wild since 1980, making it the world's most endangered canid.

The Red Wolf Recovery Plan was approved in 1982 and revised in 1984 and 1990.

The current population is descended from fourteen "pure" red wolves captured in the wild. Captive breeding of the red wolf is led by the Point Defiance Zoo and Aquarium in Tacoma, Washington, which has been involved since 1969. (Its breeding center is off-site, near Graham, Washington.)

The remote woods of Cameron Parrish in Louisiana were one of the last strongholds of the red wolf. © Robert H. Busch

The first experimental release of red wolves was in 1976 on Bulls Island, South Carolina, part of the Cape Romain National Wildlife Refuge. Eight years later, the AAZPA approved a Species Survival Plan for the red wolf. Since then, over two dozen zoos and research facilities have joined the project.

The first true release of red wolves into the wild was at Alligator River National Wildlife Refuge in North Carolina in 1987. Only one year later, these wolves reproduced and the first red wolf pups of the recovery project were born. According to former project biologist Michael Phillips, it is unlikely that the refuge can support even thirty wolves: "The primary factor limiting the size of the wolf population is the size of the reintroduction area." Many of the wolves have dispersed over large distances from the refuge, and the possibility exists of adding the nearby Pocosin Lakes National Wildlife Refuge in eastern North Carolina to the project in order to provide additional habitat.

**PARTICIPANTS IN THE RED WOLF BREEDING PROGRAM**

ALEXANDRIA ZOO (LOUISIANA)
ALLIGATOR RIVER NATIONAL WILDLIFE REFUGE (NORTH CAROLINA)
BEARDSLEY PARK ZOO (CONNECTICUT)
BREVARD ZOO (FLORIDA)
BURNET PARK ZOO (NEW YORK)
CAPE ROMAIN NATIONAL WILDLIFE REFUGE (SOUTH CAROLINA)
CHAFFEE ZOO (CALIFORNIA)
CHATTANOOGA NATURE CENTER (TENNESSEE)
CHEHAW WILD ANIMAL PARK (GEORGIA)
FORT WORTH ZOO (TEXAS)
FOSSIL RIM WILDLIFE CENTER (TEXAS)
GREATER BATON ROUGE ZOO (LOUISIANA)
GREAT PLAINS ZOO (SOUTH DAKOTA)
HENSON ROBINSON ZOO (ILLINOIS)
JACKSONVILLE ZOO (FLORIDA)
JACKSON ZOOLOGICAL PARK (MISSISSIPPI)
KNOXVILLE ZOO (TENNESSEE)
LINCOLN PARK ZOO (ILLINOIS)
LOWRY PARK ZOO (FLORIDA)
MILLER PARK ZOO (ILLINOIS)
NORTH CAROLINA LIFE AND SCIENCE MUSEUM
NORTH CAROLINA STATE UNIVERSITY
NORTH CAROLINA ZOOLOGICAL PARK
NORTH EASTERN WISCONSIN ZOO
OGLEBAY ZOO (WEST VIRGINIA)
OKLAHOMA CITY ZOO
POINT DEFIANCE ZOO AND AQUARIUM (WASHINGTON)
ROGER WILLIAMS ZOO (RHODE ISLAND)
SEWEE VISITOR AND ENVIRONMENTAL EDUCATION CENTER (SOUTH CAROLINA)
TALLAHASSEE MUSEUM (FLORIDA)
TEXAS ZOO (TEXAS)
TREVOR ZOO (NEW YORK)
VIRGINIA LIVING MUSEUM (VIRGINIA)
WESTERN NORTH CAROLINA NATURE CENTER
ENDGANGERED WOLF CENTER (MISSOURI)
WILDLIFE SCIENCE CENTER (MINNESOTA)
WOODLANDS NATURE CENTER (KENTUCKY)
WOLF HAVEN INTERNATIONAL (WASHINGTON)

Additional releases have been made on Horn Island, Mississippi; St. Vincent Island, Florida; and Durant Island, North Carolina.

In 1991, red wolves were released into Great Smoky Mountains National Park in Tennessee. Although the park receives over nine million visitors per year, biologists rather optimistically estimate that the park could support between fifty and seventy-five red wolves. The National Parks and Conservation Association in conjunction with the National Fish and Wildlife Foundation provided a compensation fund for livestock predation by red wolves within the park, primarily to appease residents of the historic farming community of Cades Cove. Livestock losses were minimal.



The adult wolves released into the park showed amazing tolerance of humans in the area, probably related to the large amount of time that these animals had spent in captivity prior to release. The juveniles have been much more wary. According to Chris Lucash, one of the project biologists, "The behavior of these wolves support the theory that younger wolves, with minimal exposure to human contact, are ideal release candidates."

The North Carolina red wolf population has been as high as 148 animals but in 2017 was at 50 wild wolves and nearly 200 in various captive breeding program facilities.

In 1976, red wolves were reintroduced into the wild in South Carolina. Julie Lawrence photo, © Wolf Haven International

Unfortunately, the reintroduction into the park was ultimately unsuccessful. The 37 reintroduced wolves were not able to find enough to eat within the confines of the park. Many eventually left the park in search of prey, and six were killed by being shot, poisoned, or hit by cars. The reintroduced wolves had a total of 33 pups, but all but four were confirmed to have died or disappeared. In 1998, the U.S. Fish and Wildlife and National Park Services made the decision to capture the final four red wolves for release elsewhere.

The recovery plan has had its share of setbacks. Interbreeding of red wolves and coyotes has blurred the recovery picture, and of the first forty-two wolves released into the Alligator River National Wildlife Refuge, twenty-two have died. The highest number of deaths was due to the wolves' being struck by cars, underlining the crucial importance of lack of human activity in potential reintroduction areas.

In 2005, project biologists were pleased with the discovery of eleven dens with fifty-five pups in the red wolf recovery area.

More recently, the recovery program came under intense political opposition that included attempts to end the recovery effort altogether. However, the U.S. Fish and Wildlife Service stepped up its public outreach efforts and the recovery program continues. But there are still major challenges as the wolf population has been declining over the past fifteen years. Some of the major problems include hybridization with coyotes and illegal shootings.



## THE NORTHERN ROCKY MOUNTAINS GRAY WOLF RECOVERY PLAN

According to L. David Mech, "Yellowstone Park is a place that literally begs to have wolves." And historically, Yellowstone did have wolves. Gray wolves have been present in North America for nearly two million years. But the Yellowstone wolves fell victim to the large-scale predator extermination programs of the late 1800s and early 1900s. The last wolf documented to have been killed in Yellowstone was in 1926.

As America's first national park, Yellowstone seemed a natural site for implementing the *Leopold Report* and restoring the predators that once roamed the area. The USFWS formulated a recovery plan for the gray wolf in the northern Rocky Mountains in 1980 and revised the plan in 1987. High

The original potential reintroduction areas for Northern Rocky Mountains Gray Wolf Recovery Plan:

1. Northwest Montana recovery area
2. Central Idaho recovery area
3. Yellowstone recovery area

(after USFWS, n.d.)

The comeback of the wolf in the northern Rocky Mountains is one of the great success stories of wildlife conservation. Julie Lawrence photo, © Wolf Haven International

on the plan's list was the reintroduction of the wolf to Yellowstone. Also recommended were two other potential reintroduction sites, the Glacier National Park Wilderness Area and the central Idaho wilderness.

> THE WHOLE WORLD . . . IS BECOMING . . . MORE FULLY PEOPLED. ALL PLACES ARE NOW ACCESSIBLE.
>
> —Tertullian, AD 337

The planned reintroduction was swamped with controversy from the beginning. It drew demonstrations in Cody, Wyoming, and Helena, Montana, by antiwolf groups, primarily local ranchers.



Public hearings and written input to recovery biologists revealed five main reasons for opposition to wolf reintroduction:

1. The impact of wolves on big game
2. The impact of wolves on livestock
3. The cost of reintroductions
4. Potential restrictions of use of public lands
5. Threat to human safety

Earth First return wolf demonstration, July 1989. Photo courtesy of the National Park Service

Many of the opponents made wild predictions about what would happen if wolves were reintroduced to Yellowstone. Montana Senator Conrad Burns stated, "There'll be a dead child within a year," and one disgruntled farmer said, "They'll want to reintroduce the saber-toothed tiger next."

Some of the ranchers' fears were allayed when the conservation group Defenders of Wildlife announced a livestock loss compensation program. (Between 1996 and 2005, the organization paid out $135,933 in compensation to ranchers who lost livestock to wolf depredation.) The group also fought hard through public information programs to overcome the fear and prejudice that have always surrounded the wolf.



Surveys showed that a majority of northwest U.S. residents supported wolf reintroduction. In 1985, 60 percent of Yellowstone visitors polled agreed with the statement, "If wolves can't return to Yellowstone on their own, then we should put them back ourselves." A 1990 poll revealed that two-thirds of Montana residents surveyed agreed with reintroducing the wolf to the Glacier National Park Wilderness Area. A 1991 Wyoming Fish and Game survey determined that 44 percent of respondents were in favor of reintroduction, 34.5 percent were opposed, and 21.5 percent were undecided. In Idaho, 72 percent of those polled supported reintroducing the wolf to the wilderness areas in the center of that state.

While humans were arguing about the Yellowstone area, the wolf was quietly reintroducing itself into some of its old haunts in Montana. One even trekked down to Yellowstone, where it was promptly shot by a hunter (who claimed he thought it was a coyote).

Some of the wolves that repopulated parts of Glacier National Park originated in southern Alberta. In 1986, one of these packs reproduced in its new home. In 1987, a USFWS study stated that the recovery of wolves in Montana would depend in part on the survival of southern Alberta wolves and their migration into Montana. Conservationists have expressed concern about the predator policies that prevail in Alberta, fearing that they might be detrimental to wolf recovery in Montana.

For example, Alberta landowners or those with the permission of landowners are allowed to kill any number of wolves at any time of the year without a license, as long as the wolves are killed on private property, leased grazing lands, or within five miles of such lands. Despite the fact that some studies have shown that the Alberta wolf population might be decreasing, the sweeping wolf-killing powers given to residents still remain in effect today.

A similar problem exists in Washington State. Jack Laufer and Peter Jenkins, in a 1989 article in the *Northwest Environmental Journal* titled "Historical and Present Status of the Gray Wolf in the Cascade Mountains of Washington," wrote that "another main concern is the *legal* killing of wolves by British Columbia residents. . . . Clearly, a treaty of comparable agreement is desirable."

By 1992, the prowolf groups such as Defenders of Wildlife and The Wolf Fund seemed to be gaining ground, as environmental impact statement hearings were overwhelmingly in support of wolf reintroduction:

| City | Present/Testifying | Percent in Favor |
|---|---|---|
| Helena | 450/142 | 60 |
| Cheyenne | 325/121 | 85 |
| Boise | 130/78 | 70 |
| Salt Lake City | 400/72 | 90 |
| Seattle | 45/28 | 90 |

In 1993, the Defenders of Wildlife began a program that pays $5,000 to any landowner in the area on whose property wolves are allowed to successfully raise pups. The program won praise from conservationists across North America who realize that farmers and ranchers are often the most severe opponents of wolf reintroduction.

The draft environmental impact statement for the recovery plan was released in July 1993. It contained proposals to reintroduce the wolf into both Yellowstone National Park and central Idaho if naturally occurring wolf packs were not found in either area before October 1994. The reintroduced animals were to be designated "nonessential experimental populations" under the Endangered Species Act in order to provide additional flexibility in their management. The reintroduction of wolves in the Glacier National Park Wilderness Area was deemed unnecessary, as wolves were successfully reproducing there without human aid.

Crystal Creek wolf pack on an elk kill in Lamar Valley, 1995. Photo courtesy of the National Park Service

The goal of the recovery plan was 30 breeding pairs with Montana, Idaho, and Wyoming each sustaining a minimum population of 100 animals for three consecutive years.

In 1995, the howling wilderness was finally returned to Yellowstone with the transplant of 14 wolves captured in central Alberta, the ultimate goal of the reintroduction being 10 breeding pairs or about 100 wolves by 2002. Fourteen other wolves were released in central Idaho. The transplants attracted international attention, with over 40,000 visitors to Yellowstone taking ranger-led walks to see the wolves. A lawsuit by a group of Montana ranchers to stop further reintroductions failed, and in 1996, thirty-eight wolves from northern British Columbia were sent to the reintroduction sites: eighteen to Yellowstone and twenty to Idaho.

In exchange for the wolves from Canada, the USFWS placed radio collars on nineteen Alberta wolves, most of which had already been shot by hunters. In British Columbia, the service provided $30,000 for research on radio-collared wolves in ten packs. Three of these wolves had also been shot by hunters already, but the rest roamed the vast wilderness in northwestern British Columbia.

The reintroductions were not without their dark side, however. In the first two years, over a dozen of the wolves have died from a variety of causes.

One was killed by a tranquilizer dart during the capture attempt in Alberta. One was humanely destroyed after it bit a biologist upon its arrival in the United States. While in an acclimation enclosure in Yellowstone, a young pup died of unknown causes. A two-year-old male had to be shot from a helicopter when it repeatedly strayed from Yellowstone, killing at least two sheep. Another died when it tangled with a mountain lion. A young pup, the offspring of two reintroduced wolves, was run over by a truck in Yellowstone. One of the British Columbia–bred males was hit by a tractor trailer, and a four-month-old pup was struck by a car. One female wolf died when she fell into a scalding hot spring. She was pregnant with six pups at the time.

A pup was caught in a trap set for another wolf that had killed some sheep, and his leg was shattered as a result. He was sent to Minnesota, where he stayed in captivity for the rest of his life.

A number of introduced wolves have already been illegally shot. In January 1995, a wolf was shot in Idaho when it was seen feeding on a dead sheep. An investigation revealed that the sheep appeared to have died from causes related to birthing and had not been killed by the wolf, which was scrounging an easy meal. When USFWS agents tried to execute a search warrant on the ranch where the shooting occurred, an ugly standoff followed, pitting the ranch owner and local sheriff against the service agents. The incident led to a congressional hearing on relationships between local, state, and federal agencies.

A yearling male wolf was found shot near Daniel, Wyoming, but his killer was never found. A cowboy near Meeteetsee, Wyoming, later shot the yearling's sister, claiming he thought she was a coyote. He turned himself in and was given a $500 fine.

An alpha male was shot near Three Forks, Montana, and his body was dumped into the Madison River. His killer remains at large.

In the most famous wolf killing to date, a hunter named Chad McKittrick shot and killed wolf Number Ten, the largest of the wolves reintroduced to Yellowstone. Number Ten was an alpha male, a proven breeder, and arguably one of the most valuable animals in the entire reintroduction program. McKittrick shot Number Ten in southern Montana, where he cut off its skull, skinned the body, and dumped the carcass in thick brush. The animal's radio collar was unbolted and thrown away and was later found by USFWS special agent Tim Eicher. The discovery of the unbolted radio collar proved that the wolf had not died of natural causes, and as a result, the Fish and Wildlife Conservation Society put up a $13,000 reward for information leading to the arrest and conviction of Number Ten's killer.

Number Ten's body was soon found by a man out looking for elk antlers. When Agent Eicher went to the site, he found one of the most heartbreaking scenes of his career: Number Ten's mate, wolf Number Nine, had dug a den beside the dead body of her mate. She was trapped and her cubs were caught by U.S. Fish and Wildlife agents.

Number Nine and her pups spent the summer in a captive pen under the care of biologists. She was then matched up with a new young mate, wolf Number Eight, and the whole family was relocated to the middle of the Lamar Valley, back in the safety of Yellowstone National Park.

McKittrick was caught and fined $10,000, sentenced to six months' imprisonment, and prohibited from hunting for one and a half years.

In addition to the wolves killed by accidents or illegal hunting, interpack aggression has led to numerous wolf deaths.

A pack known as the Druid Peak pack attacked the Crystal Creek pack and killed the alpha male. Soon after, the Druid Peak pack attacked and killed one of Number Nine's pups.

In addition to qualifying as a biological success, the reintroductions have had a pronounced economic effect. Visitors who come to the Yellowstone National Park to see wolves contribute about $70 million each year to the region's economy.

Not surprisingly, the reintroduced wolves are also having a pronounced effect on the local wildlife. A study by biologist Bob Crabtree suggests that wolf predation may decrease elk, bison, and moose numbers in the park area by 8 to 20 percent, good news for those who deplore the culling of surplus or diseased animals in the park. (In the winter of 1996–1997, over 1,000 bison were shot by park rangers, despite the park's avowed policy of "natural regulation.") During the two decades since wolves were reintroduced to the park, further research has shown that elk numbers in the northern part of the park have declined substantially—although not entirely due to wolves. (Bison numbers have been increasing, and wolves have had little impact on moose.) Observations have shown that elk are the prime large game for Yellowstone wolves in winter. In the summer, there is increased predation upon deer. As elk numbers decline in the park and bison increase, some biologists have speculated that the wolves may eventually start killing bison more frequently, although they are dangerous prey and require larger packs to attack safely.

Within eight years of wolf reintroduction, it was discovered that park elk had changed their feeding habits, avoiding streamside areas that provide abundant hiding spots for predators. The decrease in elk browsing has allowed native riparian flora such as willow and cottonwood to reestablish itself.

Beavers soon followed, and the network of dams and canals they have created made new homes for waterfowl, muskrats, and fish.

Birds have benefited as well. Studies into the relationship between Yellowstone wolves and ravens have documented that ravens often preferentially associate with wolves in order to gain access to food, and that wolves seem to tolerate this relationship (see chapter 4, "Ravens," p. 74–75).

Coyotes, however, have not fared so well. Bob Crabtree has found that at least forty-eight coyotes have been killed by wolves. "Wolves will be a lot more effective at controlling coyotes than the old park trappers ever hoped to be," he says. Coyotes have taken a second seat to wolves in many areas of the park, with notable population declines in the northern ranges. The Yellowstone coyote population has declined by half since wolves were reintroduced.

Interactions between species are never simple. Biologist Michael Phillips found that two wolves in the Blacktail Plateau of Yellowstone are now killing many more elk than expected because of a pack of six coyotes continually chasing them off kills.

Occasionally, there is food for all to share. Yellowstone National Park ranger Rick McIntyre has reported, "Grizzlies and coyotes have . . . shared in the wolves' hunts. The grizzlies take what they want, the coyotes take what's left. Everybody benefits when the wolves take their place again in the food chain."

Yellowstone biologist John Varley has echoed McIntyre's comments. "In all the studies, all the planning," says Varley, "the one thing we totally underestimated was how many other mouths the wolves would feed."

The complex interrelationships among Yellowstone species will be fodder for studies for many decades to come. Some biologists wonder, for example, if red foxes, which are often preyed upon by coyotes, will start to rebound in northern Yellowstone with the decline of the coyote.

Others have noted that because coyotes wisely avoid wolf den sites, rodent populations in those areas may boom, as they have in Grand Teton National Park, providing food for hawks, owls, and eagles.

The reintroduction of the wolf to Yellowstone has been an amazing success story, a saga of restoration and humility, an atonement for the empty decades since 1926 when the National Park Service killed the last park wolf.

With few natural predators and an abundance of game, the introduced wolves have thrived. Wolf pup survival has averaged 75 to 80 percent, significantly above that in other areas. Population growth in the first few years ranged from 40 to 50 percent annually, leveling off after five years to about 10 percent a year.

About 528 wolves roam the greater Yellowstone area in and out of the park, with 108 wolves living within the park boundaries in 11 packs. Between 2009 and 2016, the Yellowstone wolf population has ranged between 83 and 108.

Wolves are also spreading slowly to other parts of the northwest. In Washington, for example, wolves have been spotted in the Lake Chelan area, the Glacier Peak Wilderness Area, the Okanagan National Forest, the Cascade Mountains, and the Ross Lake Recreational Area. Wolves have also been dispersing westward from Idaho, and now packs have been established

IN 1909, THE SUPERINTENDENT OF ALGONQUIN PARK IN ONTARIO WROTE A MAGAZINE ARTICLE TITLED, "HOW SHALL WE DESTROY THE WOLF?"

in northeastern Washington and Oregon, in the Cascade Mountains in both states, and most recently in Northern California.

Although the reintroduction is a biological success, legally, the wrangling over the Northern Rocky Mountain gray wolf is far from over. In 2003, the USFWS announced that its recovery goals had been met, and attempted to downgrade the wolf from endangered to threatened in this area. Federal courts overturned this idea, and the matter has simmered ever since. In February 2006, the service again announced advance notice of intent to downlist, a move that was hotly contested by prowolf factions. As Steven Fritts, Northern Rocky Mountain Wolf coordinator has said, "The key to wolf population recovery in the northwestern United States lies in human tolerance—a relatively new perspective in our society." Wolves in Montana, Idaho, and parts of Oregon, Washington State, and Utah were finally removed from the endangered species list in 2011 and in Wyoming in 2017. Wolves elsewhere remain listed.



Today, at least 2,000 wolves roam the Northwest in about 300 packs with 786 wolves in Idaho, 382 in Wyoming, including Yellowstone National Park, 700 in Montana, 115 in Washington State, 112 in Oregon, and small initial population in Northern California. In the great Northwest, the wolf is back.

## THE MEXICAN WOLF

The reintroduction plan for the Mexican wolf (*Canis lupus baileyi*) is unique in that it addresses a subspecies, rather than a separate species. Many biologists today agree that the three former gray wolf subspecies *mogollonensis, monstrabilis,* and *baileyi* all actually refer to the same animal, although taxonomist Ron Nowak disagrees. He includes *mogollonensis* and

The last Mexican wolf caught in Mexico was captured in 1980. Photo courtesy of California Wolf Center

The pine scrub forests of the Sierra Madre range of north-central Mexico is one of the last habitats of the Mexican wolf. © Wolf Haven International: Paul Joslin

*monstrabilis* with *youngi* in his main southern group and believes that *baileyi* is a distinct entity.

The Mexican wolf was once a wide-ranging predator of northern Mexico and the southern portions of Arizona, New Mexico, and Texas. By 1851, strychnine was being used against wolves in Mexico. Bounties were established in Arizona and New Mexico in 1893. Within a few decades, wolf

Government predator control programs launched in 1914 helped push the Mexican wolf to extinction in the wild. Photo courtesy of California Wolf Center

The federal recovery plan for the Mexican wolf was first written in 1978. Photo courtesy of California Wolf Center

sightings became a rare event in much of the Southwest. In 1914, the wolf's fate was sealed when the federal government began a predator control program in the southwest United States.

The last wolf in Texas was killed in 1970, the last in Arizona in 1975, and the last one in New Mexico in 1976. The USFWS declared the Mexican wolf an endangered species in 1976.

In 1977, the service contracted with trapper Roy T. McBride to catch wild Mexican wolves for use in a captive breeding program. From 1977 to 1980, McBride captured four males and one pregnant female in the Durango and Chihuahua states in Mexico. These wolves were sent to the Arizona-Sonora Desert Museum (ASDA) in Tucson and the St. Louis Zoo. In 1978, the ASDA celebrated the first captive birth of a Mexican wolf.

The recovery plan for the Mexican wolf was first written in 1978 and was formally approved in 1982.

The last wolf captured in Mexico was caught in 1980, when one was trapped in Chihuahua. Prior to this wolf's capture, wolf sightings were so rare that the last wolves in Mexico were well documented.

Historic range of the Mexican wolf.
(after USFWS, 1998)

## THE LAST WOLVES TAKEN IN MEXICO

| | |
|---|---|
| –near La Flor, Durango | shot in 1977 |
| –near Penoles, Durango | shot in 1977 |
| –near Penoles, Durango | trapped in 1977 |
| –near San José, Durango | shot in 1977 |
| –near Viscaino, Durango | poisoned in 1977 |
| –near Viscaino, Durango | shot in 1977 |
| –near Las Isgalias, Durango | poisoned in 1978 |
| –near Coneto, Durango | live-trapped in 1978 |
| –near Sierra del Nido, Chihuahua | live-trapped in 1978 |

(Source: David E. Brown, *The Wolf in the Southwest: The Making of an Endangered Species*, 1983)

The reintroduction of the Mexican wolf was strongly opposed by the politically powerful ranching lobby in the southern U.S. Julie Lawrence photo, © Wolf Haven International

The USFWS estimated that the wolf population in Mexico was less than fifty by 1981. A few wild wolves may still survive; in 1985 wolf tracks were found in northern Mexico, and wolves howled back when tape-recorded howls were played in the area. However, most biologists believed that the subspecies went extinct in the wild in the late 1980s.

In 1984, the Mexican wolf recovery team released its recommendations for site selection for reintroduction:

- within the historic range of the Mexican wolf, defined as *Canis lupus baileyi, C.l. mogollonensis,* and *C.l. monstrabilis*
- minimum elevation of 4,000 feet above sea level, as most of the wolf's prey live in the high piñon-juniper forests
- human population density of less than 12 per square mile
- sufficient prey for released wolves and their first-generation progeny

This captive Mexican wolf pup at the California Wolf Center is one of many destined for future release in the southern United States. Photo courtesy of California Wolf Center

- no proposals for development or habitat destruction that would significantly harm wolf habitat
- no endangered or threatened prey populations present that would be affected negatively by wolves
- free water available in secluded areas of habitat
- mostly broken, mountainous terrain

Although the recovery team preferred "to see Mexican wolves held and bred in . . . natural-area enclosures as opposed to zoological facilities in urban or similar situations," the lack of funds and a suitable location for such enclosures negated their hopes. All the Mexican wolves bred to date have been in zoos or wolf packs.

SPACE IS AIR FOR THE GREAT BEASTS WHO ROAM THE EARTH. NOW IS THEIR FINAL BREATH.

—John Weaver, Wyoming wolf biologist

Two areas were chosen as potential reintroduction sites. The first, the White Sands Missile Range and adjacent area in New Mexico, has approximately 4,000 square miles of potential habitat. The recovery team deems this to be room for around thirty to forty wolves. Its prime drawback is the unknown quantity of wolf prey contained in the block. The other location, the huge Blue Range Area within the Apache and Gila National Forests in Arizona and New Mexico, has about 7,000 square miles of habitat.

In 1987, the military owners of the White Sands Missile Range withdrew the range as a potential reintroduction site. Conservationists were

The harsh winters in the northern reaches of the wolf's range are a supreme test of its survival instincts. Photo courtesy of California Wolf Center

stunned and disappointed. Prowolf groups mounted a massive education effort aimed at overturning the decision. In 1990, a coalition of conservation groups including the Sierra Club and the National Audubon Society filed a lawsuit against the secretary of the Interior and secretary of Defense for purported failure to implement the 1982 recovery plan. Later that year, the deputy assistant secretary of the army stated that the White Sands site could be used for wolf reintroduction.

In 1991, the Defenders of Wildlife set up a $100,000 livestock compensation fund to appease ranchers worried about predation by wolves.

In 1992, the recovery plan suffered a setback when the AAZPA initially rejected the Species Survival Plan application for the Mexican wolf on the grounds that it is only a subspecies, and not a full species.

Although a 1988 poll showed that 61 percent of Arizona respondents were in favor of wolf reintroduction, the powerful ranching lobby in the southwest United States has proved to be strongly opposed to wolf

These two female Mexican wolves were used for captive breeding in the Mexican wolf recovery plan. © Wolf Haven International: Val Halsted

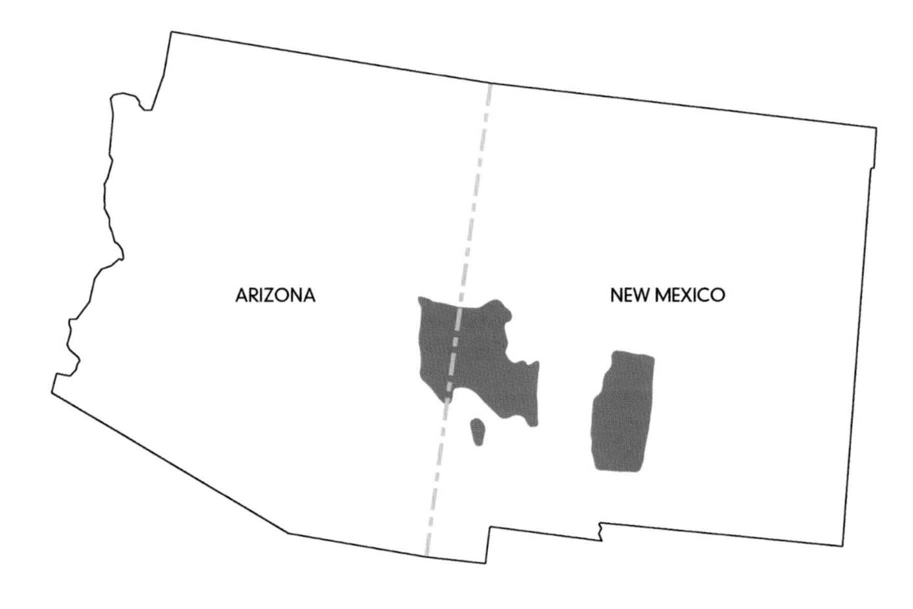


Potential reintroduction areas for the Mexican wolf. The Blue Range Area (on the left) and the White Sands Missile Range area (on the right). (after USFWS, 1988)



reintroduction. And since the USFWS will not release wolves without state approval, progress in the reintroduction effort has been slow.

In an April 17, 1991, memorandum written by the New Mexico Cattle Growers' Association, the group spread such misinformation as "Domestic livestock, particularly cattle, are the preferred diet [of wolves]" and, "Wolf attacks on humans could be expected." Once again, the old myths had raised their ugly heads.

There are now forty-nine facilities in the United States and Mexico that house Mexican wolves, with about 300 wolves in captivity. Wolves are often transferred among the facilities to facilitate genetic exchange.

## PARTICIPANTS IN THE MEXICAN WOLF BREEDING PROGRAM

African Safari (Mexico)
Alameda Park Zoo (New Mexico)
Albuquerque Biological Park (New Mexico)
Arizona-Sonora Desert Museum
Binder Park Zoo (Michigan)
California Wolf Center
Centro Ecológico de Sonora (Mexico)
Chapultepec Zoo (Mexico)
Cheyenne Mountain Zoo (Colorado)
Chicago Biological Park (Illinois)
Cincinnati Zoo and Botanical Gardens (Ohio)
Columbus Zoological Gardens (Ohio)
Dakota Zoo (North Dakota)
El Paso Zoo (Texas)
Fort Worth Zoo (Texas)
Fossil Rim Wildlife Center (Texas)
Guadalajara Zoo (Mexico)
Heritage Park Zoo (Arizona)
Hillcrest Park Zoo (New Mexico)
Houston Zoo (Texas)
Ladder Ranch Wolf Management Facility (New Mexico)
La Michilía Biosphere Reserve (Mexico)
Lincoln Park Zoo (Illinois)
Living Desert State Park (New Mexico)
Minnesota Zoo
Minnesota Zoological Garden
Navajo Nation Zoo and Botanic Park (Arizona)
Oklahoma Zoo
Parque Zoológico de San Juan de Aragón (Mexico)
Parque Zoológico de León (Mexico)
Parque Zoológico del Pueblo (Mexico)
Parque Zoológico la Pastora (Mexico)
Phoenix Zoo (Arizona)
Rancho La Mesa/Org Vida Silvestre AC (Mexico)
Rancho Los Encinos (Mexico)
Sedgewick County Zoo (Kansas)
Sevilleta Captive Wolf Management Facility (New Mexico)
Smithsonian National Zoo (Washington, DC)
Sonora Ecological Centre (Mexico)
Southwest Rehabilitation and Educational Foundation Inc. (Arizona)
The Living Desert (California)
Utica Zoo (New York)
Vallina Ranch (Mexico)
Walter D. Stone Memorial Zoo (Massachusetts)
Wild Canid Survival and Research Center (Missouri)
Wildlife Science Center (Minnesota)
Wildlife West Nature Park (New Mexico)
Wolf Conservation Center (New York)
Wolf Haven International (Washington)
Zoológico de Los Coyotes (Mexico)
Zoológico de Tamatán (Mexico)
Zoológico de Zacango (Mexico)

Despite the lack of a confined wolf population in the Southwest, reports continued to come in. Biologists examined eighty reports of wolf sightings from the southern states during the period 1983–1993. Seven of the reports were classed as "probable" wolves, but none were confirmed. It is likely that some of these were sightings of hybrid wolf-dog crosses or of pet wolves released to the wild.

On March 14, 1997, the secretary of the Department of the Interior signed a notice of record authorizing the reintroduction of the Mexican wolf into the Blue Range Area of Arizona.

On January 26, 1998, eleven Mexican wolves were reintroduced into the Blue Range. In 2000, wolves were reintroduced into the Gila Wilderness Area of New Mexico, and in 2003 into the White Mountain Apache Tribal Lands.

Human-induced mortality of reintroduced wolves dropped from seven in 2004 to zero in 2005. For this reason, the Mexican Wolf Project's Adaptive Management Oversight Committee issued a moratorium on reintroducing additional wolves during 2006, deciding to let the wild population increase naturally by itself.

While the Mexican gray wolf recovery program has been controversial and often bitterly opposed by the ranching industry, the recent news has been good. At the end of 2016 there were 113 Mexican gray wolves living in the wild, up from 97 in 2015. This includes 21 packs, with 63 wolves in Arizona and 50 in New Mexico. In 2016, 50 pups born in the wild survived through the end of the year compared to just 23 the previous year. Efforts are also underway to reintroduce the wolves back into Mexico although for now only a few are surviving there.



## THE EASTERN TIMBER WOLF RECOVERY PLAN

The lack of predators in the eastern United States has created a severe overpopulation of deer in many areas. In the upper peninsula of Michigan, for example, there is an estimated deer population of over 500,000. It is further estimated that in the winter of 1992, almost 32,000 of these deer died from starvation. Northern Michigan was one of the potential sites for reintroduction of the eastern timber wolf.

Remnants of wolf populations still existed in much of the eastern United States in relatively recent times. In the 1945–1946 trapping season, there were even enough wolves left in Iowa to sustain a catch of 388. However, the postwar boom years and attendant human expansion in the east almost destroyed the eastern wolf. Wolves were given state legal protection in Wisconsin in 1957 and in Michigan in 1965. In 1967, the

Minnesota wolf management zones. (after USFSW, 1992)

eastern timber wolf, a gray wolf subspecies (*Canis lupus lycaon*), was listed as endangered in the United States. To aid in its conservation, the Superior National Forest in Minnesota was closed to wolf hunting in 1970. The wolf received legal protection under the Endangered Species Act in 1973. The USFWS approved a recovery plan for the eastern timber wolf in 1978 and revised it in 1992.

The estimated recovery year was 2002. Under the plan, by that year, the Minnesota population had to be viable and there had to be a second population outside of Minnesota and Isle Royale, Michigan. This second population

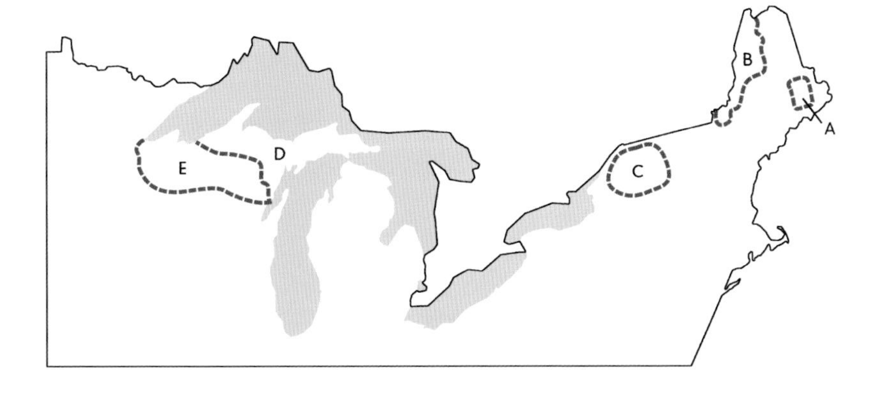


Potential reintroduction areas for the eastern timber wolf:

A. Eastern Maine
B. Northwestern Maine and portions of New Hampshire
C. Adirondack Forest Preserve
D. Michigan Peninsula
E. Northern Wisconsin

(after USFSW, 1992)



had to have at least 100 wolves in late winter if located within 100 miles of the Minnesota wolf population, or at least 200 wolves if located beyond that distance. The Wisconsin wolf would have to be downlisted to threatened if the late-winter population reached eighty wolves for three consecutive years.

Public attitudes within these areas were generally favorable to reintroduction. Yale University professor Steven Kellert in a 1985 study of Minnesotans found that 72 percent of respondents agreed with the statement, "To me, the timber wolf symbolizes the beauty and wonder of nature."

To ensure a viable wolf population within Minnesota and to stimulate new populations in the eastern United States outside of Minnesota, the plan adopted six action steps:

1. Increase public education programs on wolf restoration.
2. Monitor wolf populations, habitat, and prey.
3. Maintain suitable habitat and prey conditions.
4. Provide law enforcement activities.

5. Minimize losses of domestic livestock due to wolf predation.
6. Evaluate the need and feasibility of reintroducing wolves.

It further aims to ensure the perpetuation of wolves at the following levels in the five wolf-management zones in Minnesota:

- Zone 1: a naturally fluctuating population
- Zones 2 and 3: one wolf per 10 square miles
- Zone 4: one wolf per 50 square miles
- Zone 5: no wolves



The recovery plan has selected five sites for potential wolf reintroduction:

1. Eastern Maine, where about 2,500 square miles of uninhabited land remains
2. Northwest Maine and the adjacent portions of New Hampshire, where 11,300 square miles of sparsely populated land exists, much of it private
3. The Adirondack Forest Preserve Area of northern New York, with about 9,300 square miles of wild lands. (However, this block has been downplayed by some biologists since it lies within easy driving distance of over 20 million people.)
4. The upper peninsula of Michigan, with about 15,000 square miles of potential wolf habitat, and a small current wolf population already established
5. Northern Wisconsin, which also has a small current wolf population and may have sufficient habitat for additional wolves

The Eastern Timber Wolf Recovery Plan has been aided by natural migration of wolves from Minnesota. In 1975, the adjoining state of Wisconsin had a reproducing pack, the first in over a decade.

Canine parvovirus took a toll on Wisconsin wolves in the 1980s, but by 2000 the wolf population had grown to about 200.

In Michigan, an experimental reintroduction failed when all four wolves involved died from human causes. However, dispersing wolves from

Wisconsin and Minnesota made it to Michigan, whose wolf population reached about 190 wolves in 2000.

By that year, the wolf population goals of the Eastern Recovery Plan had been met. The total population of wolves in Wisconsin and Michigan passed the minimum of 100 wolves for five consecutive years, and the Minnesota population was well in excess of the minimum numbers cited in the plan, another success story for wolf conservation.

Ultimately, eastern timber wolves have responded very well to the recovery efforts. In 2017, there are 618 wolves in Michigan, 2,278 in Minnesota, and 866 in Wisconsin.



## Wolf Research

At the 1992 North American Symposium on Wolves, L. David Mech described the wolf as "one of the most studied of all wild species." The first scientific paper on the wolf was published in 1938. Now there are tens of thousands of books, magazines, and research journals on wolves.

Much of the early research into wolf behavior was performed by Rudolf Schenkel, who studied the wolves at the Basel Zoo in Switzerland in the 1940s.

The first man to intensively observe the wolf in the wild was Adolph Murie. Murie received his doctorate from the University of Michigan and first went to Alaska in 1922 to help his stepbrother, Olaus, in biological studies of caribou. In 1939 Murie began a two-year study of wolves in Alaska. The results were published in his 1944 book *The Wolves of Mount McKinley*, a classic in wolf literature. Murie was one of the first to describe the wolf in beneficial terms, and believed strongly in nonintrusive methods of study.

The use of radio-tracking has significantly expanded knowledge of wolf behavior. © Robert H. Busch

In Canada, Ontario Department of Lands and Forests biologist Douglas H. Pimlott's studies of wolves in Algonquin Provincial Park in the 1950s and 1960s represented the first intensive studies of Canadian wolves.

There is no question that the dean of modern wolf researchers is L. David Mech. Mech received his bachelor's degree in conservation from Cornell University and his doctorate in wildlife ecology from Purdue University. He studied under Durward Allen and was one of the first, in 1959, to use Isle Royale in Michigan as a research base. (Rolf Peterson is now directing the continuing research on Isle Royale.) Mech has served as chairman of the Wolf Specialist Group of the IUCN and as consultant to the Northern Rocky Mountain Wolf Recovery Team of the USFWS. His studies on wolves have been conducted in Minnesota, Michigan, Manitoba, Alaska, Italy, and Portugal. He is also the author of hundreds of articles on natural history. Mech describes the wolf as his "favorite animal," and perhaps no other biologist has done more to bring the plight of the wolf to public attention.

There are hundreds of other wolf researchers working across North America. Whereas the intelligent nature of the wolf and its elusive habits once made it a difficult animal to study, the use of radio collars, widely employed since the 1960s, has now made the wolf a favorite research target. In fact, for the past three decades, collar-crazy biologists have swarmed over most of the wolf's North American habitat. Unfortunately, many of the wolves caught for radio-collaring are injured during the trapping process. In one study of 109 wolves live-captured in Minnesota and Alaska from 1969 to 1976, 41 percent had skin lacerations, dislocations, or broken bones because of trap injuries. Almost half (46 percent) had tooth, lip, or gum injuries caused by the wolves' attempts to chew off the trap. Paul Joslin, former director of research at Wolf Haven International, believes "that current technologies for catching them are so traumatic that wolves should not be caught unless there is a reasonable expectation that the results will have some potential positive benefit for the animals involved." He adds that there are "some preliminary data to suggest that wolves not only remember what happens to them, but are capable of suffering from post-traumatic stress." In the rush to gather data, the humane aspects of biology are sometimes left behind.

GPS collars are commonly used to track wolves for research and management purposes. Photo courtesy of Oregon Department of Fish and Wildlife

One new tool to emerge in the past decade is the global positioning system (GPS) collar, which allows researchers to track wolves using satellite technology. GPS collars allow biologists to take position readings at various times and intervals, and download the data via satellite so that researchers can track a wolf's movements from their computers.

Today there are dozens of wolf biologists working in the United States. The reintroduction of the wolf to Yellowstone involved a number of researchers, biologists, and park rangers, including Dave Parsons, Ed Bangs, Steve Fritts, Mike Phillips, Kerry Murphy, Dan Stahler, John Varley, Debra Guernsey, Douglas W. Smith, Rick McIntyre, Dan MacNulty, and many others. (MacNulty, Smith, Stahler, and McIntyre continue to study wolves in Yellowstone.) Many of those listed continue to be involved in wolf research today. Before tragically dying in an airplane crash in 2009, Gordon Haber joined a consortium of conservation groups working to protect wolves in Alaska from being killed to increase game populations. Before his death in 2011, Erich Klinghammer was studying the social interactions of wolves.

Diane Boyd and Paul Paquet have added important information on wolf dispersal. Ron Nowak and Robert Wayne continue to tackle the puzzle of wolf taxonomy.

In Canada, at Dalhousie University's Animal Behavior Research Station in Nova Scotia, John Fentress, Jenny Ryon, and other researchers studied social interactions among captive wolves for two decades. The station closed in 2003 after the death of its last wolf. Lu Carbyn has carried out important fieldwork in Jasper, Riding Mountain, and Alberta's Wood Buffalo National Parks. Paul Paquet headed the wolf research project in Alberta's Banff National Park.



In Mexico, Julio Carrera is attempting to determine whether any Mexican wolves still survive in that country.

Despite the fact that the wolf is the most intensely studied of all North American predators, much remains to be learned. For example, there is a great need for more accurate assessments of wolf-prey relationships. As L. David Mech stated at the 1992 Symposium on Wolves, "I am not sure we'll ever answer all the questions relating to the effects of wolf predation to completely satisfy everybody." And yet, it is as a predator of big game that the wolf has suffered the most at the hands of wildlife managers.

At the same symposium, other areas cited as requiring additional research included wolf genetics, disease, inbreeding, scent marking, and dispersal. There is a dire need for long-term wolf-prey studies, including an honest evaluation of other limiting prey population factors such as hunting, logging, road construction, changes in vegetative cover, and the effects of severe winters.

The International Wolf Center sponsored a scientific symposium on wolves in Duluth, Minnesota, in October 2013 that drew scientists and people interested in wolves from around the world to attend lectures on the latest wolf research that included predator-prey interactions, preventing wolf depredation on livestock, and attempts to identify individual wolves by their howls. Interest in wolf research continues to grow as wolves naturally expand their range into former habitat, especially in Europe. The return of

A wolf biologist checks the health of a sedated wolf in Oregon. Photo courtesy of Oregon Department of Fish and Wildlife



wolves to Yellowstone National Park has been a particular boon to scientists as it has allowed them to study wolves in a natural environment where there is little or no influence by humans.

Canadian wolf biologist John Theberge states, "We need long-term research to understand the dynamics rather than short-term projects which do not allow us to understand the norms." Theberge and his assistants from Ontario's University of Waterloo studied wolves in Algonquin Provincial Park for over three decades. Their research was primarily funded by the WWF-Canada and continues the pioneer work performed by Douglas Pimlott in Algonquin in the 1950s. This makes it one of the longest continuing wolf research projects in the world. (The other two long-term wolf research programs are those on Isle Royale in Michigan and in the Superior National Forest in Minnesota, both of which began in the late 1950s.) The book, *The Wolves of Algonquin Park: A Twelve-Year Ecological Study*, by John and Mary Theberge was published in 2004 and describes what they learned about the wolves of Algonquin Provincial Park.

International wolf research has lagged far behind that performed in North America. In Europe, proper wolf censuses are badly needed in many countries and ecological evaluations are needed to preserve wolf habitat and wolf prey. Erkki Pulliainen has followed the status of the wolf in Finland for many years. Ovidiu Ionescu in Romania, Luigi Boitani in Italy, and Dimitry Bibikov in the former Soviet Union are noteworthy for their research necessary for the survival of the wolf in Eurasia. In Portugal, Francisco Álvares and his colleagues at the Centro de Investigação em Biodiversidade and at Grupo Lobo have been promoting wolf conservation and performing critical population studies. In Africa, the Ethiopian wolf has been studied extensively by Wildlife Conservation International biologists Claudio Sillero-Zubiri and Dada Gottelli. It is through the efforts of all of these dedicated biologists that what L. David Mech has termed "the puzzle we call the wolf" will be made more complete.



## Public Wolf Howls

Over the past two decades, the "greening" of the planet has led to a dramatic interest in its natural inhabitants. By far the most common of wolf-human interactions sought during this period has been public wolf howls, and by far the most famous of all public wolf-howl programs is the one running in Ontario's Algonquin Provincial Park.

As late as 1965, wolves were still being shot for "scientific purposes" in the park, but the explosive growth of the 1960s' environmental movement helped reverse the public's attitude toward animals in general and toward predators in particular. As Dan Strickland has written in *Wolf Howling in Algonquin Provincial Park*, "The public image of the wolf had been transformed from a mysterious, fearsome beast to the very symbol of the wild country people come to enjoy in Algonquin."

Wolf research in the park between 1958 and 1965 by Douglas Pimlott determined that wolves responded to recorded howls, a great aid in locating wolves in the thick woods. In fact, it has been known for a long time that wolves will answer to imitations of their howls. Tolstoy even mentioned it in his 1862 novel *The Cossacks*. Since then, researchers have determined that wolves respond more often to human howls than to tape recordings. That fact was soon used to advantage.

On August 7, 1963, Algonquin officials tried the first public wolf howl and were shocked when 180 cars and over 600 people showed up. Since then, the wolf howls have been a regular summer attraction in Algonquin. Over 82,000 people have attended these public howls and over half of them have heard wolves respond to the human howls emitted by park rangers. The event is incredibly popular; on one occasion in 1971, over 1,000 people had to be turned away.

Public wolf howl programs are popular events in many parks in Canada and the United States. Julie Lawrence photo, © Wolf Haven International



The howls are held in August and take place only when park naturalists hear wolves howl at a suitably accessible spot the night before. In August and September, wolves are gathered at rendezvous sites, and it is quite normal for them to be at the same place the next day. The presentations are preceded by a slide show and an educational talk on wolves.

The howling of wolves seems to arouse deep emotions in humans. As Dan Strickland notes, it seems to be:

> the awakening of a buried wish for the wild freedom of remote ancestors, the mystery of an animal that responds to us but which we almost never see, the thrill of direct communication with a legendary outlaw that has resisted for centuries our efforts to destroy it, [and] the magic of a night in wolf country, including even that tinge of fear carried over from childhood wolf stories.

Similar programs have now been instituted at Prince Albert, Riding Mountain, and Jasper National Parks, and in Sibley Provincial Park in Ontario. In the United States, red wolf howls are held at the Alligator River National Wildlife Refuge in North Carolina. Each of these is famed for its wild nature, but as wolf biologist Lu Carbyn notes, "The public relations and commercial gains from such interpretive activities would have to be weighed against the intrusion into the wilderness character of the landscape." On a smaller scale, public wolf howls have also been instituted in various wolf parks across the United States.

There is little question that the public appreciation of the wolf, gained in part through educational programs such as public wolf howls, has greatly aided the efforts to conserve the wolf.

CHAPTER 12

# CONCLUSION

## The Current Status of the Wolf

### NORTH AMERICA

The wolf population in both Alaska and Canada is deemed to be stable. Within the lower forty-eight states, the wolf has surprised conservationists by slowly increasing its numbers and by spreading to new patches of habitat. Furthermore, wolves have proven that they don't necessarily need large blocks of wilderness to survive and can live in close proximity to people, if people will tolerate their presence. As wolves continue to disperse from established populations in the Northern Rockies and Upper Midwest, they may well recolonize at least some of their former habitat.

There are about 5,000 wolves in the lower 48 states and an estimated 7,000 to 11,000 in Alaska, making the total US wolf population about 12,000 to 16,000. The estimates for Canada's wolf population range from 53,600 to 57,600.

### EURASIA

**Russia.** The largest wolf population in Asia is in the former Soviet Union, but political turmoil there has hampered efforts to preserve the wolf. Although the wolf was given paper protection as a threatened species in 1969, largely as a result of the publication in Russia of Farley Mowat's book *Never Cry Wolf* (which was mistranslated as *Wolves! Please Don't Cry!*), poaching of wolves is common and especially selling them across the border in China.

The wolf has had a long history of persecution in the Soviet Union; in the past seventy years, it is estimated that over 1.5 million wolves were exterminated. Currently, about 20,000 wolf skins are purchased by Soviet authorities from hunters each year; the actual number of wolves killed is known to be much higher.

Wolf numbers in the Soviet Union fluctuated from a peak of around 200,000 in the 1940s to a low of about 29,000 in 1988. Widespread poisoning programs ceased in 1985, and most areas eliminated wolf bounties in 1990. The result is that the wolf population has again risen to around 50,000. Prior to the breakup of the Soviet Union, the Commission on Large Predators of the All-Russian Teriological Society of the Academy of Sciences of the USSR was attempting to determine accurate wolf numbers across the Soviet Union.

The current numerous wildlife reserves in Russia offer limited protection and are poorly patrolled. Wolves have been observed in ninety-six different reserves, but are actively controlled in forty-one of them. The wolf is safest in the largest reserves, such as the Caucasian, Altai, and Pechyora-Ilych reserves, where they do not stray beyond reserve boundaries to prey upon livestock. The remote mountainous areas of the Caucasus, Tian Shan, and Altai still support high numbers of wolves.

Despite widespread hunting, poaching, and regional control measures, the Russian wolf population is likely large enough to be considered stable over the long term.

**Romania.** The rugged nature of Romania has preserved a strong wolf population for centuries. In 1955 the population peaked at about 4,600 wolves, after which livestock predation led to an active extermination program. In 1959 alone, 3,600 wolves were killed.

Today the wild mountainous regions of Romania hold a stable population of about 2,000 wolves. Wolves now receive full protection; however they are still often illegally killed for attacking livestock.

The saving grace for the wolf in Romania has been the rugged nature of the Carpathian Mountains, where the abundant deer and wild boar provide an ample food supply. As the wolf retreated to the high mountains, its dependency on livestock decreased: in 1960, 75 percent of the wolf's diet in Romania was estimated to be livestock, but by 1990, that portion had decreased to 22 percent.

In 1993, Euronatur began a research project in the Carpathians aimed at wolf ecology and wolf-prey relations.

**Poland.** Another large European wolf population is in Poland, where there are about 950 wolves and increasing. The largest populations there are in the Bieszczady Mountains in the south, Bialowieza National Park in the east, and in the Masurian Lakes and Biebrza marshes in the north. The Bieszczady Mountains, one of the most densely forested and least-populated areas in all of Europe, supports the largest wolf population of the three. A small population has also established itself along the border with Germany. Many of Poland's wolves immigrate into the country from the former Soviet Union.

Poland has had a long history of big-game hunting. Russian czars and Prussian generals maintained hunting lodges in Poland during the glory days of the European empires. In 1976, the wolf was declared a big-game animal, and there is a strong demand for wolf hunts, especially from German hunters. In fact, the sale of hunting licenses is still an important source of revenue for the Polish government. The hunting season went from August through March. The usual method was the battue hunt, where wolves are driven toward barriers of rope to which brightly colored flags have been attached. Once boxed in by the beaters, the wolves were shot by concealed hunters. However, now they receive full protection and it is illegal to hunt them, although there are still conflicts with humans over livestock depredation.

**Slovakia.** Czechoslovakia once had an abundant wolf population across the entire country, but by the early 1900s wolves existed only in its eastern portions.

The Slovak Republic, the eastern half of the former Czechoslovakia, holds a current population of around 350–400 wolves. Most of the population uses the mountainous habitat near the Polish border. The Czech Republic is thought to hold about 20 wolves.

The future of Slovakia's wolves is uncertain as they are subject to hunting and 100 to 160 are killed each year. This also has an effect on wolf populations in neighboring Poland and Hungary as those wolves may cross the border into Slovakia and be shot.

In the Czech Republic the wolf receives full legal protection, with exceptions made for nuisance wolves.

Much remains to be learned about the status of the wolf in Slovakia; in 1992, Pavel Hell, a wolf biologist with the Forestry Research Institute in Zvolen, stated, "We don't even know how many wolves live in our country as well as what the social structure of our wolves is like or how big the territories of packs are."

Some of the earliest wolf research conducted in Slovakia was a five-year study begun in 1994 by wolf biologist Paul Paquet, who looked at the wolf population density, influence on prey, habitat requirements, and effectiveness of guard dogs.

**Hungary.** In 1907, wolves ranged over half of Hungary, but by 1940 only one wolf was observed in the whole country.

Hungary has been without wolves for many decades, but recently two small populations have been found. One is near the border of the Ukraine and the other is in south-central Hungary. Their future and their exact numbers are uncertain, but the estimated population is about fifty.

The wolf receives paper protection year-round in Hungary, but illegal shooting remains a problem.

**Albania.** One of the poorest of European countries, Albania has long neglected its wildlife. However, under government protection, the Albania wolf population has grown to about 250.

**Slovenia, Croatia, and Bosnia-Herzegovina.** In the past, almost all of the former Yugoslav republic was wolf territory, with rugged terrain and a low human density.

However, the past war within the former Yugoslavia has had a negative effect on the wolf population, which used to number around 2,000 wolves. The wolf received no legal protection and was actively shot on sight. In Croatia, poisoning was banned in 1972, and bounties were stopped in 1975. But by that point, the Croatian wolf population had diminished to two dozen wolves. The wolf population has since grown to 400 to 600 wolves, and hunting them is prohibited.

Prior to the war, about 200 wolves were killed each year in Bosnia-Herzegovina. Since then, there have been claims by Croatian biologists that Serbian soldiers have slaughtered numerous wolves with machine guns. Other wolves are known to have been victims of land mines. The surviving population is unknown.

In Slovenia, the wolf was once present in all of the forested areas. But in the early 1800s, the Austro-Hungarian empire began a program aimed at exterminating all large predators. The success of these efforts can be seen in game statistics for the estate of Duke Karl Auersperg in Kočevje: from 1768 to 1778, eighty-two wolves were killed on the estate; from 1794 to 1808, seventy-nine wolves were killed; from 1839 to 1852 only one wolf was killed; and from 1953 to 1872, no wolves were found at all. In 1923, a Wolf Extermination Committee was formed to continue the wolf killing in Slovenia. The poisoning of wolves was stopped in 1962 after numerous accidental deaths of children. Wolf bounties in Slovenia were repealed in 1973. By 1990, only a few wolves remained in all of Slovenia, and the wolf was finally given full legal protection. The current population is about 40 to 60 wolves.

Today, numerous efforts are under way to conserve the wolf in the former republics of Yugoslavia. In Croatia, a Croatian Wolf Group has been formed under a grant from Euronatur. The aims of the group are to educate the public about the wolf and lobby for legal protection for the wolf in Croatia. The network also plans to form a joint management plan for wolves in Croatia and Slovenia and to start a research project on wolves in the Dinaric Mountains. To help support wolves and educate the public about them, an exhibition on wolves was mounted in the Natural History Museum in Zagreb, and the group printed 1,000 posters on wolves for public distribution.

**Bulgaria.** A small canid, the golden jackal (*Canis aureus*), has moved into the area as the wolf population decreased in the mid-1960s through the mid-1980s, just as the coyote has largely replaced the wolf across the plains of North America. Bulgaria now has about 1,000 wolves, a stable to increasing population and is a game species.



**Greece.** The wolf has been extinct in southern Greece since the 1930s, when it was pushed into the remote northern mountains.

About 200 wolves remain in northern Greece, but they are actively hunted and poisoned. Very little wild prey remains in the country, and many wolves have turned to taking livestock as food. Though much of the damage is believed to have been caused by wandering dogs, the wolf is often blamed. Strong populations survive in Vikos-Aoos and Valia Calda National Parks and in most of the mountainous areas of the country.

**France.** Although France has long been without wolves, wolves have dispersed into France from surrounding countries and now have a population of about 250 to 300 and are increasing. Wolves are fully protected but illegal killings when wolves attack livestock are an ongoing problem.

**Finland.** In the early 1800s wolves inhabited almost all of Finland, but by 1900 the animals bred only in the northern and eastern portions of the country. The wolf population in Finland is connected to the Russian wolf population. Since 1968, the Finnish border patrol has kept records of all wolf border crossings. Records show that the greatest numbers of wolves are entering the country from the southern portion of Finland's border, which adjoins the independent state of Karelia.

The wolf population in Finland was generally believed to be about 230 animals, but more recent research has shown that there are 150 to 180—far fewer than the 800 conservationists say are needed to maintain a healthy population.

The biggest threat to the wolf in Finland is the reindeer herder. Northern Finland, Sweden, and Norway have a combined reindeer population of about a million animals, and laws have long existed to protect these herds. Reindeer are left unattended for much of the year, making them easy prey to wolves. As a result, the Finnish government issues hunting permits to cull the wolf population to protect reindeer and game animals, and is opposed by wolf conservation groups.

Hunting is even sometimes allowed in nature preserves. Landowners also have the right to kill wolves to protect their livestock. Compensation for livestock predation is paid by the state.

According to Föreningen Varggruppen (the Wolf Group), the Swedish prowolf organization, "Attitudes to wolves are worse in Finland than in the rest of Scandinavia."



**Norway and Sweden.** Wolves were common in both Norway and Sweden until 1900, when active persecution began. The last wolf in Sweden was killed in 1966, and in Norway in 1973. Wolves did not return and breed again in these areas until 1978.

Both Norway and Sweden harbor small populations of wolves, but their survival is threatened by poor public attitudes in Scandinavia toward the wolf.

Swedish farmers may shoot wolves to protect livestock, but aside from this exception, wolves have received full legal protection since 1966. The courts, however, are extremely lenient; in 1985, when a breeding female was shot and the hunter taken to court, he was not punished. Sweden's wolf population has grown to about 340 animals. There is a compensation program for owners of livestock killed by wolves. Potential wolf prey is abundant; the moose population in Sweden is estimated at one million.

Sweden is fortunate in having a strong prowolf group, Föreningen Varggruppen, working to preserve the wolf in Sweden, Norway, and Finland. The group was formed in 1983 and is now one of the strongest prowolf organizations in all of Eurasia. The group's headquarters are in

Stockholm, and it now has over 1,800 members. Its activities include the production of a quarterly newsletter, educational wolf exhibits, lectures, and political lobbying.

In Norway, about 70 wolves are known to exist. The wolf received legal protection in Norway in 1983. Attitudes toward wolves are poor in Norway; over two million sheep freely graze the forests, and ranchers fear predation upon their animals. The Norwegian government sometimes authorizes hunts to reduce wolf attacks on livestock. In 2015 11,000 hunters applied for licenses to shoot 16 wolves.



However, the abundant deer and moose population ensures that wolves could face a bright future in Scandinavia if public attitudes toward their existence improves.

**Spain.** Wolves were found over all of Spain and Portugal until the beginning of the 19th century.

Despite active hunting of wolves as a game animal, over 1,500 to 2,000 wolves live in Spain today. Strong populations exist in the mountains of Galicia, and in Asturias and León. Small populations live in northern Andalusia and the Álava-Logroño area of northeast Spain. Andalusia is unique in Spain for paying compensation for livestock predation by wolves. The National Conservation Branch of the Ministry of Agriculture has found that livestock predation is primarily a problem where proper agricultural practices are not followed. Efforts are under way to educate the local farmers in order to reduce wolf predation on their livestock.

Despite these efforts, it is estimated that between 500 and 750 wolves are killed in Spain each year.

The wolf receives paper protection in Spain, and the central government is supposed to enforce the wolf's protection. In practice, however, each regional government sets its own policies, and prosecutions for illegal wolf killings are rare.

**Portugal.** The wolf in Portugal once roamed the entire country, but is now restricted to the northern third. About 200 to 300 wolves remain in the country, and theoretically they have received full legal protection since

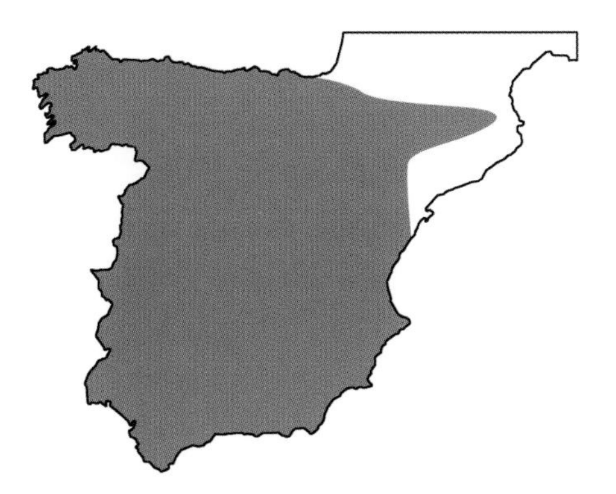

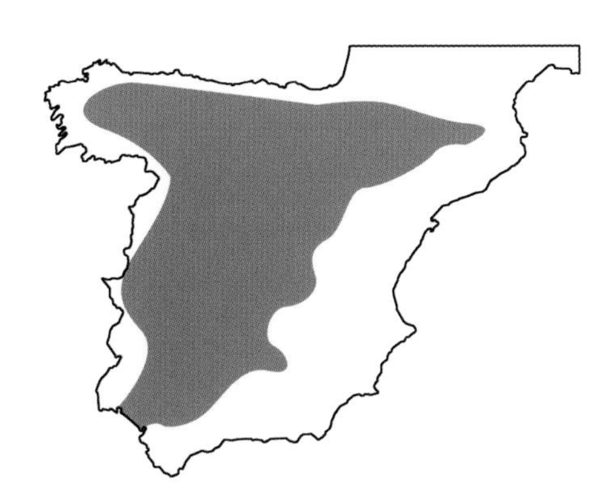

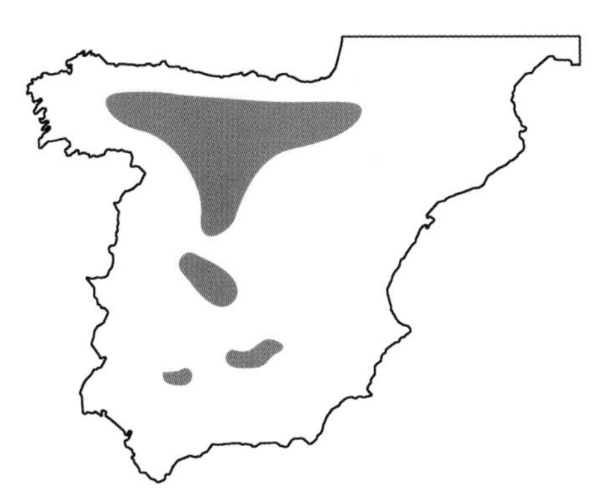

The shrinking range of the wolf in Spain. (after Vila et. al, 1992)

1988. Unfortunately, illegal hunting and poaching are common. The first prosecution for the unlawful killing of a wolf did not occur until 1992, and most infractions still go unpunished. The government has stated that it will pay for livestock predation by wolves, but the slow processing of claims has angered farmers. It is estimated that 65 percent of the wolf's diet in Portugal is livestock. Portugal has one prowolf group, Grupo Lobo, which has a traveling educational exhibit and maintains a recovery center where it is attempting to rehabilitate zoo wolves. As a result of strong lobbying by Grupo Lobo and other organizations, Portuguese citizens voted the wolf Favorite Animal of the Year in 1992.



**Italy.** The last wolves in the western Italian Alps were killed in the 1920s, and the last Sicilian wolf died in the 1940s. The stronghold of the Italian wolf has been the Apennine Mountains, which run like a central spine through almost the entire length of the country.

Currently about 1,000 wolves live in Italy, primarily in the central and southern Apennines. The exact number is highly debated; experience has indicated that many Italian hunters and foresters have mistaken dogs for wolves, and therefore many wolf sightings are thought to be spurious. Regional laws provide compensation for verified livestock losses by wolf predation. There is a great need for protected areas in which to preserve the wolf; only 3 percent of Italy is currently protected as parks or preserves. There is also a need for more efficient agricultural practices. Many Italian farmers now just leave livestock carcasses in place, and open garbage dumps litter the countryside. Luigi Boitani, a wolf biologist with the University of Rome, found in 1982 that 60 to 70 percent of the wolf's diet in the area he studied was human garbage.

Although the wolves in Italy have received paper protection since 1971, they are actively hunted as a pest. And according to Boitani, "Local authorities have never shown any real willingness to enforce the protection and to follow up on dead wolves findings and prosecute poachers." Vittorio Guberti, of the Instituto Nazionale per la Fauna Selvatica stated in 1992, "Not one of at least two hundred wolves denounced as illegally-killed since 1971 produced guilty verdicts" in ensuing investigations.

Compounding the problem in Italy is the huge number of stray and feral dogs, which roam in packs, attacking livestock and destroying property. Much of the damage they do is attributed to wolves, and the wolf's public image suffers. There is also some evidence that a large number of wolf-dog hybrids have been produced, which are a threat to the genetic integrity of the wild Italian wolf. Italian biologists have begun a captive breeding program to preserve genetic integrity, but additional controls on the domestic dog population are badly needed. However, the predominant Catholic religion frowns upon spay/neuter programs, the only viable solution to domestic dog overpopulation.



**Germany.** Wolves were almost exterminated in Germany by 1900, but a few stragglers were able to survive in the remote forests of East Germany. The population was very small; from 1945 to 1991, there were only twenty-five reports of wolves killed by hunters in all of Germany. The wolf received protection in 1990. Today there are about 150 wolves in Germany with most of the population located in the Lusatia region in the eastern part of the country.

In 1993, the state government of Brandenburg announced that four wolves had taken up residence near the border of its jurisdiction. The wolves probably emigrated from Poland and have raised pups successfully in their new home. Brandenburg has five large nature reserves and the lowest human population density in all of Germany. German authorities are working to protect the wolves, and Euronatur has launched a massive media campaign to inform and educate the public about wolves. The network has also worked on a wolf management plan for Brandenburg. As the network has stated, "What seemed impossible 15 years ago might become reality in a few years: the wolf could have a future in one of the most developed countries on this planet."

**Switzerland.** In 1995, wolves were spotted in Switzerland, likely having traveled over the border from Italy. The population is now at about 30 to 35. Although they are a protected species, the government sometimes permits them to be killed for repeated livestock depredations. Between 2000 and

2013 the Swiss government allowed eight problem wolves to be shot. Illegal shooting is also an ongoing problem.

**Turkey.** There are an estimated 7,000 wolves living in Turkey. The hunting of wolves is forbidden within nature reserves and national parks, but elsewhere, the wolf is actively hunted as a deemed threat to livestock. Since over 16 percent of the country is protected as parks or preserves, the outlook for the wolf in Turkey is generally positive.

**Iran.** Iran has a strong wolf population spread almost everywhere across the country, but the wolf is treated as a pest and a serious threat to livestock. Livestock guard dogs are widely used as a predator deterrent.

**Israel.** Israel is unique in that it harbors three subspecies of wolves: *Canis lupus lupus*, *Canis lupus pallipes*, and *Canis lupus arabs* (although some authorities doubt that *arabs* extends so far north). Conflicts with farmers are a serious problem, and recently the Israel Nature Reserves Authority has given livestock guard dogs to shepherds to help protect their flocks. Israel gives full legal protection to the wolf.

**India.** Perhaps 1,000 wolves survive in India, but the population is under severe pressure. The booming human population, habitat destruction, and lack of wild prey have combined to systematically kill off the wolf in many parts of India. At present, only 3 percent of India is protected as parks or preserves. However, India's national parks and reserves offer little protection, as they are severely understaffed and poaching is rampant. As H. S. Panwar, director of the Wildlife Institute of India, has said, "India has so many continuing crises that wildlife is a low priority."

The wolf received full legal protection in India in 1991 under the Wildlife Protection Act, with exceptions for protection of property. However, Raghunandan S. Chundawat reported in 1992 that wolves were widely hunted and that "most hunting is either illegal or in protection of livestock."

**Mongolia.** Wolves are considered a pest in Mongolia, and active control measures are in place throughout the country. However, the wild nature of the region and extremely low human population density (less than three people per square mile) have aided in preserving the Mongolian wolf. At least 10,000 wolves, and perhaps twice as many, remain in Mongolia today.

**China.** The huge human population in China has long waged war on wolves, with large-scale poisoning, trapping, and bounty programs. Habitat loss has been severe. Scattered packs survive across northern China, but there are no wolves in Hainan or the southern portions of the country. There are perhaps up to 12,000 wolves in China that legally have protection; however, there is no enforcement. The Chinese government is considering opening wolf hunting to attract foreign tourists.

## The Legal Status of the Wolf

The legal status of the wolf is crucial to its survival. Species conservation often only becomes a serious issue after an animal is officially declared threatened or endangered.

### NORTH AMERICA

**United States.** As of 2017, the gray wolf is listed as Endangered under the federal Endangered Species Act throughout the United States except in Minnesota where they are listed as Threatened. They have been delisted from the ESA in Montana, Idaho, Wyoming, eastern Washington, eastern Oregon, and northern Utah. Red wolves in the southeastern United States also listed as Endangered.

The relevant legislation is the Endangered Species Act (see Appendix I).

**Canada.** In Canada, threatened species are managed by the Committee on the Status of Endangered Wildlife in Canada (COSEWIC). The committee is composed of federal, provincial, and territorial wildlife biologists and managers, in addition to representatives of conservation organizations such as the WWF-Canada.

Threatened species are listed under one of three categories:

- Endangered: any indigenous species of fauna or flora that is threatened with imminent extirpation or extinction throughout all or a significant portion of its Canadian range
- Threatened: any indigenous species of fauna or flora that is likely to become endangered in Canada if the factors affecting its vulnerability do not become reversed
- Vulnerable: any indigenous species of fauna or flora that is particularly at risk because of low or declining numbers, occurrence at the fringe of its range or in restricted areas, or for some other reason, but is not a threatened species

The North American wolf has been extirpated from 95 percent of its historic range. Photo courtesy of William E. Rideg

COSEWIC currently deems the Canadian population of wolves to be generally stable and has not listed it under any of the three categories above. The status of the wolf, and that of all other Canadian species, is reviewed on a regular basis.

## EUROPE

The wolf is listed in Appendix II to the 1979 Convention on the Conservation of European Wildlife and Natural Habitats (the Bern Convention) and designated a "strictly protected fauna species" deserving to be "specially protected."

Signees agree to prohibit the killing and capture of wolves, to prohibit the destruction of dens, and to prevent the trade in wolves and wolf skins. The legislation lacks real power since it allows signees to make specified exclusions.

Although Greece, Norway, Sweden, Portugal, Spain, Romania, and Finland are all signees, many have chosen to exempt the wolf from their legislative protection.

## INTERNATIONAL STATUS

**IUCN.** The International Union for the Conservation of Nature and Natural Resources maintains a large database on endangered species, areas, and ecosystems. It is best known for its published species analyses and for its red data books listing threatened species throughout the world and protected area directories.

The union was first formed in 1948 as the International Union for the Protection of Nature. After World War II, a number of biologists realized that an international effort would be required to protect the world's natural resources. The original union was a group of 18 governments and 114 nature organizations. It changed its name to the International Union for the Conservation of Nature in 1956, and later added "and Natural Resources." It is also known now as the World Conservation Union, a somewhat less unwieldy title.

The union hosts international technical meetings on endangered species and manages over 500 field conservation projects around the world.

Despite the endangered status of the Ethiopian wolf, the Ethiopian government has yet to permit any captive breeding of the animal. (Patricio Robles Gil)

The IUCN officially lists *Canis lupus* on its red list of species vulnerable in the wild. Both the red wolf and the Ethiopian wolf are listed as endangered.

The IUCN adopted a Manifesto on Wolf Conservation in 1973 (see Appendix II).

In 1992, a workshop, Wolves in Europe—Current Status and Prospects, was held in Oberammergau, Germany. At this meeting it was decided to form Euronatur to improve communication among European wolf biologists and aid in conserving European wolves. The network has become a subgroup of the IUCN Wolf Specialist Group and a strong force in preserving the wolf in Europe. In 2013 it was officially folded into the IUCN Canid Specialist Group.

**CITES.** The Convention on International Trade in Endangered Species of Wild Fauna and Flora is an international agreement dating from 1973. Its purpose is to regulate international trade in endangered species, their parts and derivatives, and any articles made from those species or their parts.

Species are listed in one of the three appendixes, depending on their rarity and the effects that international trade would have on their numbers. Once listed, all countries that are signees to CITES agree to certain conditions regarding the issuance of trade permits.

**Appendix I** species are very rare or endangered. Trade is not permitted for purely commercial purposes. If an animal is to be exported, the importer must have a permit issued by the government of the exporting country and an import permit issued by the government of the importing country. The gray wolf is listed as an Appendix I species for the countries of Bhutan, Pakistan, India, and Nepal. The red wolf is also listed under Appendix I for the United States.

**Appendix II** species are not deemed to be rare or endangered but may become so if trade is not regulated. Any species traded must be covered by an export permit issued by the government of the exporting country before export is allowed. The gray wolf is listed as an Appendix II species in all other signee countries to CITES except those listed in Appendix I.

**Appendix III** species are not endangered and are managed within the listing country. If the species is to be traded, it must be covered by an export permit if trade is with a CITES signee country, or by a certificate of origin or reexport certificate if trade is with any other country. No wolf population is listed within Appendix III.

Trade in an Appendix I or II species theoretically may be allowed only if that trade will not be detrimental to the survival of the species. However, the "nondetrimental" label is not applied as rigorously as it should be. In addition, many countries are not parties to CITES, and many exporters reroute goods through these countries. The illegal trade in various species and their parts is still common.

With respect to the wolf, almost all parts of the body have been sold. Wolf feet, teeth, claws, meat, pelts, heads, and live wolves have all been reported by CITES authorities.

## The Future of the Wolf

In 1970, L. David Mech wrote in *The Wolf: The Ecology and Behavior of an Endangered Species*: "In all other areas of the country, excluding Alaska, the few remaining wolves left no doubt will soon be gone." Luckily, Dr. Mech was wrong. The increasing population of the wolf in the lower 48 is not only a testament to the wolf's survival skills, but also a measure of the maturing public attitudes toward predators.

The *IUCN RedData Book* states that the wolf "must be considered as highly vulnerable until human attitudes toward the species change." As late as 1987, the director of USFWS, Frank Dunkle, told Wyoming ranchers that the only wolves his service would ever bring to Yellowstone National Park were the ones decorating his tie. Since then, the growth of the environmental movement has spawned a more positive attitude toward the wolf and all other creatures we share the planet with. In 1993, L. David Mech admitted that "attitudes about wolves may be shifting for the better." Since then, surveys have shown that large percentages of the public support returning wolves to their former range in both North America and Europe where they were formerly killed off.



## THE ROLE OF EDUCATION

Education is clearly one of the keystones of wolf conservation. USFWS studies have shown that people with a fuller knowledge of wolves tend to have a more positive attitude toward them. Thus, there is a great need for continuing education programs aimed at erasing the pervasive myths that still surround wolves.

Currently, there are over two dozen wolf conservation organizations in the United States alone. Some groups, such as Defenders of Wildlife and The Wolf Fund, have produced education kits aimed at erasing negative wolf mythology. In Canada, Wolf Awareness, Inc., tours grade schools with factual information on the wolf, hoping to instill a better attitude in our future generations.

Despite these efforts, there will always be some individuals who hate the wolf and who refuse to accept updated knowledge about its place in nature.

In one Italian survey, researchers found, "The farther we were from the areas in which wolves lived, the more dangerous they were believed to be." Typically, those with the worst attitudes about wolves are hunters, trappers, ranchers, and those living in remote areas. Luigi Boitani found that in Italy,

An uneasy peace now exists between wolves and humans in much of the United States. Julie Lawrence photo, © Wolf Haven International



"Town and city people show a general positive attitude, while modern farmers . . . show the highest opposition to the wolf presence."

In a 1986 study by S. R. Kellert, almost a third of Minnesota farmers, hunters, and trappers surveyed stated that they might shoot a wolf on sight even if they knew it was illegal.

In 1990, two of Paul Paquet's research wolves in the Southern Rockies Canine Project were shot by hunters. That same year, five of the ten Kootenay, British Columbia, wolves destined for relocation to the United States were shot by hunters.

In March 1994, someone shot a three-year-old wolf outside Algonquin Provincial Park and nailed its head to a pole at the local community center. The wolf was part of a wild pack being studied by biologist John Theberge and was killed in response to a request by a conservation group that local citizens stop killing wolves in the area. As the WWF-Canada commented, "There continue to be individuals who harbor a deep-seated hatred of wolves, and other large carnivores such as bears and cougars, despite the fact that we are beginning to understand their vital ecological role in natural systems."

**THE MOST TRADED WOLF PARTS**

1. WOLF PELTS
2. WOLF-SKIN GARMENTS
3. TROPHIES
4. LIVE WOLVES
5. BODIES
6. SKIN SCRAPS AND PIECES

(Source: CITES)

Illegal killing of wolves continues to be a significant problem. The U.S. Fish and Wildlife Service estimates that illegal killing by humans accounts for 24 percent of wolf mortality the Northern Rockies, 70 percent in Minnesota, and 50 percent of Mexican gray wolves in the Southwest.



## PRESERVATION OF WILDERNESS

The other half of the equation for preserving the wolf is preservation of wilderness. The most serious problem facing wildlife today is loss of habitat. In 1986, the Wolves in American Culture Committee wrote that "it is the preservation of wilderness that will prove to be the single most important factor in insuring that wolves will survive."

It is clear that "wilderness" must be defined as an area that is almost totally inaccessible to humans. Barry Lopez, in his essay "Yukon-Charley: The Shape of Wilderness," wrote, "We often come to wilderness to find animals; we are less sure about the presence of people. In the Wilderness Act humans are construed as aliens."

In a 1975 study, T. F. Weise noted that the approximate number of wolves remaining in Minnesota correlated well with the low density of humans in those areas. In Italy, M. Apollonio stated at the 1992 WWF Wolf Conference that there was a significant relationship between wolf population increases in the northern Apennine Mountains and the decreased human presence in the area.

And the wilderness should ideally be complete, unscarred by logged-out clearcuts and unpenetrated by roads or trails. Many studies have shown that poaching increases dramatically when trails of any sort penetrate a wilderness area. Barbara Scott, a Vancouver Island wolf researcher, said that "once there's a road, it makes the wolves really vulnerable." As L. David Mech wrote in *The Wolves of Isle Royale,* "Just as a drained pond cannot support fish, a destroyed wilderness cannot support wolves."

Parks and preserves are the best place to conserve animals in a natural habitat, but all too many jurisdictions still allow hunting in these "protected areas."

And wolves unfortunately do not understand the artificial boundaries that humans have drawn around parks and reserves. It is very common for them to leave these refuges, at which point they are promptly shot. In Algonquin Provincial Park in Ontario, it was found that up to 60 percent of the annual wolf mortality was caused by wolves straying outside park boundaries and being shot by hunters or farmers or struck by cars. In 1992, one of the first wolves to naturally return to Yellowstone National Park was shot when it strayed outside the park's southern boundary. Many conservationists have suggested that no-hunting buffer zones be set up around parks to aid in wolf survival.

The most severe problem facing wildlife today is habitat loss. © Robert H. Busch



But in a larger view, parks are just isolated islands of hope, large-scale zoos harboring their precious inhabitants.

One solution to the problem of isolated patches of wilderness is the Wildlands Project. Promoted by biologist Michael Soulé and ex-environmental activist Dave Foreman, the project envisions an interlinked system of wilderness reserves connected with habitat corridors. The mission's statement for the project asserts: "Our vision is simple: we live for the day when grizzlies in Chihuahua have an unbroken connection to grizzlies in Alaska, when gray wolves' populations are continuous from New Mexico to Greenland." The same principle was recognized by Euronatur in its Wolf Conservation Strategy for Europe: "Travelling corridors are important.

Gazing toward an uncertain future. Photo courtesy of William E. Rideg

Corridors support the existence of other wildlife and can serve as a base for a metapopulation of wolves in which subpopulations are connected via occasional migrants. This significantly enhances the viability of scattered populations and their genetic quality." Paul Joslin, former director of conservation and research at Wolf Haven International has written that in the northwestern United States, "the corridors of travel . . . run mostly north and south along the predominant drainage systems, between the mountain ranges." Unfortunately, these same drainage valleys are in high demand for logging and road construction. He concludes that "we must learn to work together in ways that will enable wolves and other large carnivores to move between their population centers."

Another approach is the Conservation Strategy for Large Carnivores in Canada adopted in 1990 by the WWF-Canada. The aim of the strategy is to conserve Canada's large carnivore population of wolves, bears, cougars, and wolverines. The strategy has seven steps of action that could serve well for wolves everywhere:

1. Determine population conservation goals.
2. Establish Carnivore Conservation Areas.
3. Control killing by humans.

4. Manage impacts on habitat.
5. Broaden public education.
6. Strengthen conservation research.
7. Improve cooperation between provincial, federal, and international agencies.

In Canada, the WWF proposed the establishment of five Carnivore Conservation Areas, locations especially dedicated to preserving their large predators. The WWF defines these territories as "areas of sufficient size and managed in such a way to ensure long-term survival for free-ranging, minimum viable populations of large carnivores."

There is no question that the future of the wolf looks brighter today than it did even a decade ago. The animal's high intelligence and natural survival skills have stacked the odds in its favor, but the ultimate deciding factor is man.

Humans are responsible for wolf mortality more than any other agents, and only humans can alter that. Through education and preservation of wilderness, we can save the wolf. We must educate our children about the wolf's place in the natural world. We must fight for more parks and reserves to save a place for the wolf. We must push our politicians to enact biologically responsible laws and to enforce animal-protection legislation. We can once again boast of a "howling wilderness" if we establish that as a prime goal for our generation. The fate of the wolf is up to us. And the time to act is now.

# APPENDIX I

## The Endangered Species Act of 1973

The Endangered Species Act (ESA) of 1973 is a strong tool for the protection of American endangered species. A species may be listed as *endangered*: in danger of extinction throughout all or a significant portion of its range; or as *threatened*: likely to become endangered within the near future without protection. The gray wolf is listed as endangered in all lower 48 states except for Minnesota, where it is listed as threatened. The gray wolf is deemed to be stable within Alaska.

The ESA contains two sets of prohibitions against actions that may affect a listed species. The first is the so-called no-jeopardy standard in Section 7.

**Section 7:** This section imposes obligations on federal agencies that deal with the listed species. First, it imposes the obligation on those agencies to conserve threatened and endangered species. Second, those agencies must "insure that actions authorized, funded, or carried out by" an agency are "not likely to jeopardize the continued existence of any (listed) species or result in the destruction or adverse modification" of the species' critical habitat.

The act requires that stringent precautions be taken before any federal agency commits any action that may affect a listed species. The agency must first determine whether a listed species "may be present" in an area and then whether that species "is likely to be affected" by the proposed action. If so, the agency must consult with the USFWS to obtain a written opinion on whether the proposal will jeopardize the listed species.

All activities requiring federal funding, authorization, or permits are subject to these Section 7 requirements.

The second is Section 9, a group of restrictions on any person or entity taking, harming, or harassing an endangered species.

**Section 9:** This section states that it is illegal for "any person subject to the jurisdiction of the United States" to "take" an endangered species. The term "take" is broadly defined as "harass, harm, pursue, hunt, shoot, wound, kill, trap, capture, or collect, or attempt to engage in any such conduct." Any activity that negatively affects the normal behavior of a listed species is prohibited. In at least one instance, the alteration of habitat critical to the recovery of a listed species has been deemed to constitute "taking."

Any violation of a prohibition involving a listed species subjects the individual or entity to fines up to $50,000 and one year in jail. Additional civil penalties of up to $25,000 may also be assessed, and all federal permits and licenses possessed by the individual or entity are revoked.

The only exception to this section is a clause allowing otherwise prohibited activities "for scientific purposes or to enhance the propagation or survival of the affected species." The act also allows exceptions in documented cases of self-defense against the listed species. The secretary of the interior may also allow the taking of a threatened species if it is deemed "necessary and advisable to provide for the conservation" of that species.



**Other clauses:** The ESA requires all federal agencies to further the conservation of endangered species. The term "conservation" is defined as "the use of all methods and procedures which are necessary to bring any endangered or threatened species to the point at which the measures provided pursuant to this Act are no longer necessary."

The act also generally requires that the secretary of the interior develop any and all plans to achieve the delisting of a listed species.

A 1982 amendment to the ESA allows the designation of introduced populations as "experimental," which allows greater flexibility in their biological and political management.

# APPENDIX II

## The IUCN Manifesto on Wolf Conservation

This manifesto on wolf conservation, along with recommended guidelines for conservation, was adopted by the International Union for the Conservation of Nature and Natural Resources Wolf Specialist Group at its meeting in Stockholm, Sweden, in 1973. It has been endorsed by the Survival Service Commission and the Executive Board of IUCN.

The 1973 meeting was attended by delegates and observers from twelve countries that had significant wolf populations.

### DECLARATION OF PRINCIPLES FOR WOLF CONSERVATION

1. Wolves, like all other wildlife, have a right to exist in a wild state. This right is in no way related to their known value to mankind. Instead, it derives from the right of all living creatures to co-exist with man as part of the natural ecosystems.

2. The wolf pack is a highly developed and unique social organization. The wolf is one of the most adaptable and important mammalian predators. It has one of the widest natural geographical distributions of any mammal. It has been, and in some cases still is, the most important predator of big-game animals in the northern hemisphere. In this role, it has undoubtedly played an important part in the evolution of such species and, in particular, of those characteristics which have made many of them desirable game animals.

3. It is recognized that wolf populations have differentiated into subspecies which are genetically adapted to particular environments. It is of first importance that these local populations be maintained in their natural environments in a wild state. Maintenance of genetic purity of locally adapted races is a responsibility of agencies which plan to reintroduce wolves into the wild as well as zoological gardens that may prove a source for such reintroductions.

4. Throughout recorded history man has regarded the wolf as undesirable and has sought to exterminate it. In more than half of the countries of the world where the wolf existed, man has either succeeded, or is on the verge of succeeding, in exterminating the wolf.

5. This harsh judgment on the wolf has been based first on fear of the wolf as a predator of man and second on hatred because of its predation on domestic livestock and on large wild animals. Historical perspectives suggest that to a considerable extent the first fear has been based on myth rather than on fact. It is now evident that the wolf can no longer be considered a serious threat to man. It is true, however, that the wolf has been, and in some cases, still is, a predator of some consequence on domestic livestock and wildlife.

6. The response of man, as reflected by the actions of individuals and governments, has been to try to exterminate the wolf. This is an unfortunate situation because the possibility now exists for the development of management programs which would mitigate serious problems, while at the same time permitting the wolf to live in many areas of the world where its presence would be acceptable.

7. [Later modified to the following:] It is required that occasionally there may be a scientifically established need to reduce non-endangered wolf populations; further it may become scientifically established that in certain endangered wolf populations specific individuals must be removed by appropriate conservation authorities for the benefit of wolf populations. Conflict with man sometimes occurs from undue economic competition or from imbalanced predator-prey ratios adversely affecting prey species and/or the wolf itself. In such cases, temporary reduction of wolf populations may become necessary, but reduction measures should be imposed under strict scientific management. The methods must be selective, specific to the problem, highly discriminatory, and have minimal adverse effects on the ecosystem. Alternative ecosystem management, including alteration of human activities and attitudes and non-lethal methods of wolf management,

should be fully considered before lethal wolf reduction is employed. The goal of wolf management programs must be to restore and maintain a healthy balance in all components of the ecosystem. Wolf reduction should never result in the permanent extirpation of the species from any portion of its natural range.

8. The effect of major alterations of the environment through economic development may have some serious consequences for the survival of wolves and their prey species in areas where wolves now exist. Recognition of the importance and status of wolves should be taken into account by legislation and in planning for the future of any region.

9. Scientific knowledge of the role of the wolf in ecosystems is inadequate in most countries in which the wolf still exists. Management should be established only on a firm scientific basis, having regard for international, national and regional situations. However, existing knowledge is at least adequate to develop preliminary programs to conserve and manage the wolf throughout its range.

10. The maintenance of wolves in some areas may require that society at large bear the cost, e.g. by giving compensation for the loss of domestic stock; conversely there are areas having high agricultural value where it is not desirable to maintain wolves and where their introduction would not be feasible.

11. [Later modified to the following:] In some cases there has been a marked changed in public attitudes towards the wolf. This change in attitudes has influenced governments to revise and even to eliminate archaic laws. It is recognized that education to establish a realistic picture of the wolf and its role in nature is most essential to wolf survival. Education programs, however, must be factual and accurate.

12. Socio-economic, ecological and political factors must be considered and resolved prior to reintroduction of the wolf into biologically suitable areas from which it has been extirpated.

# WOLF CONSERVATION ORGANIZATIONS AND NEWSLETTERS

## ORGANIZATIONS

*Alaska Wildlife Alliance,* P.O. Box 202022, Anchorage, AK 99520; http://akwildlife.org

*California Wolf Center,* P.O. Box 1389, Julian, CA 92036; www.californiawolfcenter.org

*Clan des loups d'Amérique du Nord,* 1232 Chute Planet, St-Raymond, QU, Canada G3L 4P3; www.clanloups.com

*Colorado Wolf and Wildlife Center,* P.O. Box 713, Divide, CO 80814; www.wolfeducation.org

*Defenders of Wildlife,* 1130 17th St. NW, Washington, DC 20036; www.defenders.org

*Deutsche Wolfsgemeinschaft,* Am Stege 43, D-34123 Kaissel, Germany

*Earthroots Wolves Ontario Project,* 401 Richmond St. W, Ste. 410, Toronto, ON, Canada M5V 3A8; http://earthroots.org

*Endangered Wolf Center,* 6750 Tyson Valley Rd., Eureka, MO 63025; www.endangeredwolfcenter.org

*Euronatur,* Westendstrabe 3, 78315 Radolfzell, Germany, www.euronatur.org

*Foreningen Våre Rovdyr,* Postboks 17, 195, 2151 Arnes, Norway; www.fvr.no

*Föreningen Varggruppen,* Box 15061, S-104, 65 Stockholm, Sweden; www.timberwolfinformation.org

*Gesellschaft zum Schutz der Wölf,* Blasbacher Str. 55, 6330 Wetzlar 26, Germany; www.gzsdw.de

*Grand Canyon Wolf Recovery Project,* P.O. Box 233, Flagstaff, AZ 86002-0233; www.gcwolfrecovery.org

*Grupo Lobo,* da Universidade de Lisboa, Edificio C2, Campo Grande, 1749-016 Lisbon, Portugal; http://lobo.fc.ul.pt/UK/

*Haliburton Wolf Research Centre,* RR #1, Haliburton, ON, Canada K0M 1S0

*International Wolf Center,* 1396 Hwy. 169, Ely, MN 55731; www.wolf.org

*Kerwood Wildlife Education Center,* RR 3, Kerwood, ON, Canada N0M 2B0; http://wolveswhisperaz.tripod.com

*Les Loups du Gévaudan,* 48100 Saint-Léger-de-Peyre, France; www.loupsdugevaudan.com

*Maine Wolf Coalition,* 30 Meadow Wood Dr., South China, ME 04358; http://mainewolfcoalition.org

*Mission: Wolf,* 13388 County Rd. 634, Westcliffe, CO 81252; www.missionwolf.org

*New Hampshire Wolf Alliance,* P.O. Box 498, Rumacy NH 03266

*Northwest Wildlife Preservation Society,* 30958, RPO James Bay, Victoria, BC V8V 4M3, Canada; http://northwestwildlife.com

*Restore: The North Woods,* P.O. Box 1099, Concord, MA 01742; www.restore.org

*Richard E. Flauto Wildlife Foundation,* P.O. Box 9452, Youngstown, OH 44512; rfwf@wolfcountry.org

*Timber Wolf Information Network,* Waupaca Field Stn., E110 Emmons Crk. Rd., Waupaca, WI 54981; www.timberwolfinformation.org

*UK Wolf Conservation Trust,* UK Wolf Centre, Butlers Farm, Beenham, Reading, Berkshire, RG7 5NT; https://ukwct.org.uk

*White Wolf Sanctuary and Educational Facility,* 10095 East Alsea Hwy., Tidewater, OR 97390; www.whitewolfsanctuary.com

*Wild Canid Survival and Research Center*, P.O. Box 760, Eureka, MO 63025; wildcanidcenter@onemain.com

*Wildlife Science Center*, 5463 West Broadway, Forest Lake, MN 55025; www.wildlifesciencecenter.org

*Wild Sentry: The Northern Rockies Ambassador Wolf Program Inc.*, P.O. Box 172, Hamilton, MT 59840; www.wildsentry.org

*Wild Spirit Wolf Sanctuary*, 378 Candy Kitchen Rd., Ramah, NM 87321; www.wildspiritwolfsanctuary.org

*Wolf Awareness, Inc.*, 21-514 Anderson Rd., Golden, BC, Canada V0A 1H1; http://wolfawareness.org

*Wolf Conservation Center*, P.O. Box 421, South Salem, NY 10590; https://nywolf.org

*Wolf Education and Research Center*, 1721 Forest Rd., Winchester, ID 83555; www.wolfcenter.org

*Wolf Haven International*, 3111 Offut Lake Rd., Tenino, WA 98589; https://wolfhaven.org

*Wolf Hollow (North American Wolf Foundation, Inc.)*, 114 Essex Rd., Rte. 133, Ipswich, MA 01938; www.wolfhollowipswich.org

*Wolf Mountain Sanctuary*, 7520 Fairlane Rd., Lucerne Valley, CA 92356; www.wolfmountainsanctuary.net

*Wolf Park*, 4004 E 800 N, Battle Ground, IN 47920; http://wolfpark.org

*Wolf People*, P.O. Box 246, Cocolalla, ID 83813; http://wolfpeople.com

*Wolf Recovery Foundation*, P.O. Box 444, Pocatello, ID 83204; www.forwolves.org

*Wolf Society of Great Britain*, Moon Cottage, Kingswood Lane, Hindhead, Surrey, England GU26 6D

*Wolf Song of Alaska*, P.O. Box 770950, Eagle River, AK 99577-0950; www.wolfsongalaska.org

*Wolfwatch U.K.*, Rivendell, The Hollow, Meltham, Holmfirth, HD9 5LA, England; www.wolfwatch.uk

## NEWSLETTERS

*International Wolf.* International Wolf Center, 1396 Hwy. 169, Ely, MN 55731

*Wolf Tracks.* Wolf Haven International, 3111 Offut Lake Rd., Tenino, WA 98589

*Wolves.* Haliburton Forest Wolf Center, RR #1, Haliburton, ON, Canada K0M 1S0

# GLOSSARY

**AAZPA:** American Association of Zoological Parks and Aquariums
**AHA:** American Humane Association
**canine:** referring to any member of the dog family
**carnassial:** the last upper premolar and first lower molar tooth of certain predators
**carnivore:** an animal that feeds on flesh
**carrion:** dead and decaying flesh
**CITES:** Convention on International Trade in Endangered Species of Wild Fauna and Flora
**COSEWIC:** Committee on the Status of Endangered Wildlife in Canada
**ESA:** Endangered Species Act (United States)
**estrus:** the period of sexual receptivity of a female
**extirpated:** referring to a species once extant in an area, but now extinct, and surviving elsewhere
**feline:** referring to any member of the cat family
**foveal pit:** a small depression at the back of the eyeball that permits focusing at a distance
**gestation:** the carrying of young in the womb from conception until delivery
**holarctic:** a geographic term for the areas north of the Tropic of Cancer
**hybrid:** an animal or plant produced from the mixture of two species
**IUCN:** International Union for the Conservation of Nature and Natural Resources
**lycanthropy:** a mental illness in which the patient believes he or she is a wolf
**miacid:** a primitive carnivore distributed from the Paleocene to the Oligocene epochs
**olfactory:** relating to the sense of smell
**precaudal gland:** a gland on the dorsal surface of a wolf's tail; function unknown

**prey efficiency:** the percentage of pursued prey animals that are successfully captured

**range:** area in which a particular species is normally found

**sanitation effect:** the removal of biologically weak or inferior animals from a prey population

**territory:** area which a particular species uses for feeding and will defend as its own

**ungulate:** referring to any hoofed, four-legged mammal

**USFWS:** U.S. Fish and Wildlife Service

# BIBLIOGRAPHY


"Aerial Wolf Hunt Delayed in Alaska." 1993. *Animals* 126(1):5.

Alardice, Pamela. 1991. *Myths, Gods, and Fantasy*. Bridport, England: Prism Press.

"Alaska Bags a Boycott." *Vancouver Province*, September 24, 1993, p. 6.

"Alaska to Reconsider Aerial Wolf Hunts." 1993, *Animals* 126(3):4.

Alberta Fish & Wildlife Division. 1984. *Status of the Fish & Wildlife Resource in Alberta.* Edmonton, Alberta, Canada: Alberta Environmental Protection, Natural Resources Service, Wildlife Management Division.

Allen, Durward L. 1979. *The Wolves of Minong: Their Vital Role in a Wild Community.* Boston: Houghton Mifflin.

——. and L. David Mech. 1963. "Wolves versus Moose on Isle Royale." *National Geographic* 123(2):200–219.

Allen, Thomas B. 1974. *Vanishing Wildlife of North America.* Washington, DC: National Geographic Society.

"Alligator River National Wildlife Refuge." 1994. *Wolf!* 12(1):8.

Almberg, Emily S., Paul C. Cross, Peter J. Hudson, Andrew P. Dobson, Douglas W. Smith, & Daniel R. Stahler. "Infectious Diseases of Wolves in Yellowstone." https://www.nps.gov/yell/learn/ys-24-1-infectious-diseases-of-wolves-in-yellowstone.htm.

Angier, Bradford. 1956. *How to Stay Alive in the Woods.* New York: Collier Books.

Ausband, David E., Lindsey N. Rich, Elizabeth M. Glenn, Michael S. Mitchell, Pete Zager, David A.W. Miller, Lisette P. Waits, Bruce B. Ackerman, Curt M. Mack. "Monitoring Gray Wolf Populations Using Multiple Survey Methods." *The Journal of Wildlife Management* 78(2):335-346; 2014; DOI: 10.1002/jwmg.654.

"A Wolf Kill at Any Cost." 1993. *Nature Alert* 3(2):1.

Bailey, Paul, 1988. "Vancouver Island Wolf Control." *B.C. Outdoors* 44(6):25–27.

Banfield, A. W. F. 1974. *The Mammals of Canada.* Toronto: University of Toronto Press.

Bangs, Ed. 1991. *Return of a Predator: Wolf Recovery in Montana*. Helena, MT: U.S. Fish and Wildlife Service.

——. and Steven Fritts, 1993. *Reintroduction of Gray Wolves to Yellowstone National Park and Central Idaho.* Endangered Species Technical Bulletin, 28(3): 18-20.

Barbour, Laura, Brittni Brown, Betsaida Chavez-Garcia, Arnaulde Irangabiye, Kare Tonning, and Yan Xu. "The Biological, Social, Cultural, Political and Economic Aspects of Wolf Reintroductuon in Idaho & Yellowstone National Park." *Environmental Studies Capstone,* Spring 2013, College of Idaho.

Barron, Hannah. *Earthroots.* Personal Communication.

Bass, Rick. 1993. *The Ninemile Wolves.* Livingston, MT: Clark City Press.

Bath, Alistair. 1991. "Public Attitudes in Wyoming, Montana, and Idaho Toward Wolf Restoration in Yellowstone National Park." In *Transactions of the 56th North American Wildlife and Natural Resources Confederation*, pp. 91–94.

Bergman, Charles. 1989. *Wild Echoes: Encounters with the Most Endangered Animals in North America.* New York: McGraw-Hill.

Bishop, N. A., comp. 1991. *Yellowstone Wolf Answers: A Second Digest.* Yellowstone National Park.Washington DC: U.S. National Park Service.

Bomford, Liz. 1993. *The Complete Wolf.* New York: St. Martin's.

Bouchner, Miroslav. 1982. *A Field Guide in Color to Animal Tracks & Traces.* London: Octopus Books.

Boyd, D., J. Gude, B. Inman, N. Lance, A. Messer, A. Nelson, T. Parks, M. Ross, T. Smucker, J. Steuber, and J. Vore. 2017. *Montana Gray Wolf Conservation and Management 2016 Annual Report.* Montana Fish, Wildlife & Parks. Helena, Montana, p. 71.

Bradley, L., J. Gude, N. Lance, K. Laudon, A. Messer, A. Nelson, G. Pauley, K. Podruzny, M. Ross, T. Smucker, and J. Steuber. 2014. *Montana Gray Wolf Conservation and Management. 2013 Annual Report.* Montana Fish, Wildlife & Parks. Helena, Montana, p. 54.

——. J. Gude, N. Lance, K. Laudon, A. Messer, A. Nelson, G. Pauley, M. Ross, T. Smucker, and J. Steuber. 2013. *Montana Gray Wolf Conservation and Management 2012 Annual Report.* Montana Fish, Wildlife & Parks. Helena, Montana, p. 55.

———. J. Gude, N. Lance, K. Laudon, A. Messer, A. Nelson, G. Pauley, M. Ross, T. Smucker, J. Steuber, and J. Vore. 2015. *Montana Gray Wolf Conservation and Management. 2014 Annual Report.* Montana Fish, Wildlife & Parks. Helena, Montana, p. 60.

Brandenburg, Jim. 1988. *White Wolf: Living with an Arctic Legend.* Minocqua, WI: Northword Press.

———. 1991. "My Dances with Wolves." *International Wildlife* 21(4):30–36.

Brown, David E. 1983. *The Wolf in the Southwest: The Making of an Endangered Species.* Tucson: University of Arizona Press.

Bruce, David. 1971. *Bird of Jove.* New York: Ballantine.

Bryner, Jeanna. "Africa's Lone Wolf: New Species Found in Ethiopia." *Livescience*, January 28, 2011.

Burton, Robert. 1979. *Carnivores of Europe*. London: B. T. Basford.

Busch, Robert H. 1992. "That Clever Coyote: A Natural History of Charlie." *Country Journal* 19(2):29–31.

———. ed. 1994. *Wolf Songs: The Classic Collection of Writing about Wolves.* San Francisco: Sierra Club Books.

"Captive Wolf Research in the Netherlands." 1992. *Wolf News* 10(3):3.

Carbyn, Ludwig N. 1987. "Gray Wolf and Red Wolf." In *Wild Furbearer Management and Conservation in North America,* edited by M. Novak, J. A. Baker, M. E. Obbard, and B. Malloch. North Bay, Ontario: Ontario Trappers Association and Ontario Ministry of Natural Resources.

———. 1988. "Descriptions of Wolf Attacks on Bison Calves in Wood Buffalo National Park." *Arctic: Journal of the Arctic Institute of North America* 41(4):297–302.

———. 1988. "Wolves in Riding Mountain National Park. Ecosystem protection and thoughts on a holistic conservation strategy." Paper presented at the Wolf Symposium, University of British Columbia, Vancouver, May 9, 1988.

———. and T. Trottier. 1987. "Responses of bison on their calving grounds to predation by wolves in Wood Buffalo National Park." *Canadian Journal of Zoology* 65:2072–2078.

——, Steven Fritts, and Dale Seip, eds. In press. *Ecology and Conservation of Wolves in a Changing World: Proceedings of the Second North American Symposium on Wolves.* Edmonton, Alberta: Canadian Circumpolar Institute.

Carlson, Delbert G., and J. M. Griffin. 1980. *Dog Owner's Home Veterinary Handbook.* New York: Howell Book House.

Cassidy, Kira A., Douglas W. Smith, L. David Mech, Daniel R. MacNulty, Daniel R. Stahler, & Matthew C. Metz. "Territoriality and Inter-Pack Aggression in Gray Wolves: Shaping a Social Carnivore's Life History." *Yellowstone Science* 24(1) 2016.

Chadwick, Douglas H. 1992. "Denali, Alaska's Wild Heart." *National Geographic* 182(2):63–87.

Coltrane, J., J. Gude, B. Inman, N. Lance, K. Laudon, A. Messer, A. Nelson, T. Parks, M. Ross, T. Smucker, J. Steuber, and J. Vore. 2015. *Montana Gray Wolf Conservation and Management 2015 Annual Report.* Montana Fish, Wildlife & Parks. Helena, Montana, p. 74.

"Compound 1080 Banned in U.S.A. but Still Used in Alberta & B.C." 1989. *Wolf News* 7(2):5.

Connolly, Guy E. 1978. "Predators and Predator Control." In *Big Game of North America: Ecology and Management*. Harrisburg, PA: Stackpole Books.

"Conserving a Coyote in Wolf's Clothing?" 1991. *Science News* 139(24): 374–375.

"Coyote Interaction." 1993. *Wolves and Related Canids* 6(3):5.

Crane, Candace, 1989. "Last of the Lobos." *Animals* 122(4):18–24.

Crisler, Lois. 1958. *Arctic Wild.* New York: HarperCollins.

——. 1968. *Captive Wild.* New York: HarperCollins.

Curtis, Patricia. 1992. "Help Wanted for Exotic Pets." *Animals* 125(5):22–25.

"Debate Over Wolf Control Held at U.B.C." 1988. *Working for Wildlife,* World Wildlife Fund-Canada (Summer/Fall):4.

*Defending the Wolf*. 1993. Washington, DC: Defenders of Wildlife.

Diamond, Seth, 1994. "The Prairie Wolf Returns." *WolfTracks* 11(2):8–9.

Dufresne, Frank. 1991. *No Room for Bears*. Seattle: Alaska Northwest Books.

Durrell, Gerald. 1973. *Beasts in My Belfry*. London: William Collins.

Durrell, Lee. 1986. *State of the Ark.* New York: Doubleday.
Eliot, John L., ed. 1993. "As Forests Fall, the Iberian Wolf Dwindles." *National Geographic* 183(2):139.
Elliot, John, 1988. "Balance of Nature in British Columbia's Northeast." In *Big Game Records of B.C.* Trophy Wildlife Records Club of B.C. Nanoose, British Columbia: Trophy Wildlife Records Club of B.C.
"Ethically Incorrect." *Vancouver Sun,* March 18, 1993, p. A19.
Eyck, Laurie T. 1989. "Dogs: Origin of a Species." *Animals* 122(6):5–9.
——. 1994. "Endangered in Europe: The Big Bad Wolf." *Animals* 127(1):8–13.
*Fact Sheet: Wolf Hybrids.* 1992. Washington, DC: Humane Society of the United States.
"Fear and Loathing: The Persecution of Algonquin's Wolves." 1993. *Nature Alert* 3(3):3.
Fiennes, Richard. 1976. *The Order of Wolves.* Indianapolis: Bobbs-Merrill.
Fischer, Hank, 1993. "Wolves for Yellowstone." *Defenders* 63(2):12–17.
Forstenzer, Martin. 1993. "Fit to Kill?" *Audubon* 95(2):18–20.
Fox, Michael W. 1971. "Possible Examples of High Order Behavior in Wolves." *Journal of Mammalogy* 52:640–641.
——. 1980. *The Soul of the Wolf.* New York: Lyons & Burford.
——. 1993. "Wolf-Dog Hybrids." *Wolves and Related Canids* (Summer):21–22.
Frazer, James G. 1949. *The Gold Bough: A Study in Magic and Religion.* New York: Macmillan.
Fritts, Steven H. 1991. *Wolf Recovery Efforts in the Northwestern United States.* Washington, DC: U.S. Fish and Wildlife Service.
——. 1992. *Gray Wolf Recovery in the Northwestern United States.* Washington, DC: U.S. Fish and Wildlife Service.
——, William J. Paul, L. David Mech, and David P. Scott. 1992. *Trends and Management of Wolf-Livestock Conflicts in Minnesota.* USFWS Resource Publication 181. Washington, DC: U.S. Fish and Wildlife Service.
Furber, Debbie. "Wolves of the West." *Canadian Cattlemen,* October 21, 2015.

Gannon, Megan. "North America Has Only 1 True Species of Wolf, DNA Shows." *LIVESCIENCE,* July 29, 2016.

——. "Yellowstone Wolves Hit by Disease." *LIVESCIENCE,* September 10, 2012.

Ginsberg, J. R., and D. W. Macdonald, eds. 1990. *Foxes, Wolves, Jackals, and Dogs: An Action Plan for the Conservation of Canids*. Gland, Switzerland: International Union for the Conservation of Nature and Natural Resources.

"Glacier Park Wolf Shot in Canada, 700 km Away." 1987. *Wolf News* 5(3):6.

Glen, Barb. "Wolves have a taste for Alberta Beef." *The Western Producer.* April 14, 2011.

Glubok, Shirley. 1975. *The Art of the Northwest Coast Indians.* New York: Macmillan.

Grainger, David. 1978. *Animals in Peril.* Toronto: Pagurian Press.

Grambo, Rebecca. 2005. *Wolf: Legend, Enemy, Icon*. Richmond Hill, Ontario: Firefly Books.

Gray, David R. 1987. *The Muskoxen of Polar Bear Pass*. Toronto: Fitzhenry & Whiteside.

*Gray Wolf EIS Planning Update Report*. April 1993. Washington, DC: U.S. Fish and Wildlife Service.

Grimm, David. "Dogs may have been domesticated more than once." *Science,* June 2, 2016.

Grzimek, Bernhard, ed. 1972. *Grzimek's Animal Life Encyclopedia*. New York: Van Nostrand Reinhold.

Gunson, J. R., ed. *Management Plan for Wolves in Alberta.* Edmonton, Alberta: Fish and Wildlife Division, Alberta Department of Forests, Lands, and Wildlife.

Hall, Wayne, 1993. "Alliance Helps Commission Wolf Research by Dr. Gordon Haber." *The Spirit* (October/November):3.

Hamilton, Susan. 1992. "Call of the Wild." *International Wildlife* 22(6):29.

Hammill, Jim. 1992. "Wolf Recovery." *Michigan Natural Resources Magazine,* (November/December). First published in 1992 by Michigan Department of Natural Resources.

Hanauska-Brown, L., L. Bradley, J. Gude, N. Lance, K. Laudon, A. Messer, A. Nelson, M. Ross, and J. Steuber. 2012. *Montana Gray Wolf Conservation and Management 2011 Annual Report.* Montana Fish, Wildlife & Parks. Helena, Montana, p. 54.

Harvey, Fiona. "Finland has far fewer wild wolves than previously thought, census shows." *The Guardian*. Monday, June 26, 2017.

Hayes, R.D., A.M. Baer & D.G. Larsen. *Population Dynamics and Prey Relationships of an Exploited and Recovering Wolf Population in the Southern Yukon.* Yukon Fish and Wildlife Branch Final report TR-91-1, 1991.

Homer, Stephen. 1987. "Conversations with Lupus." *Equinox* 6:3(33):58–71.

Houk, Rose. 1993. *Great Smoky Mountains National Park: A Natural History Guide*. Boston: Houghton Mifflin.

"How Often are Wolves Injured During Live-Capture?" 1992. *Wolf News* 10(2):4–5.

"How to Live with the Wolf." *Alberta Report,* November 13, 1989, pp. 54–55.

"Howls across the Border." *Alberta Report,* May 14, 1990, p. 26.

http://fieldguide.mt.gov/speciesDetail.aspx?elcode=AMAJA01030

http://pacificwild.org/take-action/campaigns/save-bc-wolves

http://voices.nationalgeographic.com/2016/09/27/solving-the-mystery-of-the-18th-century-killer-beast-of-gevaudan/

http://www.carnivores.cz/threats-for-large-carnivores/wolf-hunting-in-slovakia/

https://pacificwolffamily.org/theroguepack/

https://www.fws.gov/redwolf/docs/the-challenges-of-red-wolf-conservation-and-the-fate-of-an-endangered-species-recovery-program.pdf

https://www.nps.gov/yell/learn/nature/gbearinfo.htm

https://www.nps.gov/yell/learn/nature/wolves.htm

https://www.yellowstonepark.com/things-to-do/brothers-that-dont-get-along

Hummel, Monte, and Sherry Pettigrew. 1991. *Wild Hunters: Predators in Peril.* Toronto: Key Porter Books and World Wildlife Fund-Canada.

"Hunters' Victims Include Gray Wolves." 1990. *Animals* 123(1):1.

Idaho Department of Fish and Game. 2015. 2015 *Idaho wolf monitoring progress report*. Idaho Department of Fish and Game, 600 South Walnut, Boise, Idaho. p. 71.

International Wolf Center. 1992. *Wolves of the High Arctic.* Ely, MN: International Wolf Center.

Johnson, Terry B. 1990. "Nongame Field Notes: Mexican Wolf." *Arizona Wildlife Views*, September, p. 18.

——. 1990. "Preliminary Results of a Public Opinion Survey of Arizona Residents and Interest Groups about the Mexican Wolf." Tucson: Arizona Game and Fish Dept.

——. 1992. "Just How Big & Bad is the Wolf?" *Wildlife Views,* May, pp. 1–3.

——. Debra C. Noel, and Laurie Z. Ward. 1992. "Summary of Information on Four Potential Mexican Wolf Reintroduction Areas in Arizona." Tucson: Arizona Game and Fish Dept.

Joslin, Paul. 1994. "Wolf Corridors and Other Concepts Learned by Monitoring Radio-Collared Wolves." *WolfTracks* 11(3):8–9.

Junkin, Elizabeth Darby. 1991. "Wolf." *Buzzworm* 111(1):47–53.

Karnowski, Steve. "Wolf's recovery seen in livestock loss payouts." *MPR News*, Sept. 5, 2012.

"Kelly Creek Wolf." 1993. *Wolves and Related Canids* (Summer):5.

Krebs, John W., Tara W. Strine, and James E. Childs. 1993. "Babies Surveillance in the U.S. during 1992." *Journal of the American Veterinary Medical Association* 203(12):1718–1731.

Krueger, Steve. 1991. "What Would Darwin Say?" *Nature Canada* 20(1):12–17.

Kunelius, Rick, 1983. *Animals of the Rockies*. Banff, Alberta: Altitude Publishing.

Laufer, Jack, and Peter T. Jenkins. 1989. "Historical and Present Status of the Gray Wolf in the Cascade Mountains of Washington." *The Northwest Environmental Journal* 5(2):313–327.

Lawrence, R. D. 1980. *Secret Go the Wolves.* New York: Ballantine.

——. 1986. *In Praise of Wolves.* Toronto: Totem Books.

——. 1990. *Wolves.* Toronto: Key Porter.

——. 1993. *Trail of the Wolf.* Toronto: Key Porter.

Lee, David. 1993. "Are Wolves Already in Yellowstone?" *Wildlife Conservation* 96(1):11.
Leopold, Aldo. 1949. *A Sand County Almanac.* New York: Oxford University Press.
Leslie, Robert Franklin, 1974. *In the Shadow of a Rainbow.* New York: Norton.
"Long Distance Trek Ends." 1992. *Wolf!* 10(2):25.
"Longevity in Wolves." 1988. *Wolf News* 6(3):5.
Lopez, Barry H. 1978. *Of Wolves and Men.* New York: Charles Scribner's Sons.
———. 1989. *Crossing Open Ground.* New York: Vintage.
———. 1991. "Making Animals Dance." Letter to the editor. *Outside* 16(11):20–21.
Lorenz, Konrad, 1952. *King Solomon's Ring.* New York: Thomas Y. Crowell.
MacNulty, Daniel R., Daniel R. Stahler, C. Travis Wyman, Joel Ruprecht & Douglas W. Smith. "The Challenge of Understanding Northern Yellowstone Elk Dynamics after Wolf Reintroduction." *Yellowstone Science* 24(1) 2016.
"Man Fined for Releasing Wolves." 1991. *Wolf News* 9(3):8.
Marshall, Anthony D. 1994. "Zoo Story." *Wildlife Conservation* 97(3):78–79.
Matthiessen, Peter. 1959. *Wildlife in America.* New York: Viking.
Mauer, Richard. "Pilot tried to save wolf biologist after crash in Denali park." *Alaska Dispatch News,* October 16, 2009.
McBride, Chris. 1977. *The White Lions of Timbavati.* London: Paddington Press.
McCracken, Harold. 1959. *George Catlin and the Old Frontier.* New York: Bonanza Books.
McHargue, Georgess. 1976. *Meet the Werewolf.* New York: Lippincott.
McHugh, Tom. 1972. *The Time of the Buffalo.* New York: Knopf.
Meador, Ron. "Does wolf hunt reduce livestock losses? Maybe not, lawmakers are told." *MINNPOST.* 01/31/14. www.hybridlaw.com.
Mech, L. David. 1966. *The Wolves of Isle Royale.* Fauna of the National Parks of the United States, Fauna Series 7. Washington, DC: U.S. Government Printing Office.

———. 1970. *The Wolf: The Ecology and Behavior of an Endangered Species.* Minneapolis: University of Minnesota Press.

———. 1977. "Where Can the Wolf Survive?" *National Geographic* 152(4):518–537.

———. 1988. *The Arctic Wolf: Living with the Pack.* Stillwater, MN: Voyageur Press.

———. 1990. "Who's Afraid of the Big Bad Wolf?" *Audubon* 92(2):82–85.

———. 1991. "Meet the Wolf." *Defenders* 66(6):28–32.

———, and L. D. Frenzel. 1971. *Ecological Studies of the Timber Wolf in Northeastern Minnesota.* North Central Forest Experimental Station, Forest Research Paper NC-52. St. Paul, MN: U.S. Department of Agriculture.

"Mexican Wolf EIS Delayed Until Summer." 1992. *Wolf!* 10(2):18.

Miot, Christine. "Two wolves survive in the world's longest running predator-prey study." *Science,* April 18, 1017.

"Montana Wolf Population Growing Steadily." 1994. *Wolf!* 12(10):30.

Montaner, Michaela. "UPDATE: Wolf kill numbers nearly double in 2016." *Pacific Wild.* May 3, 2016.

Morgan, Jody. 1990. "Canine Vision." *Equinox* 9:3(51):29.

Morris, D. 1990. *Animal Watching: A Field Guide to Animal Behavior.* London: Jonathan Cape.

Mowat, Farley. 1963. *Never Cry Wolf.* Toronto: McClelland & Stewart.

Muggeridge, Kitty, trans. 1973. *Fables from La Fontaine.* London: William Collins & Sons.

Murie, Adolph. 1944. *The Wolves of Mount McKinley.* Fauna of the National Parks, No. 5. Washington, DC: U.S. Government Printing Office.

Murie, Olaus. 1954. *A Field Guide to Animal Tracks.* Boston: Houghton Mifflin.

Murray, Dennis L., Guillaume Bastille-Rouseau, Jennifer R. Adams, & Lisette P. Waits. *The Challenges of Red Wolf Recovery and the Fate of an Endangered Species Recovery Program.* Conservation Letters, September/October 2015: 8(5), 338–344.

Murray, J. A., ed. 1993. *Out Among the Wolves.* Seattle: Alaska Northwest Books.

Nash, Roderick. 1967. *Wilderness and the American Mind.* New Haven, CT: Yale University Press.

O'Connor, Jack. 1961. *The Big Game Animals of North America.* New York: Outdoor Life/E. P. Dutton.

Ormond, Clyde, 1962. *The Complete Book of Hunting.* New York: Outdoor Life/Harper Bros.

Orning, Elizabeth. Personal Communication. Oregon State University. 2014.

——, and Katie M. Dugger. *Competitive Interactions Between Wolves and Cougars in the Mt. Emily Wildlife Management Unit, Northeast Oregon.* Wolf-Cougar Study in Northeast Oregon – Project Update: 1 January 2017. Oregon Cooperative Fish and Wildlife research Unit, Department of Fisheries and Wildlife, Oregon State University.

Parr, Sadie. Wolf Awareness, Inc. Personal Communication.

Parsons, David R. 1993. *Proposed Action for Reintroduction of the Mexican Wolf* (Canis lupus baileyi). Albuquerque, NM: U.S. Fish and Wildlife Service.

Peters, Roger. 1985. *Dance of the Wolves.* New York: Ballantine.

Peterson, Brenda. 2001. *Build Me an Ark: A Life with Animals.* New York: Norton.

Peterson, Rolf O. 1977. *Wolf Ecology and Prey Relationships on Isle Royale.* National Park Service Scientific Monograph Series No. 11. Washington, DC: National Park Service.

Phillips, Mike. 1994. *Activities of Reintroduction Project during March 1994.* U.S. Government Memorandum.

"Playing with Nature a Dilemma." *Calgary Herald,* November 25, 1988, p. C12.

"Poachers Slaughter East Kootenay Wolves." *Calgary Herald,* April 22, 1991, p. A3.

Poglayen, Giovanni, Francesca Gori, Benedetto Morandi, Roberta Galuppi, Elena Fabbri, Romolo Caniglia, Pietro Milanesi, Marco Galaverni, Ettore Randi, Barbara Marchesi , Peter Deplazes. "Italian wolves (Canis lupus italicus Altobello, 1921) and molecular detection of taeniids in the Foreste Casentinesi National Park, Northern Italian Apennines." *International Journal for Parasitology: Parasites and Wildlife* 6 (2017) 1e7.

Promberger, Christoph, and Wolfgang Schroder, eds. 1992. *Wolves in Europe: Status and Perspectives*. Ettal, Germany: Munich Wildlife Society.

"Protecting the Predators." *Alberta Report,* March 21, 1988, pp. 25–26.

Quammen, David. 1993. "Only Connect." *Outside* 18(12):29–35.

Quebec Forests, Wildlife and Parks. http://www.mffp.gouv.qc.ca/faune/statistiques/chasse-piegeage.jsp.

"Red Wolf: Great Smoky Mountains." 1994. *Wolf!* 12(1):7.

Runtz, Michael W. P. 1991. *Moose Country*. Toronto: Stoddart Publishing.

Russell, Andy. 1967. *Grizzly Country*. New York: Ballantine.

Russell, Franklin. 1983. *The Hunting Animal*. Toronto: McClelland & Stewart.

Rutter, R. J., and Douglas Pimlott. 1968. *The World of the Wolf*. Philadelphia: Lippincott.

Savage, Candace. 1988. *Wolves*. Vancouver, British Columbia: Douglas & McIntyre.

Siino, Betsy. 1991. "Wolf Hybrids: The Newest Fad." *The Advocate* 9(2):12–15.

Sime, Carolyn A., V. Asher, L. Bradley, K. Laudon, N. Lance, and M. Ross, and J. Steuber. 2009. *Montana gray wolf conservation and management 2008 annual report.* Montana Fish, Wildlife & Parks. Helena, Montana, p. 154.

——. 2010. *Montana gray wolf conservation and management 2009 annual report*. Montana Fish, Wildlife & Parks. Helena, Montana, p. 173.

——. 2011. *Montana gray wolf conservation and management 2010 annual report*. Montana Fish, Wildlife & Parks. Helena, Montana, p. 168.

Singh, Arjan. 1984. *Tiger! Tiger!* London: Jonathan Cape.

Smith, Douglas W. "Ten Years After: What We're Learning About Wolves in Yellowstone." *Yellowstone Science,* 13(1) Winter 2005.

——, and Gary Ferguson. 2005. *Decade of the Wolf: Returning the Wolf to Yellowstone*. Guilford, CT: Lyons Press.

——, Daniel R. Stahler, Matthew C. Metz, Kira A. Cassidy, Erin E. Stahler, Emily S. Almberg, & Rick McIntyre. "Wolf Restoration in Yellowstone: Reintroduction to Recovery." *Yellowstone Science*, 24(1) 2016.

Smits, Lee. 1963. "King of the Wild." *Michigan Conservation* 32(1):45–50.

"So You Want to Own a Wolf or Wolf/Dog Hybrid?" 1988. *Wolf News* 6(3):6.

Sparks, John. 1982. *The Discovery of Animal Behavior*. Boston: Little, Brown.

Spence, Lewis. 1988. *Encyclopedia of the Occult*. London: Bracken Books.

Stanwell-Fletcher, J. F. 1942. "Three Years in the Wolves' Wilderness." *Natural History* 49:136–147.

Stanwell-Fletcher, Theodora C. 1946. *Driftwood Valley*. New York: Little, Brown.

Stewart, Darryl. 1978. *From the Edge of Extinction: The Fight to Save Endangered Species.* Toronto: McClelland & Stewart.

——. 1981. *The Canadian Wildlife Almanac*. Toronto: Lester & Orpen Dennys.

Stewart, Hillary. 1990. *Totem Poles*. Vancouver, British Columbia: Douglas & McIntyre.

Stewart, Miller, & Margaret Stewart. 1971. *Bright World Around Us*. Richmond Hill, Ontario: Simon & Schuster.

Strickland, Dan. 1992. *Wolf Howling in Algonquin Provincial Park.* Algonquin Technical Bulletin No. 3. Whitby, Ontario: Friends of Algonquin Park, in cooperation with the Ontario Ministry of Natural Resources.

"Stronger Protection for Algonquin's Wolves." 1993. *Working for Wildlife.* World Wildlife Fund-Canada (Fall): 4.

Struzik, Ed. 1993. "Managing the Competition." *Nature Canada* 22(4):22–27.

——. 1994, "The Art of Loving Wolves." *International Wildlife* 24(1):18–23.

"Summary of Revised Eastern Timber Wolf Recovery Plan." 1992. *Wolf!* 10(2):7.

Tarpy, Cliff. 1993. "New Zoos: Taking Down the Bars." *National Geographic* 184(1):2–37.

Theberge, John. 1994. "Why Fear the Wolf?" *Equinox* 13:1(73):42–53.

"They're Not Just Crying Wolf." *B.C. Report*, February 15, 1993, pp. 34–36.

Tolstoy, Nikolai. 1985. *The Quest for Merlin*. London: Hamish Hamilton.

*Treasury of Aesop's Fables*. 1973. New York: Crown Publishers.

*2017 Fur Prices: NAFA May Auction Results*. http://trappingtoday.com/2017-fur-prices-nafa-may-auction-results/.

*2016 Mexican Gray Wolf population Survey Reveal gains for Experimental Population*. News Release, US Fish and Wildlife Service, Southwest Region. February 17, 2017.

U.S. Fish and Wildlife Service. *The Mexican Wolf: Natural History and Recovery Efforts*. Albuquerque, NM: U.S. Fish and Wildlife Service.

———. 1982. *Mexican Wolf Recovery Plan*. Albuquerque, NM: U.S. Fish and Wildlife Service.

———. 1987. *A Summary of the Northern Rocky Mountain Wolf Recovery Plan*. Washington, DC: U.S. Fish and Wildlife Service.

———. 1988. *The Mexican Wolf: Biology, History, and Prospects for Reestablishment in New Mexico*. Endangered Species Report No. 18. Albuquerque, NM: U.S. Fish and Wildlife Service.

———. 1989. *An Evaluation of the Ecological Potential of White Sands Missile Range to Support a Reintroduced Population of Mexican Wolves*. Endangered Species Report No. 19, Albuquerque, NM: U.S. Fish and Wildlife Service.

———. 1989. *Red Wolf Recovery Plan*. Atlanta, GA: U.S. Fish and Wildlife Service.

———. 1992. *Recovery Plan for the Eastern Timber Wolf*. Twin Cities, MN, U.S. Fish and Wildlife Service.

———. 1992. *Summary of Public Comments on Reintroduction of the Wolf to Yellowstone National Park and Central Idaho*. Washington, DC: U.S. Fish and Wildlife Service.

———. 1993. *Draft Environmental Impact Statement: The Reintroduction of Gray Wolves to Yellowstone Park and Central Idaho—Summary*. Helena, MT: U.S. Fish and Wildlife Service.

———. 1993. *Status Report for the Mexican Wolf Recovery Program*. Albuquerque, NM: U.S. Fish and Wildlife Service.

———. 1994. *Red Wolf Bibliography*. Red Wolf Management Series Technical Report 9. Atlanta, GA: U.S. Fish and Wildlife Service.

U.S. National Park Service and U.S. Fish and Wildlife Service. 1990. *Yellowstone Wolf Questions: A Digest. Extracts from Wolves for Yellowstone? A Report to the United States Congress.* Washington, DC: U.S. National Park Service.

Vila, Carlos, Javier Castroviejo, and V. Urios. 1992. "The Iberian Wolf in Spain." In *Wolves in Europe: Status and Perspectives.* Ettal, Germany: Munich Wildlife Society.

Walker, Roberta. 1993. "Return of the Wolves." *Reader's Digest*, April, pp. 78–82.

Ward, Geoffrey C. 1992. "India's Wildlife Dilemma." *National Geographic* 181(5):3–29.

Weaver, John. 1978. *The Wolves of Yellowstone*. Natural Resources Report No. 14. Washington, DC: National Park Service.

"What Is a Livestock Guard Dog?" 1990. *Northwest Wildlife Focus,* Northwest Wildlife Preservation Society (Spring): 2.

"What on Earth Is a Public Wolf Howl?" 1994. *Algonquin Provincial Park Parkway Corridor*. Whitney, Ontario: Friends of Algonquin Park.

Wheeler, Timothy B. "Effort to Return Red Wolves to Great Smoky Mountains Ends in Failure." *Baltimore Sun,* December 13, 1998.

"When Wolf and Cougar Meet." 1990. *Wolf News* 83:6.

Whitaker, John O., ed. 1980. *Audubon Society Field Guide to North American Mammals*. New York: Knopf.

White, Connie. 1994. "Wolf Head Impaled to Post in Round Lake Centre." *Barry's Bay This Week* 24(11):1–2.

Wildlife Committee of the Rio Grande Chapter of the Sierra Club and Mexican Wolf Coalition. 1993. *The Mexican Wolf.* Albuquerque, NM: Wildlife Committee of the Rio Grande Chapter of the Sierra Club and Mexican Wolf Coalition.

Williams, Ted. 1988. "Bringing Back the Beast of Lore." *Modern Maturity,* June/July, pp. 44–51.

——. 1993. "Alaska's War on the Wolves." *Audubon* 95(3):44–50.

Wilson, Ian, and Sally Wilson 1989. *Wild & Free: Living with Wildlife in Canada's North*. West Vancouver, British Columbia: Gordon Soules Books.

Wise, Carla, Jeffrey J. Yeo, Dale Goble, James M. Peck, and Jay O'Laughlin. 1991. *Wolf Recovery in Central Idaho: Alternative Strategies and Impacts.* Report 4. Boise, ID: Idaho Forest, Wildlife and Range Policy Analysis Group.

*Wolf!* 1986. Ashland, WI: Northword Inc. and Wolves in American Culture Committee.

"Wolf Debate Reflects Split on Resources." *Albuquerque Journal,* January 31, 1993, p. B4.

"Wolf Howling in Algonquin Park." 1989. *Wolf News* 7(3):4–5.

"Wolf Killer Wants Endangered Animal Back." 1994. *Wolf!* 12(1):11.

"Wolf Revival in Michigan." 1994. *Wolf!* 12(1):34

Wolok, Mimi. 1993. *Reported Wolf Observations in New Mexico, Texas, and Mexico*. Albuquerque: U.S. Fish and Wildlife Service.

"Wolves and Lions Natural Enemies?" 1994. *Wolf!* 12(1):29.

"Wolves and Ungulates: Separating Myth From Reality." 1988. *Working for Wildlife* (Summer/Fall):4.

"Wolves Doing Well in Spain." 1990. *Wolf News* 8(3):8.

"Wolves in Europe." 1988. *Wolf News* 6(3):4.

"Wolves Increasingly Threatened in Ontario." 1992. *Working for Wildlife,* (Winter):8.

"Wolves: Past Story Updates." 1991. *Buzzworm* 111(2):15.

"Wolves Seen Attacking Bears Near Glacier." 1994. *Wolf!* 12(1):30.

"Wolves Sought to Help Manage Elk Population." 1994. *Wolf!* 12(1):10.

"Wolves Surviving in Turkey." 1989. *Wolf News* 7(3):8.

*World Book Encyclopedia,* s.v. "Werewolf."

Wormington, H. M. 1957. *Ancient Man in North America*. Denver, CO: Denver Museum of Natural History.

"Yellowstone Wolf Release Favored." 1992. *Defenders* 67(5):4.

Young, S. P., and E. A. Goldman. 1944. *The Wolves of North America.* Washington, DC: American Wildlife Institute.

Young, Steven B. 1989. *To the Arctic: An Introduction to the Far Northern World*. New York: Wiley.

"Yukon Wolf Control." 1993. *Working for Wildlife* (Spring):4.

Yuskavitch, Jim. *In Wolf Country: The Power and Politics of Reintroduction.* Lyons Press, Guilford, CT. 2015.

Zimmer, Carl. "DNA Study Reveals the One and Only Wolf Species in North America." *The New York Times*, July 27, 2016.

Zumbo, Jim. 1994. "Wolf Wars." *Outdoor Life*, February, pp. 59–84.

# INDEX

*Note: Italicized page references indicate illustrations.*

**B**

## C

**D**

## E

**F**



**G**

## H

## N



## O

**P**

## Q



## R

**S**